Chinua Achebe

Contemporary World Writers

SERIES EDITOR   JOHN THIEME

ALREADY PUBLISHED IN THE SERIES

Peter Carey   BRUCE WOODCOCK
Amitav Ghosh   ANSHUMAN MONDAL
Maxine Hong Kingston   HELENA GRICE
Kazuo Ishiguro   BARRY LEWIS
Hanif Kureishi   BART MOORE-GILBERT
Doris Lessing   SUSAN WATKINS
David Malouf   DON RANDALL
Rohinton Mistry   PETER MOREY
Timothy Mo   ELAINE YEE LIN HO
Toni Morrison   JILL MATUS
Alice Munro   CORAL ANN HOWELLS
Les Murray   STEVEN MATTHEWS
R. K. Narayan   JOHN THIEME
Michael Ondaatje   LEE SPINKS
Caryl Phillips   BÉNÉDICTE LEDENT
Caryl Phillips, David Dabydeen and Fred D'Aguiar:
Representations of Slavery   ABIGAIL WARD
Salman Rushdie   ANDREW TEVERSON
Amy Tan   BELLA ADAMS
Ngugi wa Thiong'o   PATRICK WILLIAMS
Derek Walcott   JOHN THIEME

Chinua Achebe

JAGO MORRISON

Manchester University Press

Copyright © Jago Morrison 2014

The right of Jago Morrison to be identified as the author of this work has been asserted by him in accordance with the Copyright, Designs and Patents Act 1988.

Published by Manchester University Press
Oxford Road, Manchester M13 9PL
www.manchesteruniversitypress.co.uk

British Library Cataloguing-in-Publication Data
A catalogue record for this book is available from the British Library

Library of Congress Cataloging-in-Publication Data applied for

ISBN 978 1 5261 1679 6 *paperback*

This edition first published 2017

The publisher has no responsibility for the persistence or accuracy of URLs for any external or third-party internet websites referred to in this book, and does not guarantee that any content on such websites is, or will remain, accurate or appropriate.

Typeset in Aldus
by Koinonia, Manchester

For Lily

Contents

ACKNOWLEDGEMENTS	viii
SERIES EDITOR'S FOREWORD	ix
ABBREVIATIONS	x
CHRONOLOGY	xi
1 Speaking from the middle ground: contexts and intertexts	1
2 *Things Fall Apart* and *No Longer at Ease*	55
3 *Arrow of God*	93
4 *A Man of the People* and the Biafran writings	135
5 *Anthills of the Savannah*	183
6 The balance of stories: critical overview and conclusion	224
NOTES	239
SELECT BIBLIOGRAPHY	258
INDEX	272

Acknowledgements

Many friends and colleagues have helped in the writing of this book, in formal and informal ways. For their advice and help in finding difficult-to-access resources, I am particularly indebted to Bernth Lindfors and Lyn Innes. Expert staff at SOAS Special Collections, as well as the archives of the Foreign and Commonwealth Offices at the UK Public Records Office, gave invaluable advice. Thanks to David Chioni Moore for giving me pre-print access to his illuminating 2009 interview with Achebe, and to Wendy Knepper for her suggestions on the book's conclusion. John Thieme's editorial guidance on my first draft was invaluable, making me think in new ways about several aspects of Achebe's work. Throughout, Matthew Frost has been as easy and supportive as an editor can be. Thanks to Lily and Bevan Morrison for keeping me sane, and to Alison for her unfailing love and support.

Series editor's foreword

Contemporary World Writers is an innovative series of authoritative introductions to a range of culturally diverse contemporary writers from outside Britain and the United States or from 'minority' backgrounds within Britain or the United States. In addition to providing comprehensive general introductions, books in the series also argue stimulating original theses, often but not always related to contemporary debates in post-colonial studies.

The series locates individual writers within their specific cultural contexts, while recognising that such contexts are themselves invariably a complex mixture of hybridised influences. It aims to counter tendencies to appropriate the writers discussed into the canon of English or American literature or to regard them as 'other'.

Each volume includes a chronology of the writer's life, an introductory section on formative contexts and intertexts, discussion of all the writer's major works, a bibliography of primary and secondary works and an index. Issues of racial, national and cultural identity are explored, as are gender and sexuality. Books in the series also examine writers' use of genre, particularly ways in which Western genres are adapted or subverted and 'traditional' local forms are reworked in a contemporary context.

Contemporary World Writers aims to bring together the theoretical impulse which currently dominates post-colonial studies and closely argued readings of particular authors' works, and by so doing to avoid the danger of appropriating the specifics of particular texts into the hegemony of totalising theories.

List of abbreviations

AWS	African Writers Series
BBC	British Broadcasting Corporation
BOFF	Biafran Organization of Freedom Fighters
BP	British Petroleum
CMS	Church Missionary Society
EAEC	East African Examinations Council
ENBS	Eastern Nigeria Broadcasting Service
NBC	Nigerian Broadcasting Corporation
NBS	Nigerian Broadcasting Service
NCNC	National Council of Nigeria and the Cameroons
NPN	National Party of Nigeria
PRP	People's Redemption Party
WAEC	West African Examinations Council
WNBC	Western Nigeria Broadcasting Corporation

Chronology

1930 Chinua Achebe born 16 November, in Nnobi, South East Nigeria
1944 Attends Government College Umuahia
1948 Attends University College, Ibadan
1954 Gains employment with the Nigeria Broadcasting Service (Nigerian Broadcasting Corporation from 1957)
1957 Attends staff training at the BBC, London, and makes contact with London publishers
1958 Promoted to Controller of Broadcasting for Eastern Nigeria
Things Fall Apart published by Heinemann
1960 Nigeria gains independence from Great Britain
No Longer at Ease published by Heinemann
1961 Appointed Director of the Voice of Nigeria external broadcasting service
Marries Christie Okoli
1962 Appointed General Editor of Heinemann's African Writers Series
1964 *Arrow of God* published by Heinemann
1966 Appointed President of the Society of Nigerian Authors
A Man of the People published by Heinemann
Chike and the River published by Cambridge University Press
January coup led by Igbo officers kills Prime Minister Abubakar Balewa – end of the First Republic
July counter-coup heralds wave of anti-Igbo pogroms – the Achebe family are forced to flee to South East Nigeria
1967 Secession of Biafra, outbreak of Nigerian Civil War
Founds the Citadel Press with Christopher Okigbo

1968 Appointed Chairman of the National Guidance Committee for Biafra, by Head of State General Emeka Ojukwu
1969 Publication of *The Ahiara Declaration: The Principles of the Biafran Revolution* by the government of Biafra
1970 Defeat of Biafra
1971 *Beware Soul Brother* published by Nwankwo-Ifejika
1972 Moves to the United States
Girls at War and Other Stories published by Heinemann
How the Leopard Got His Claws published by Nwamife
1975 *Morning Yet on Creation Day* published by Heinemann
1976 Returns to Nigeria
Appointed Professor in the Department of English at the University of Nigeria, Nsukka
1977 *The Flute: A Children's Story* and *The Drum: A Children's Story* published by Fourth Dimension
1979 Democracy restored in Nigeria – beginning of the Second Republic
1982 Joins the People's Redemption Party (PRP) under Aminu Kano
1983 *The Trouble with Nigeria* published by Fourth Dimension
Return to military rule in Nigeria
1987 *Anthills of the Savannah* published by Heinemann
1988 *Hopes and Impediments: Selected Essays* published by Heinemann
1990 Seriously injured in a car accident in Akwa, Nigeria
Moves permanently to the United States – appointed Professor of Literature at Bard College, New York State
1993 Nigeria briefly returns to civilian rule
1994 End of the Third Republic and re-establishment of military rule
1999 Democratic elections in Nigeria – beginning of the Fourth Republic
2001 *Home and Exile* published by Anchor
2005 *Collected Poems* published by Carcanet
2009 *The Education of a British-Protected Child* published by Penguin
2012 *There Was a Country: A Personal History of Biafra* published by Penguin
2013 Dies in Boston, United States

1

Speaking from the middle ground: contexts and intertexts

In 1954 a graduate, one year out of college, was recruited to the Talks Department of the Nigerian Broadcasting Service (NBS). By the age of twenty-eight, he was one of the most powerful media professionals in Nigeria. Before independence in 1960 he had established a second career as a fiction writer with the international publisher Heinemann – in due course, his first novel alone would sell an extraordinary ten million copies. Sponsored by the Rockefeller Foundation, he celebrated his thirtieth birthday by embarking on an international tour that would help to establish him as one of the most influential voices in contemporary world literature. How should Chinua Achebe's spectacular rise to prominence be understood?

In Nigeria in the 1950s, the cultural field was undergoing profound, multidimensional change, as practices, values and assumptions previously taken for granted by producers and consumers in the media and the arts were rapidly redefined. With the systematic withdrawal of the British from public institutions, opportunities presented themselves to that first cohort of Nigerian graduates that must have seemed incredible to their parents' generation. In this sense, from a historical point of view Achebe arrived on the scene at precisely the right moment. In broadcasting, the process of 'Nigerianisation' that preceded independence had produced an urgent demand for young, well-educated, home-grown talent, in exactly the form he exemplified. At the same time, in international publishing, decolonisation posed major challenges for big companies such as Longman and Oxford University Press. Both were comparatively slow to respond to the reality that, especially in the educational field, postcolonial markets would present demands quite different from those of the colonial era. Heinemann, a comparatively smaller player with an aggressive and entrepreneurial attitude, was the first to recognise that African writing could be promoted to education ministries and examination boards as a new canon for the postcolonial world. Achebe became their standard bearer in a way no writer before or since was able to do.

Within five years of independence, his status within the African arts world was unparalleled. At consultant editor for Heinemann's ground-breaking African Writers Series, he became the gatekeeper to international attention for a generation of emerging writers. As Director of the Voice of Nigeria, the nation's international broadcasting service, he was the media professional most directly responsible for shaping Nigeria's image abroad. When the Society of Nigerian Authors partied into the night of 14 January 1966 to celebrate the launch of his fourth novel *A Man of the People*, therefore, it would have been easy to assume that Achebe's status was unassailable. From that moment, however, his position began rapidly to unravel. The new novel depicted a coup – overnight, one had taken place almost exactly as he had described. Nigeria's first attempt at democratic self-government was at an end, and the following weeks and months saw a rapid unravelling of its political fabric, with escalating ethnic violence against Igbo professionals and their families. The Achebes, who narrowly escaped with their lives, were forced to flee from Lagos to their native South East, while an estimated 30,000 Igbo, who were not so lucky, died in the pogroms.

From his first novel onwards, as we will see throughout this book, the image of Nigeria Achebe had created in fiction was always a deeply troubled and problematic one. In 1966, *A Man of the People* presented a nation in fundamental crisis, and events on the ground seemed to have confirmed that diagnosis. When his native East announced its departure from the Nigerian Federation and declared itself a sovereign state the following year, Achebe made the decision to become a secessionist and a citizen of Biafra. In his new nation, as part of the rebel leader Emeka Ojukwu's inner circle, his writing would take a different turn, when he became the lead author of Biafra's defining statement of values *The Ahiara Declaration*. War was soon upon him and, as his memoir *There Was a Country* shows, this experience was also a defining one. As UK Commonwealth and Foreign Office records of the period show, Nigeria's violent response to the secessionists was energetically encouraged by the British who, anxious to safeguard their oil rights in the Niger Delta, supplied the Federation with quantities of armaments that were unprecedented in Britain's history as an arms trading nation. Their action enabled a complete siege of the rebel republic that cost over two million lives. Militarily overwhelmed, and in the face of mass starvation and disease, Achebe's new nation held out for three years before being forced to a comprehensive defeat. For him, from a creative as well as personal and political point of view, the experience was disastrous. Three years previously, he had had to abandon his fifth novel uncompleted, and in the event it was twenty years before he was able to find the peace of mind and emotional stability to complete *Anthills of the Savannah*. By that time, Nigeria had once again become his homeland. As that novel revealed, however, his relationship to it was as painful and difficult as ever.

Growing up with Nigeria

Nigeria is a nation-state encompassing a range of cultures as diverse as those of Europe. Those cultures have never cohered particularly harmoniously under a single national banner, and in the periods in which Achebe was active in Nigeria as a broadcaster and writer, it is important to recognise that ethnic and regional agendas defined the political landscape in fundamental ways. In common with many of his contemporaries, Achebe's own relationship to Nigeria was, from the first, an awkward one. In his fictional and critical writings, anti-colonial sentiment is everywhere to be found, and it is clear that he was strongly committed to seeing the end of British rule. As too few critics have recognised, however, his relationship to nationalism and to Nigeria itself is a rather different question. In an essay entitled 'What Is Nigeria to Me?', membership of the Igbo nation is offered as his primary affiliation:

> My earliest awareness in the town of Ogidi did not include any of that British stuff, nor indeed the Nigerian stuff. That came with progress in school. Ogidi is one of a thousand or more 'towns' that make up the Igbo nation, one of Nigeria's (indeed Africa's) largest ethnic groups. But the Igbo, numbering over ten million, are a curious 'nation.' They have been called names like 'stateless' or 'acephalous' by anthropologists; 'argumentative' by those sent to administer them. But what the Igbo are is not the negative suggested by such descriptions but strongly, positively, in favor of small-scale political organization so that (as they would say) every man's eye would reach where things are happening. So every one of the thousand towns was a mini state with complete jurisdiction over its affairs. A sense of civic attachment to their numerous towns was more real for precolonial Igbo people than any unitary pan-Igbo feeling. This made them notoriously difficult to govern centrally, as the British discovered but never appreciated nor quite forgave. Their dislike was demonstrated during the Biafran tragedy, when they accused the Igbo of threatening to break up a nation-state they had carefully and laboriously put together.[1]

Although statist nationalism – in the sense of commitment to the One-Nigeria project – was a key channel for anti-colonial sentiment during his formative years, it does not seem to have been something that penetrated deeply into the lives of families like Achebe's. As his autobiographical writings make clear, the cultural dialectic that structured his upbringing was between the world of the Christian mission, on the one hand, and Igbo traditional culture, on the other. In an interview with Dennis Duerden in 1965, the author described some of the typical evangelising activities in which he was expected to participate as a child (evidently pursued with less vigour than expatriate missionaries would have liked):

> When I was growing up it was not very common to see people converted. I know we used to go out, every fourth Sunday, into the village – the Christians I mean – and sing and preach, you see, and the 'pagans' as they were called would assemble and listen. The idea was that way you could covert a few more, but I don't remember that we met with any great success. In fact, many of the people who turned up were what you might call backsliders, some who had been in the church and given it up, and they put some rather embarrassing questions to the catechist or pastor.[2]

Achebe's mother, the daughter of a village blacksmith, had worked as a servant for the principal of St Monica's Girls School in Ogidi in exchange for an education. His father was a stalwart of the Church Missionary Society (CMS) based regionally at Onitsha, and travelled as a preacher between the surrounding towns and villages. The churches within whose ambit the Achebe family existed were staffed and congregated by local Igbo: white people, and people from outside the locality, were a comparatively rare sight. As Achebe makes clear in *The Education of a British-Protected Child*, then, the church and the Igbo community which surrounded it were the defining cultural contexts of his childhood. In political terms, the very idea of thinking of oneself in terms of 'national' identity, rather than as being from Ogidi or as an Igbo, was not even on the radar until introduced into his consciousness at Government College Umuahia. This is not altogether surprising: from a historical point of view the idea of dividing the whole of Africa into national political units was a comparatively recent development.

The name 'Nigeria' itself was first proposed by Flora Shaw (later Lady Lugard, wife of the first colonial Governor General) in a letter to *The Times* newspaper of 8 January 1897. Given the diverse and sprawling nature of, as she put it, 'the agglomeration of pagan and Mahommedan states which have been brought by the exertions of the Royal Niger Company', some common name needed to be agreed on so that people at all levels of the colonial enterprise could properly understand which territories they were speaking of. Some in the Royal Niger Company favoured the name of 'Goldesia', in recognition of the colonial entrepreneur George Goldie, who had played a key role in subjugating the region to Britain's economic interests. Eventually, however, Shaw's less controversial proposal, taking the name of the Niger river, was agreed upon as the title for the area controlled by the company in the Southern territories. Later it was adopted as the nomenclature for a larger area, extending to the colony of Lagos and Britain's interests in the primarily Islamic, Northern region as well. Though perhaps incidental in itself, this story of naming has become emblematic of the arbitrary and haphazard manner in which the outlines of the modern nation were arrived at, for Achebe and many other Nigerians.

In 1914, while Achebe's father was building his reputation within the CMS, the Colony and Protectorate of Nigeria was established, as a step toward amalgamating Britain's vast and unwieldy dominions in the area as a single administrative entity. Even at that time, however, the idea of creating structures to promote 'national' cultural cohesion were not on the agenda. As the historian Gary Diamond argues in his study *Class, Ethnicity and Democracy in Nigeria*:

> While the British established over Nigeria a common political authority, transportation grid, and monetary system, they did not rule it as a single nation. In 1900, separate protectorates were proclaimed for Northern and Southern Nigeria, and a Native Authority System was constructed to rule indirectly in the North through traditional authorities. Even after formal amalgamation in 1914, the British continued to rule Nigeria, in effect, as two countries. In the South, Western education and religion were vigorously promoted and English was employed as the language of administration. Elective representation was introduced there 25 years before it would appear in the North. By contrast, British officials administered the North through the Hausa language and, seeking to preserve that region's social structure and institutions, effectively sealed off the North, especially the Muslim emirates, from Western

influences, even in the person of Southern Nigerians. Those Southerners who migrated to the North were forced to live in segregated housing and to educate their children in separate schools, and were prevented from acquiring freehold title to land. Northern Muslims were forbidden on both religious and administrative grounds to associate with Southerners, whom they were taught to regard as 'pagans' and 'infidels'. As a crucial component of this policy, Christian missionaries were forbidden in the emirates and Western education was severely restricted ... This separate administration of North and South not only profoundly hindered the development of a common national identity but also generated an immense development gap.[3]

Without doubt, the establishment and administration of Nigeria by the British had, from the outset, far more to do with the expediencies of colonial economic policy than it did with fostering national development or cultural consensus among its peoples. Therefore it is unsurprising if – while anti-colonial sentiment steadily grew during the whole period of colonisation – mass enthusiasm about the 'national idea' did not manifest itself nearly so strongly or consistently. Because of the North's comparative cultural isolation from the South East and South West, because of its distinct Islamic identity, and also because Britain's policy was to keep local structures of power in place as far as possible, regional identity rather than a common bond of 'Nigerian-ness' emerged as the pre-eminent political force in the last phase of colonial control. In 1946, Britain's 'Richards Constitution' for Nigeria formalised the already-established divisions between the regions by establishing separate Houses of Assembly for each one; over the following decade, these acquired an increasing amount of power. Increasingly, therefore, the struggle for influence in these regions became the focus of political attention.

In the South East where Achebe grew up, as well as in the South West, the colonial education system was rapidly expanded in the 1940s and 1950s, partly in an effort to supply the civil service and other public institutions with clerks and other workers. As Obi Nwakanma's account of the experience at Achebe's own school, Government College Umuahia, illustrates, the objective of the colonial education system at that time was a straightforward one: to produce functionaries, or intermediaries between the imperial centre and its subject populations:

> It was conceived by the British colonial administration to educate a select category of 'natives' who were to be recruited into the colonial administration, following the loss of some of England's most talented young men in the First World War. Administrators of the empire created local equivalents of Eton, Harrow and Winchester, to train the elite who would assist in running the colony ... They had teachers drawn mostly from English men who themselves had been educated at Cambridge and Oxford. These teachers were employed through the colonial civil service as education officers rather than through the missions. Their mandate was to provide the best English education to a select elite, trained and prepared in the English mould.[4]

In the North, significantly, there was no such expansion: as Diamond observes, no 'higher' schools comparable to Achebe's were established there at all in this period. When he proudly enrolled as one of the first cohort of the new University College Ibadan in 1948, moreover, only 6 per cent of his fellow students were northerners, despite the fact that the Northern region accounted for four-fifths of Nigeria's landmass and more than half of its population.

During Achebe's education, the philosophy of democratic nation-statism certainly seems to have informed the curriculum he was offered, even if it was not presented in the form of 'political theory'. As Benedict Anderson suggests in his classic study of nationalism *Imagined Communities*, this was true throughout the colonised world. In French Vietnam, for example, it was considered normal for schoolchildren to learn about the 1789 Revolution as an aspect of general knowledge about France. Similarly, he argues, 'Magna Carta, the Mother of Parliaments, and the Glorious Revolution, glossed as English national history, entered schools all over the British Empire.'⁵ Undoubtedly, then, the idea that the independent, democratic nation-state was the political goal to be striven for would have been familiar to the generation who came of age with Achebe, as anti-colonial agitation in Africa was reaching its height.

During his time at Umuahia and then at University College Ibadan, political engagement among students was the norm, and it would have been unusual if Achebe had not taken a keen interest in Nigeria's progress towards independence. Judging by his own published output and the evidence provided by biographer Ezenwa-Ohaeto,⁶ however, there is little sign that, as a student, he took any special interest in proselytising the Nigerian national project. Achebe's most active involvements during his time at the University College were in the Dancing Club and as a contributor of creative, critical and philosophical pieces to student periodicals. In his period as editor of the *University Herald*, his published pieces were strikingly a-political in tone:

> There was a young man in our Hall
> Who said that because he was small
> His fees should be less
> Because he ate less
> Than anyone else in the Hall⁷

and

> The behaviour of students during the performance of *Hiawatha* last Sunday was, quite frankly, disgraceful. Unintelligent and rude laughter, clapping and similar 'pit' reactions are out of place in a University. They exasperate the few who are prepared to appreciate great works of art in a sober manner.⁸

The nationalist rhetoric of the time was, as he says in *The Trouble with Nigeria*, 'of a dream-Nigeria in which a citizen could live and work in a place of his choice anywhere, and pursue any legitimate goal open to his fellows'.⁹ Almost a decade before the British withdrawal, however, it is clear that Achebe himself was already doubtful about the real prospects for this ideal. The idea of the nation uniting harmoniously at independence was, he writes, 'an unrealistic dream at the best of times' even if 'some young, educated men and women of my generation did dream it'.[10]

Many of the major public figures in Nigeria were invited to speak to the student body while Achebe was at Ibadan, and he would have been exposed to the full cut and thrust of political argumentation in the period. Tellingly, he writes in *The Trouble with Nigeria*, for him the most memorable political moment of that time was the symbolic defeat of nationalism's leading proponent Nnamdi Azikiwe in the regional elections of 1951. 'Zik', editor of the radical *West African Pilot* and a long-time agitator for independence, had led an eight-month tour of Nigeria to build a national consensus around the campaign for self-government. According to the political historian Richard L. Sklar, however, by the beginning of the 1950s much of the political energy surrounding the Nigerian nationalist project had already dissipated. Indeed, the faltering of Zik's own career in this period neatly illustrates the way in which the political climate was changing.[11] In the 1950 elections, he had attempted – as an Igbo, brought up in the North – to become leader of the Western Region. If successful, his achievement would have provided an iconic achievement for the project of national integration. In actuality, as Achebe writes, his defeat had an enormous deflationary effect on the One-Nigeria campaign:

> I was an eye-witness to that momentous occasion when Chief Obafemi Awolowo 'stole' the leadership of Western Nigeria from Dr. Nnamdi Azikiwe in broad daylight on the floor of the Western House of Assembly and sent the great Zik scampering back to the Niger 'whence [he] came.' Someday when we shall have outgrown tribal politics, or when our children shall have done so, sober historians of the Nigerian nation will see that event as the abortion of a pan-Nigerian vision.[12]

Nigerian nationalism – understood as a commitment to the establishment and maintenance of the Nigerian nation-state – was undoubtedly, in the early years, fuelled and defined by the powerful anti-colonial sentiment that Achebe and most of his contemporaries shared. Nevertheless, as we have seen, Nigeria's genesis as a relatively recent, somewhat arbitrary and certainly unwieldy colonial construct meant that it was always locked in tension with deeply embedded regional and ethnic loyalties in the various territories it encompassed. In 1947, the example of India had demonstrated to all concerned that the geo-political *status quo* was not the only option for postcolonial nations: in response to pressure from the predominantly Islamic north, British India had been divided at independence into the separate sovereign states of India and Pakistan. In Nigeria before 1960, in the years when the nature of the independence settlement remained a matter of public debate, there was every reason to expect that a very similar pattern might be followed. The nation-state bequeathed by the activities of the Royal Niger Company, self-divided and problematic as it was in social and cultural terms, did not by any means represent the only possible political construction which could be imagined.

During Achebe's time as a student at Ibadan, when anti-colonial agitation was at its popular height, the proposition that a united Nigeria embodied the inevitable political destiny of the people was still, therefore, something that had to be argued and fought for by its political proponents. Indeed, as late as 1958, Zik was still having to plead to the divided interests of the Legislative Council, that One-Nigeria remained the region's best bet for independence:

> This country, Nigeria, can no longer be regarded as a mere geographical expression. It is also an historical expression. The various communities or nationalities inhabiting this country have great traditions and a rich heritage of culture which, if pooled together, can make Nigeria great and enable her to take her rightful place among the family of nations. I have great respect for the Hausa-speaking peoples. Studying their historical background, which goes back through centuries of medieval and ancient history, one is proud of the achievements of the Ghana, Melle, Mellestine and Songhay empires. The same is applicable to the Nupe, the Tiv, the Kanuri, not to speak of the Yoruba, Ibo, Edo, Ibibio, Ijaw and other tribes and nationalities

forming the various communities in Nigeria. It is essential that ill-will be not created in order to encourage a Pakistan in this country. The North and the South are one, whether we wish it or not. The forces of history have made it so. We have a common destiny; so, too, have the East and the West. Any attempt from any source to create dissension and make the North feel that it is different from the South and the West from the East, or to make any particular nationality or tribe in Nigeria feel it is different from the others, should be deprecated. It is from these points of view that I feel that this House should place on record their condemnation of such a practice, and I have in mind the New Year's message of Your Excellency when you appealed to the various communities of Nigeria to appreciate the need to live in harmony so as to make Nigeria a worthy place for all to live in.[13]

Although, in 1960, the independence settlement brokered by the British did retain the one-nation model of Nigeria they had developed as the colonial power, it was one which in many ways enshrined, rather than transcended, ethnic and regional divisions. By then, according to Achebe's own account, the notion of a truly united Nigeria, in which all citizens could live and work where they wanted and where opportunities would be open to all regardless of ethnic or regional background, had been put aside as an 'unrealistic dream' for almost a decade.

Immediately after independence, being a free Nigerian rather than a 'British Protected Person' was undoubtedly intoxicating, especially if one travelled to other African states which were still governed by European powers. For Igbo people, even the youngest and most idealistic among them, however, the glamour of that new national identity was to be short lived. In his essay 'What Is Nigeria to Me?' Achebe writes:

> At the time we were proud of what we had just achieved. True, Ghana had beaten us to it by three years, but then Ghana was a tiny affair, easy to manage, compared to the huge lumbering giant called Nigeria. We did not have to be vociferous like Ghana; just our presence was enough. Indeed, the elephant was our national emblem;

our airline's was the flying elephant! Nigerian troops soon distinguished themselves in a big way in the United Nations peacekeeping efforts in the Congo. Our elephant, defying aerodynamics, was flying!

Traveling as a Nigerian was exciting. People listened to us. Our money was worth more than the dollar. When the driver of a bus in the British colony of Northern Rhodesia in 1961 asked me what I was doing sitting in the front of the bus, I told him nonchalantly that I was going to Victoria Falls. In amazement he stooped lower and asked where I came from. I replied, even more casually, 'Nigeria, if you must know; and, by the way, in Nigeria we sit where we like in the bus.'

Back home I took up the rather important position of director of external broadcasting, an entirely new radio service aimed primarily at our African neighbours. I could do it in those days, because our politicians were yet to learn the uses of information control and did not immediately attempt to regiment our output. They were learning fast, though. But before I could get enmeshed in that, something much nastier had seized hold of us all.

The six-year-old Nigerian federation was falling apart from the severe strain of regional animosity and ineffectual central authority. The transparent failure of the electoral process to translate the will of the electorate into recognizable results at the polls lead to mass frustration and violence.[14]

Achebe's fiction in the 1950s and early 1960s, certainly, is strongly Igbo in focus, with little attempt to explore the differential experiences of, for example, the Yoruba, Fulani or Hausa peoples. Can the Igbo experience explored in these novels be taken as representative of Nigeria as a whole? Hardly, given that within six years of independence, ethnic conflict had escalated to a point that most Easterners no longer felt they could continue to exist as 'Nigerians', and a bloody civil war was on the horizon. Achebe's fourth novel *A Man of the People* is set more clearly in a 'national' space, a kind of not-Nigeria, and explores the national political scene with a sceptical, deeply questioning eye. Read as an exhortation to Nigeria to reform itself, to realise its lost potential, this novel could be seen as a kind of sceptical dalliance with statist nationalism. Even if this is accepted, however, it is certainly very far from the nationalism of Benedict Anderson's 'deep horizontal comradeship'. In the wake of the political eruption that coincided with its publication, moreover, any ambivalent hopes Achebe may have harboured for the nation were shaken further. In 'What Is Nigeria to Me?' he recalls:

> My feeling towards Nigeria was one of profound disappointment. Not because mobs were hunting down and killing in the most savage manner innocent civilians in many parts of northern Nigeria, but because the federal government sat by and let it happen. The final consequence of this failure of the state to fulfil its primary obligation to its citizens was the secession of Eastern Nigeria as the Republic of Biafra. The demise of Nigeria at that point was averted only by Britain's spirited diplomatic and military support of its model colony. It was Britain and the Soviet Union which together crushed the upstart Biafran state. At the end of the thirty-month war, Biafra was a vast smoldering rubble. The cost in human lives was a staggering two million souls, making it one of the bloodiest civil wars in human history. I found it difficult to forgive Nigeria and my countrymen and women for the political nonchalance and cruelty that unleashed upon us these terrible events, which set us back a whole generation and robbed us of the chance, clearly within our grasp, to become a medium-rank developed nation in the twentieth century.[15]

Nine years after the civil war, when military dictatorship was coming to an end, and the establishment once again recognised Achebe with the Nigerian National Merit Award, his commentary in the Lagos *Daily Times* showed a continuing ambivalence: 'I think I am on safe ground if I say that Nigerian writers are not planning to send a delegation to President Shehu Shagari to pledge their unflinching support. Flinching support is more in their line of business.'[16]

In the mid-1980s, during the preparation of *Anthills of the Savannah*, Achebe used the high profile Regent's Lecture at the

University of California, Los Angeles to address the question of his relationship to Nigeria. Once again, he took the opportunity to define himself in terms of Igbo traditions (Mbari and Afikpo), while questioning the possibility of a culture that could call itself 'Nigerian':

> Who is my community? The *mbari* and the Afikpo examples I referred to were clearly appropriate to the rather small, reasonably stable and self-contained societies to which they belonged. In the very different, wide-open, multicultural and highly volatile condition known as modern Nigeria, for example, can a writer even begin to know who his community is let alone devise strategies for relating to it?[17]

As we see here, Achebe's own account of himself and his work in *The Education of a British-Protected Child* explicitly contradicts the thesis put by influential critics such as Simon Gikandi that his work can be read in terms of a consistent commitment to nationalism.[18] Instead, in this volume, Achebe situates himself in a very different way that usefully illuminates the strategies we find in his fiction. Neither an ideologue, nor an agitator in the foreground of political struggle, he wants to characterise himself as speaking from a 'middle ground', a space of negotiation between two poles: on the one hand, the culture bequeathed by colonialism and, on the other hand, the Igbo civilisation of his native South East. As Achebe writes:

> That middle ground is, of course, the least admired of the three. It lacks lustre; it is undramatic, unspectacular. And yet my traditional Igbo culture, which at the hour of her defeat had ostensibly abandoned me in a basket of reeds in the waters of the Nile, but somehow kept anxious watch from concealment, ultimately insinuating herself into the service of Pharaoh's daughter to nurse me in the alien palace; yes, that very culture taught me a children's rhyme which celebrates the middle ground as most fortunate:
>
> Obu-uzo anya na-afu mmo
> Ono-na-etiti ololo nwa
> Okpe-azu aka iko

The front one, whose eye encounters spirits
The middle one, the dandy child of fortune
The rear one of twisted fingers.

Why do the Igbo call the middle ground lucky? What does this place hold that makes it so desirable? Or, rather, what misfortune does it fence out? The answer is, I think, Fanaticism. The One Way, One Truth, One Life menace. The Terror that lives completely alone ... The middle ground is neither the origin of things nor the last things; it is aware of a future to head into and a past to fall back on; it is the home of doubt and indecision, of suspension of disbelief, of make-believe, of playfulness, of the unpredictable, of irony ... When the Igbo encounter human conflict, their first impulse is not to determine who is right but quickly to restore harmony. In my hometown, Ogidi, we have a saying, *Ikpe Ogidi adi-ama ofu onye:* The judgement of Ogidi does not go against one side. We are social managers rather than legal draftsmen. Our workplace is not a neat tabletop but a messy workshop.[19]

In this passage, Achebe playfully presents himself as a Moses figure, referring to the Old Testament prophet who would have been a recurring figure in his missionary education. To gloss this story briefly: in the book of *Exodus*, Pharaoh orders that all of the boys born to Israelite women should be cast into the Nile. Moses' mother cannot bear to drown her baby son, and instead sets him floating on the river in a basket of reeds. While bathing with her handmaids, Pharaoh's daughter sees the child and takes pity on him. Moses' sister, who is watching nearby, asks if she should call a wet nurse. Ironically, Moses' mother is then employed by Pharaoh's daughter to rear the boy until he is ready to enter Pharaoh's palace as her son. Moses grows up, to all appearances, as an Egyptian. His ultimate role, however, is to become the guide of his enslaved people. For Achebe, the very act of making a comparison between 'my own puny story' and that of the Israelite leader is, he is aware, 'sheer effrontery'.'[20] What it does bring out, however, are important elements of the writer's self-conception. In the book of *Exodus*, of course, Moses is not a formulator of nationalist slogans, but a carrier of messages between fearful authorities – Pharaoh and Jehovah – to whom his double-sided history gives him unique rights of access. He is not an architect of grand schemes and ideologies but a go-between, a broker between rival systems of power, a reader of tablets, a navigator across new and unknown times. Certainly, these are useful ideas to take to Achebe's fiction.

One thing that is clear here is that, in the analogy above, the 'people of Israel' whose freedom Achebe might help to realise are not the Nigerians but the Igbo. As he says in the essay 'What Is Nigeria to Me?' for him and his generation, growing up in the 1940s and 1950s, the idea of being a 'Nigerian' was, he says, only ever 'an acquired taste',' much like the colonial entertainment of ballroom dancing. Nationalism, in other words, even in the period of most intense excitement surrounding independence, was always more of a required performance than an ideological commitment. As he comments tellingly: 'I found, however, that once I had overcome my initial awkwardness I could do it pretty well.'[21] Should Achebe therefore be read as an Igbo nationalist? It is true that his works explore and, in some ways, celebrate the ethnic culture of the Igbo. As we will see in the following chapters, however, he is also very far indeed from ideologising the 'Igbo nation' as the goal or prize of struggle. Indeed, in *Arrow of God* particularly, Igbo culture is treated to quite a scathing analysis. In this sense, as we will see, it is much more useful to see Achebe's novels as questioning, troubling works which incite debate over questions of ethnic and national identity, rather than as expressions of political orthodoxy in themselves.

Broadcasting

In the late 1950s and 1960s, as we have seen, Achebe emerged as a major figure in broadcasting and, at the same time, as an important presence in African writing and publishing. As I will argue below, these roles were inextricably related, in terms of the way they shaped his sensibility as a public intellectual. In this sense, I will be challenging the unexamined assumption made by the vast majority of critics, that Achebe's role at the centre of the Nigerian media establishment, throughout the period of the country's emergence from colonial control, has nothing significant to tell us about him as a writer, commentator and critic. The aim of this section is to go some way towards redressing that critical tendency by exploring the field within which Achebe found himself as a broadcaster in these years, setting out some important ground work for the more detailed discussions of his writing offered in subsequent chapters.

Achebe's unexpected entry to the broadcast industry followed closely on the decision of Tom Chalmers, the British Director of the Nigerian Broadcasting Service in 1954, to begin concerted recruitment of Nigerian staff to his organisation. As independence approached, Chalmers recognised that a national broadcaster comprised entirely of colonial expatriates would soon lose leverage and credibility. Although there were many seasoned professionals working across the Nigerian media at that time, Chalmers' belief was that recruiting fresh graduates without previous experience, and training them in-house, would best fulfil the on-going aims of the service.

From its inception, as a relay for the London BBC's Empire Service in the 1930s, broadcasting had been seen by the British establishment as an instrument of effective government in its colonies: in Nigeria, as elsewhere, the NBS was developed as a collaboration between the BBC and the Colonial Office. From the end of the 1940s, efforts to develop the service proceeded with particular rapidity. As Charles Armour, head of the Schools Broadcasting Unit in Nigeria, says in a report on broadcasting developments during this period:

> In 1949 the desire to take speedy counter measures against Communism provided a powerful, immediate inducement to enhance UK funds specifically for broadcasting developments. In the background was the rising tide of new forces in Africa – the new 'Africanism' described by Lord Hailey in his revised African Survey of 1956; but perhaps more realistically labelled 'African Nationalism' by Thomas Hodgkin whose ear was sympathetically tuned to the

elemental, revolutionary forces building up in post-war Africa. The writings, newspapers and utterances of Dr Nnamdi Azikiwe, Chief Obafemi Awolowo and Kwame Nkrumah were having their impact and resonances outside Nigeria and the Gold Coast. Colonial Governments were pondering over their response; for some officials these nationalists could be dismissed as troublemakers. Riots in Accra in February 1948 sparked off a reaction, perhaps an excessive one in proportion to the small scale of the disturbances, but sufficient for [Secretary of State] Creech Jones in his May Circular to draw attention to the great potential value of broadcasting in 'correcting false impressions and rumours in times of civil disturbance' as recent events in the Gold Coast had underlined.[22]

In Ghana in 1951, Nkrumah's overwhelming victory for nationalists in elections to the new National Legislative Assembly further focused the minds of colonial governments on the need to develop broadcasting as a means of shaping African opinion. At that time, as Armour says, the clear view of Colonial Secretary Arthur Creech Jones was that broadcasting in Britain's subject territories would require 'close governmental supervision'.[23] From the point of view of the BBC, his insistence on direct political control of the service's output was seen as running entirely counter to its ethos of editorial independence, and the corporation was unwilling to operate in Nigeria on that basis. Instead, as a compromise, the BBC agreed to supervise and facilitate the development of a service which would be owned by the colonial regime, with the expectation that the corporation's own involvement would be time-limited, and that the new organisation would eventually be staffed entirely by Nigerians. From the early 1950s, therefore, 'the BBC now concentrated its energies on meeting the Nigerian requirement to establish broadcasting as a department of Government'.[24]

On the evidence of Armour's and others' accounts, recruitment to the service worked through the 'old boy' network and personal recommendation by senior expatriates. In Achebe's case, Professor James Welch from University College Ibadan, who had tried and failed to get his young student a postgraduate scholarship at Trinity College Cambridge, put his name forward directly to NBS Director Tom Chalmers. Achebe started at the makeshift headquarters in Lagos, working within the Talks Department under the well-known broadcaster Angela Beattie. His responsibilities included both production work and interviewing for the radio. Key assignments for the service included hosting the 'Lugard Lectures', a series of talks by eminent Nigerians such as the Director of the National Archives at Ibadan, Kenneth Dike, whose chosen topic was 'One Hundred Years of British Rule in Nigeria'. The Queen's visit in 1956 and the regional elections of that year provided other important highlights. In *Another Africa*, Achebe recalls interviewing the legendary colonial anthropologist Sylvia Leith-Ross, who 'conceded the many good, new things in the country, like Ibadan University College, and asked wistfully: "But where is my beloved bush?"'[25]

In Lagos, a circle of recent graduates had begun to gather, occupying a number of civil service and media positions, and many of Achebe's contemporaries supplied content for him and his colleagues. As Ikpehare Aig-Imhokhuede, a *Daily Times* journalist within this group, describes: 'It was made up of a little circle of educated friends and colleagues; close peers really. Most of us were recently from the University College, Ibadan, and doing things in Lagos. I was writing leaders for the *Times*. Chinua was talks producer at NBC. Chris [Okigbo] was just busy having fun. He had moved to the Federal Ministry of Information. Ralph Opara arrived in Lagos and started in Radio ... It was an intense place.'[26] Supplementing his newspaper work, Aig-Imhokhuede provided book reviews for Achebe in the Talks Department and co-scripted the popular serial *Safe Journey* with radio announcer Ralph Opara.

Despite the quasi-colonial 'club' atmosphere all of this suggests, Achebe's role within the NBS also undoubtedly exposed him to the cut and thrust of Lagos politics in the mid-1950s.[27] The Talks Department had the responsibility of handling NBS coverage of all key broadcasts by government ministers and addresses by the Governor General. By the time Achebe commenced employment with the service, as media analyst Ebele Ume-Nwagbo shows, these were already politically charged events. In 1953, for example, when in a statement of resistance Action Group politicians had withdrawn from the Western House of Assembly, the NBS itself became the subject of major political controversy. With flagrant bias, the service had given free airtime to the colonial Governor General John Stewart MacPherson, allowing him publically to denounce the Action Group, while denying the party any right of reply.[28] By the time of Achebe's appointment in the following year, the service's handling of all subsequent political developments had already become the subject of intense public scrutiny. According to Ian MacKay, who succeeded Chalmers at the head of the organisation, government expectations from the service were that it would not only provide entertainment and topical commentary, but also fulfil a broader cultural role, to 'raise standards and appreciation'.[29] As material from London was progressively supplanted by programming produced in Nigeria itself, the Talks Department was increasingly responsible for developing educational and literary content as well as maintaining coverage of the political sphere. As Achebe explains to Ezenwa-Ohaeto: 'Broadcasting at that point was a very exciting thing to do. And I learnt a lot by handling scripts. I was involved with the spoken word programme, although I was never an announcer but a producer. So I learnt a lot. We did short stories, short fifteen-minute talks, debates, current affairs and so on. But the short story was really my special interest and I encountered a lot of ideas just handling that.'[30]

This cultural role, umbilically linked as it was to the established modes of colonial paternalism that informed the whole of the service, was also shaped by a distinct political agenda. That agenda, pursued through programming both directly and indirectly, was to promote Britain's preferred, 'one-nation' model of post-independence Nigeria. As Ian MacKay, its last expatriate Director, writes in his study *Broadcasting in Nigeria*, the conscious intention of senior figures in the NBS was that it should 'play a dominant and vital role in spreading knowledge and understanding', including bringing pleasure to a wide variety of listeners, but 'without losing sight of the *One Nigeria* ideal'.³¹ While, as we have seen, there is little evidence to suggest that Achebe had any special, personal commitment to that particular model of independence for his area of West Africa, like all staff, he would have had to work within the organisation's priorities.

As the voice of the regions came to dominate the political agenda more and more powerfully in the run-up to independence, the broadcaster's role as a force for national cohesion was stressed increasingly strongly by the British establishment. From the start, as Ume-Nwagbo points out, it had been run directly from the Public Relations Department of the Nigerian government, with technical support from the Posts and Telegraphs Department, a division of the civil service. While the political climate in Nigeria during the 1950s forced the service to provide more and more regionally focused content – for example, in major regional vernaculars such as Hausa, Yoruba and Igbo – the organisation clung strongly to its core aim of disseminating centrally produced material 'intended to stress a sense of national unity'.³² As part of the 'national programme', regardless of his personal affiliations or political perspective, Achebe's work within the Talks Department would have been essentially defined by that objective.

In 1954 a motion was put to the Federal House of Parliament by Alahaji Adegbenro, a subsequent premier of the Western Region, arguing that the only way to remove press criticism of the NBS as a puppet of the Nigerian government was to legislate for its complete abolition, and replacement by an independent corporation. The motion received widespread support and a period of negotiation began, concerning the structure and remit of the new broadcaster. This question was to dominate debate around the Nigerian media throughout Achebe's first three years in radio. Once again, the voices of the regions were a powerful influence, and when the Nigerian Broadcasting Corporation (NBC) was formally established in 1957, it was set up under joint control of the state and the regions, with the Northern, Western and Eastern arms of the organisation given a substantial amount of autonomy over programming in their areas. Although the national organisation based in Lagos, where Achebe was employed, continued to supply a proportion of the broadcasted content across the whole country, it increasingly struggled to compete with the popularity of new, rival stations set up completely independently of the NBC in each of the three regions.

One of Chalmers' key strategies in attempting to build the credibility and resilience of this national service was to invest in the training of young Nigerian producers, including Achebe, who would increasingly be relied on to present the public face of the corporation. After a period of learning-on-the-job under senior British staff, each of them was sent to London for an extended period of training provided by the BBC. As Armour writes:

> This gave opportunity for such trainees as Cyprian Ekwensi, Chinua Achebe, Muhammadu Ladan, Victor Badejo (later the first Nigerian director general of NBC), Sam Nwaneri, the cousins 'Yinka and Michael Olumide, Joe Atuona and many others to establish personal contacts in Britain which had wider implications for building them up as Nigerian national figures than narrowly local experience and training might have yielded.[33]

For Achebe, the secondment to London in 1957 had the effect of fulfilling Chalmers' ambition to 'build them up as national figures' in a somewhat indirect way, in that the visit was to lead directly to the breakthrough that launched his literary career. Victor Badejo, his contemporary, was ultimately to take Chalmers' own position at the head of the NBC.

Returning to Nigeria after the secondment, Achebe was promoted to a senior position that, according to biographer Ezenwa-Ohaeto, had long been marked out by Chalmers. As Controller for the Eastern Region, his role was to manage the provision of programming aimed specifically at Igbo and other Eastern listeners, including in local vernaculars, while upholding the NBC's overarching ethos, to promote the 'One-Nigeria' ideal. According to J. F. Wilkinson, an expatriate programme officer in Northern Nigeria and later head of the BBC African Service:

> The Regional Controllers and Regional Boards carried very considerable power and responsibility for the Regional services, each of which had their own particular interests and problems. The task ... was, first, to create a regional identity in the minds of the listener and try to widen the range of interest from purely local affairs ... and then to go on to try and use the NBC to create a national consciousness. The overall programme plan therefore involved opting in and out of the National Programme at frequent intervals each day.[34]

Arguably, fulfilling the NBC's ambition to be a significant unificatory force for Nigeria was bound to be an uphill struggle for Achebe and his staff. Wireless sets remained too expensive for an average household at that time, with radio listening still largely confined to community centres and other public places, and the cultural and linguistic heterogeneity of the audience made programming inherently difficult. Despite the fact that the new corporation had been formed precisely to remove the criticism that the national broadcaster was simply an arm of central government, opposition towards the NBC continued to grow in the regions, while public interest in actually listening to its output remained quite weak. Revealing something of the challenge Achebe faced as the corporation's senior face in the Eastern Region, media historian Ebele Ume-Nwagbo writes:

> It was not surprising that between 1959 and 1962 three rival broadcasting services, owned and operated by the regional governments, were established. And the speed with which the services sprang up and expanded was clearly indicative of how resolutely the governments had gone to dump the NBC.
>
> The Western Nigerian government was the first to set up an independent service, the WNBC (Western Nigeria Broadcasting Corporation) in 1959.... Also out of favor with the NBC, the government of Eastern Nigeria formed the ENBS (Eastern Nigeria Broadcasting Service) to handle its radio and television services. Earlier, the region's minister of Information and Welfare, B.C. Okwu, had remarked disparagingly that the NBC 'does what it likes

... and although it exists here to serve the Eastern Region, its position is rather innocuous.'³⁵

Perhaps unsurprisingly, according to J. F. Wilkinson, the late 1950s and 1960s saw an exodus of skilled staff from the National Service, with the predictable result that the NBC's regional services were painfully squeezed. In his analysis, the inability of the NBC in the regions to check the growth and popularity of the new independent stations was a key strategic failure for the Nigerian project around the time of independence. While his conclusions might very well be questioned by subsequent historians of Nigerian politics in the 1960s, they are striking and interesting for the importance they ascribe to radio broadcasting, and the (failed) role of the NBC during Achebe's employment there, as an apparatus for holding the fragmenting nation together:

> In the Nigerian Constitutional Conference leading up to independence it was decided that broadcasting should be a 'concurrent' subject, that is, it could be the responsibility of both the Federal government and the Regional governments. This resulted in the Premiers of the North, East and West setting up their own radio – and later TV – stations in Regional headquarters in parallel to and in competition with the regional stations of the NBC. The Sardauna of Sokoto, the Premier of the North, 'persuaded' practically all the talented NBC North Regional staff who had been assembled and trained over a period of years to resign and join his new station. The standard of NBC regional broadcasting tended to decline and the net result was that the divisive influences in Nigeria were given their head and allowed to ferment feeling through these new regional stations. It is my belief that this step, which undermined the unifying influence of a single Nigerian Broadcasting Corporation, played an important part in leading Nigeria to the tragedy of the civil war from which the country is only now recovering. This development illustrates the power of radio and great importance of ensuring that it is in responsible professional hands.³⁶

On a day-to-day level, according to Ezenwa-Ohaeto, Achebe's role as Controller involved such responsibilities as intervening in employment disputes between engineers and programme staff, helping to support the NBC staff canteen and hearing petitions for changes in working conditions and pay – including from one Christie Chinwe Okoli, a university student on a holiday placement, who later became his wife.

The programming he oversaw ranged from jazz and classical music through documentary pieces on such subjects as the Igbo caste system, children and women's programmes, cultural and religious features and coverage of current affairs. After three difficult years under Achebe's management, however, the NBC Eastern service had yet to find a mass listenership in the face of competition from the locally based ENBS, with its populist, regionalist stance. Whether for this or other reasons, Achebe was invited to return to Lagos as the Director of a new broadcasting venture, the Voice of Nigeria. If the objective of the NBC in the Eastern region had been to promote national feeling through regionally targeted programming, the corporation's ambitions for this new external service constrained its content even more closely to the national governmental agenda.

The service was targeted at African listeners outside Nigeria itself. As Director, Achebe's priority was to stress its credibility and commitment to journalistic values of independence and impartiality. Speaking on the programme *Nigeria Today*, he was keen to persuade listeners that 'Nigeria occupies a very important position in contemporary Africa, and what she says or does is of enormous significance, and ought to become known and understood.' He went on to stress that the service was 'not the voice of the schoolmaster but the voice of a friend. Our news broadcasts will strive to be accurate and our commentaries objective. We shall attempt to portray our country as truly as we can so that anybody who wishes to know about her may have a true guide.'[37] The potential for tension between these democratic aspirations and those of the service's funder, the federal government, is not difficult to see, however. Federal Minister of Information T. O. S. Benson's official broadcast to mark the establishment of the Voice of Nigeria struck a rather more didactic note, for example, asserting that its purpose was 'to ensure that the country's policies and views are better understood by her neighbours'.[38]

Achebe's own appointment as a (by then) recognised and established public figure was itself no doubt intended to bolster the impression that the external service would be more than an extended advertisement for Nigeria's domestic and foreign policies. However, there can be little doubt that in agreeing to take on the role, he would have to accept significant limitations on his own right to speak, especially on political affairs, and that the remit of the service itself would be tightly circumscribed. Certainly, the head of the NBC during these years, Ian MacKay, viewed the project in that light, arguing quite simply that 'the purpose of external broadcasting is to secure long or short term advantages for the originating country'.[39] While reflecting many of the liberal broadcasting principles of the BBC, and while being actively expected to represent a variety of voices from across Nigeria's cultural spectrum, the *raison d'être* of the service in the minds of senior managers and of the federal government was to promote Nigeria and its interests abroad.

In this context, it is perhaps unsurprising that in his contributions to public debates in this period, Achebe's tone is marked by a noticeably 'committed' and ambassadorial tone. In a much-quoted address to the Commonwealth Writers Conference in Leeds, England in 1964, for example, he distinguished his position sharply from what he regarded as the prototypical stance of the European writer who is both suspicious of, and an object of suspicion for, his society. For such a writer, he says disparagingly, '[t]he last thing society would dream of doing is to put him in charge of anything'.[40] An African writer such as himself, he argues, must be prepared to assume greater public responsibilities in the task of public 're-education and regeneration'.[41]

In a perverse way, and arguably because of its attractive ideological clarity, this public address made by Achebe in the mid-1960s, and later published under the title 'The Novelist as Teacher', has become one of the most widely reproduced and anthologised of all his critical and political writings. A comparison with the fictional work he was developing at the same time, especially the novel *A Man of the People*, however, shows a contrast of attitude that is very interesting indeed. In his novels, as we will see in the following chapters, we see such a questioning and troubled sensibility that it is almost difficult to believe that they were authored by the same person as texts like this address. Fiction, it seems, was the space where orthodoxy and 'commitment' were allowed to fall away.

In many critical interpretations that try to find a doctrinaire 'cultural nationalist' Achebe, this is the central tension or contradiction within his work that tends to be missed. As I will be arguing in this book, the reason why the development of Achebe's fiction in the 1960s should not be separated from the constraints of his high-profile position with the national broadcaster (as well as his privileged relationship to Heinemann) is not because his creative writing blindly reflects those organisations' priorities and predispositions, but rather because it does not. In the case of *A Man of the People*, what he presents seems to be precisely the image of Nigeria that could *not* be aired on the 'Voice of Nigeria', or offered to schoolchildren as a lesson in liberation struggle. If, in his role as a broadcaster and public commentator, Achebe was constrained to reflect a certain kind of affirmative political agenda in this period, in other words, it is clear that in his fictional writings, he felt no compunction whatsoever to do the same.

This is not to suggest that, within the overarching remit of representing Nigeria in a positive light to the outside world, and working on the understanding that the service should never acknowledge dissent from the country's official foreign policy, Achebe enjoyed no editorial freedom as head of the 'Voice of Nigeria'. A variety of prominent literary and cultural figures were invited onto the air, and the service endeavoured to promote intercultural understanding between Nigeria and the neighbouring countries of West Africa. As Director, one of his prime responsibilities was to recruit and train staff for international placements. Another was to manage the incredible technical challenges of establishing an international broadcasting service with a minimum of equipment in hastily acquired, temporary studios and, for the first two years, a completely inadequate transmission infrastructure. By 1963, some of these initial difficulties had been surmounted and, as MacKay reported:

> The pattern was now emerging. In the planning and content of programmes the NBC tried to publicize the policies, development, culture, and way of life in Nigeria ... Recruitment of qualified staff is always difficult in a multilingual service, particularly on a continent where rapid development in adjoining countries provides many opportunities. NBC concentrated on securing competent Nigerians with professional standards. People who could speak for the nation and be accepted in the country whose audience it wishes to attract.[42]

The driving context of these efforts was clear, however. In 1961, a Bill had been passed restoring formal ownership of the entire NBC to the national government, a radical centralising move which strongly accorded with MacKay's conception of the corporation as a force for promoting national cohesion. Defending his own record in the study *Broadcasting in Nigeria,* he 'unhesitatingly advocates a point of view which I battled for during my service with the NBC. I recall – and reject – the smiling admonition from a friendly Western Region politician who said, "Mr. McKay. You are before your time. The First Nigerian has not been born yet."'[43]

Soon after the publication of *A Man of the People*, the contradictions between Achebe's role as a leading broadcaster and proselytiser of the Nigerian project, and his position as a writer forcing uncomfortable political truths onto the table of public debate, sharply manifested themselves. By the end of 1966 he had resigned from the NBC and returned to Onitsha amid Nigeria's mounting political crisis. Within a few months, war had commenced between the Nigerian Federation and his native East, now self-declared as the sovereign state of Biafra. As we will see in chapter 4, that conflict would propel Achebe to the upper echelons of the new republic, as one of Emeka Ojukwu's most trusted advisers. On 9 July 1967, less than seventy-two hours after the declaration of hostilities, it must have been with bitter irony that Achebe heard the Voice of Nigeria's broadcast to the region:

> A friend in need is a friend indeed. A more suitable adage can hardly be found for measuring the depth of the perfidy of some of Nigeria's so-called friends in the current situation. Foremost on the list of those who want Nigeria divided is the new clique led by Ojukwu. It is clear that without a group of misguided fellow travellers encouraging him, the rebel leader alone could not have singlehandedly embarked upon his hopeless gamble ... But now external forces, some of them old friends of Nigeria, are not only deserting and playing the double game, some have even jumped on the band wagon of the rebel Ojukwu ... Nigeria, however, knows how the minds of these economic exploiters are working.[44]

As Ebele Ume-Nwagbo argues, one of the effects of the outbreak of civil war in relation to the NBC was to demonstrate how completely it had become the media mouthpiece of the Nigerian Federal agenda. During the conflict, courtesy of the British and the Soviets, Nigeria was to enjoy vast superiority of arms over Biafra. It was the infrastructure and culture developed under colonial stewardship and built up by Achebe and his colleagues, however, that facilitated the Federation's equally aggressive campaign for control of the international media agenda. As Ume-Nwagbo suggests, the civil war 'brought to maturity the use of broadcasting by leadership as an instrument of secular and national mobilization'.[45] For the following twenty-five years, all broadcasting in Nigeria was to remain a jealously guarded monopoly of the state government.

The literary and cultural field

In critical introductions to his work, Achebe is routinely presented to students as the 'founding father' of African literature. Before his appearance, readers are encouraged to believe, Africa had been badly represented by colonial writers such as

Joseph Conrad and Joyce Cary; with *Things Fall Apart* in 1958, Achebe broke new ground by presenting things from an African perspective. In this way, according to (for example) David Whitaker and Msiska Mpalive-Hangson, *Things Fall Apart* essentially created the field of postcolonial writing, becoming 'the progenitor of a whole movement in fiction, drama and poetry that focuses on the revaluation of traditional African cultures and the representation of culture conflicts that had their genesis in the colonial era'.[46] According to the critic Nahem Yousaf, similarly, 'Achebe began to create Nigeria's literary landscape in the years preceding Independence in 1960.'[47] Once again, in the critical essay that prefaces *Things Fall Apart* in Heinemann's new 'Classics in Context' edition, we are informed by the influential African American scholar Simon Gikandi that:

> Achebe is that man who invented African Literature because he was able to show, in the structure and language of his first novel, that the future of African writing did not lie in simple imitation of European forms but in the fusion of such forms with oral traditions. Achebe is the conscience of African literature because he has consistently insisted on the power of storytellers to appeal to the morality and humanity of their readers and to give their life fuller meaning.[48]

As I will be arguing here, the assumptions that underpin these assessments of Achebe's significance are deeply unhelpful in terms of positioning his work in literary and cultural terms. Inadvertently, they help to reproduce a Western habit of perception about Africa as a *tabula rasa* or cultural vacuum before Europeans (in this case, Heinemann Books) discovered it. In fact, Heinemann were quite late on the scene. Certainly, interest in recovering and revaluing traditional cultures in Nigeria and elsewhere was a major intellectual preoccupation throughout the period of Achebe's upbringing and education. Publishing, in a variety of forms and genres, and for audiences both local and international, had also been a feature of Nigerian public life since its foundation in the early years of the twentieth century. Among notable literary forerunners, Pita Nwana's *Omenuko*

(1932), published while Achebe was still a small child, is regularly credited with the distinction of pioneering the novel in Igbo. Amos Tutuola's *The Palm Wine Drinkard*, published by Faber in 1952, fused traditional tales drawn from Yoruba orature with European Modernist aesthetics in ways that excited substantial interest and controversy. Cyprian Ekwensi's work, depicting the energies of urban Lagos in a more popular idiom, had established a major fan base in Nigeria before being taken up by the international publisher Longman in 1954. With some notable exceptions, including Niyi Osundere and Stephanie Newell, the mainstream of Achebe criticism has generally failed to recognise the ways in which his work emerges from, rather than 'founding', this already established literary tradition in Nigeria.

In terms of early intertexts for Achebe's work, the first writer to represent Igbo culture widely in print was almost certainly the slave-turned-celebrity Olaudah Equiano, whose autobiographical *The Interesting Life of Olaudah Equiano, or Gustavus Vassa, the African, Written by Himself* became an international bestseller after its publication in 1789. While for more than two centuries, Equiano's work was received as a 'founding' text in representations of slavery and the middle passage, subsequent scholarship cast new questions over it, with the emergence of baptismal and naval records suggesting that, rather than having been born in Igboland and surviving the Middle Passage as his text suggests, Equiano/Vassa may well actually have been born in South Carolina around 1747. Seen in a crude light, such revelations might seem to negate the value of his text. As Vincent Carretta suggests in *Equiano, the African: Biography of a Self-Made Man*, however, in fact this shift in our perception of the narrative's provenance can be seen as deepening and enriching our understanding of his text as a document of its time.[49] In this light, the *Interesting Life* can be seen as occupying an interesting in-between position, seeking to accord dignity and value to a culture with which its author became strongly identified but which he may never have known first hand.

An anti-racist *avant la letter*, Equiano represents the Igbo as a people who, though lacking some of the 'refinements'[50] of

Europe, deserve to be treated as the moral equals of Westerners. At the same time, his articulate performance as a writer works, in itself, to combat contemporary claims associated with such illustrious figures as Thomas Jefferson, principal author of the American *Declaration of Independence*, that blacks were incapable of uttering a thought 'above the level of plain narration'.[51] While he does often represent Africans as the *cultural* inferiors of Europeans, his fundamental contention is that all peoples are morally equal in the sight of God:

> Are there not causes enough to which the apparent inferiority of an African may be ascribed, without limiting the goodness of God, and supposing he forebore to stamp understanding on certainly his own image, because 'carved in ebony?' Might it not naturally be ascribed to their situation? When they come among Europeans, they are ignorant of their language, religion, manners, and customs. Are any pains taken to teach them these? Are they treated as men? Does not slavery itself depress the mind, and extinguish all its fire, and every noble sentiment? But, above all, what advantages do not a refined people possess over those who are rude and uncultivated? Let the polished and haughty European recollect, that *his* ancestors were once, like the Africans, uncivilized, and even barbarous. Did nature make *them* inferior to their sons? [A]nd should *they too* have been made slaves? Every rational mind answers, No.[52]

Regardless of how one assesses the (in some ways opaque) question of his early history, Equiano's writing makes an interesting comparison with Achebe's, in that both traverse an ideological 'middle ground' in which Igbo culture is partly refracted through the lens of Christianity. As critics like Rhonda Cobham have argued, the imprint of biblical motifs – such as the sacrifice of the son in *Things Fall Apart* – is unmistakeable in Achebe's work. For her, Achebe's reading of Igbo culture in his first novel is inextricably shaped by his Christian consciousness and the need to 'find a way of synchronizing the qualities he wishes to represent with the values he has internalized'.[53] In Equiano's portrait of Igbo life, written two centuries before, this hybridisation is even more strongly marked, as the author seeks to represent his ancestral culture in Edenic terms, as an unspoilt haven of Christian values. If in Achebe's novel the alien-ness of polygamy to Christian eyes is softened through his stress on the unique emotional bond between Okonkwo and Ekwefi, Equiano's account of marital customs strongly stresses the fidelity and monogamy of Igbo women, and the 'sacred ... honour of the marriage bed'.[54] If Okonkwo's honest industry is contrasted in Achebe's novel to the laziness and improvidence of his father, Equiano's account is keen to emphasise that 'we are unacquainted with idleness [and] have no beggars'.[55] If the deity Chukwu is characterised in *Things Fall Apart* as, in many ways, analogous to the Christian God-the-Father, in Equiano's work the complexity of Igbo cosmology is trimmed equally violently to fit with monotheistic, European assumptions:

> As to religion, the natives believe that there is one creator of all things, and that he lives in the sun ... They believe that he governs events, especially our deaths or captivity.[56]

Like Achebe's, Equiano's writing is explicitly directed against colonial oppression, especially (in his case) in the form of the Atlantic slave trade. The enthusiastic take-up of Equiano's work by British readers was intimately connected to heightened public interest in relations between Europe and Africa, as debates over the ethical basis of slavery heated up in the late eighteenth century. As Akito Ito points out in an essay on Equiano's work, subscribers to his first self-published edition included the Prince of Wales, the Bishop of London and numerous members of the British aristocracy.[57] Vassa was a popular commentator in London newspapers such as the *Morning Chronicle* and the *Public Advertiser* in the late 1780s, and much of the appeal of the *Interesting Life* to his contemporaries may well be attributable to the skilfulness with which, in framing his own self-presentation as a multiply enslaved, multiply displaced black African, he negotiates the imperialist assumptions of his readership. The nature of Achebe's hybridity is clearly very different from this. Despite being separated by almost two centuries of history, nevertheless, something the two writers share is the way they situate their work in a mediating position between colonised and coloniser, Igbo and Christian culture.

In Achebe's case, growing up within the fold of the Anglican Church Missionary Society, the anthropologist George Basden was undoubtedly a significant early influence. Basden's work in the church was closely associated with that of Achebe's father and he was held in high esteem throughout the Christian community in the Onitsha area. As biographer Ezenwa-Ohaeto records, Basden was Isaiah Achebe's tutor at Akwa College, where the latter trained to be a catechist, and later presided over his wedding to Janet Anaenechi, Chinua Achebe's mother. Basden was, in Ezenwa-Ohaeto's words, 'a welcome visitor and a man to treat with respect in the home of Isaiah Achebe' throughout the author's youth.[58]

As a college student interested in exploring the indigenous culture of his people, reading back over Basden's writings on the Igbo must have been a strange and painful experience for Achebe. Basden's *Among the Ibos of Nigeria: An Account of the Curious and Interesting Habits, Customs and Beliefs of a Little Known African People by One Who Has for Many Years Lived Amongst Them on Close & Intimate Terms* (1921)[59] is a pure sample of colonial anthropology, written with the same distinctive mixture of interest in 'native customs' and unshakeable belief in European superiority found in the work of contemporaries such as Sylvia Leith-Ross, whose *African Women*[60] was published by Faber in 1939. Basden may have been a familiar presence at the Achebe family table, but in his work the idea of Africa's opacity or inaccessibility to the white man, famously explored in Joseph Conrad's *Heart of Darkness*, remains a dominant motif. For him, as for Conrad, there is something inexplicable and threatening in the heart of the African, that turns itself against the European:

> [I]t is a practical impossibility for the European to comprehend fully the subtleties of the native character. Some white men claim to have done this, but my experience leads me to think that the claim can rarely, if ever, be substantiated with definite assurance. The depths may be

sounded at times, but only by accident, and on most of such occasions the inquirer does not recognise that he has actually tapped the inner consciousness of the native. Let not this be thought strange, for the black man himself does not know his own mind. He does the most extraordinary things, and cannot explain why he does them. He is not controlled by logic: he is the victim of circumstance, and his policy is very largely one of drift. The will of the tribe or family, expressed or implied, permeates his whole being, and is the deciding factor in every detail of his life. It is a sort of intangible freemasonry; the essence of the primary instincts of the people. Men constantly act contrary to their better judgment, and, at times, even wrongly, because they firmly believe they have no alternative: they dare not oppose the wishes of their people. Consequently though there may be independent thought, there is seldom independent action, probably never where other members of the tribe or family are involved, however remotely. A further result, and one which must always be borne in mind by the foreign inquirer into primitive customs, is that the ideas of the native are indefinite. He has no fixed thoughts. He is under the influence of an atmosphere which emanates from the whole tribe. This subliminal consciousness, by which all his movements are controlled, becomes practically a sixth sense. It is inexpressible in words but, nevertheless, extremely powerful in action.[61]

Basden's admission that, after seventeen years of anthropological work, he remains 'puzzled'[62] by the Igbo does not, of course, prevent him from expounding on their culture and customs for some 300 pages. In chapter 1, the reader is invited to laugh with him at the violent treatment of Africans on transports along the West African coast, and the excitement of journeying up the swampy Niger Delta. In chapter 2, we are introduced to the British settlement at Onitsha, still at the time of his arrival 'an attractive field for investigation in which the native could be studied in his primitive environment'.[63] One can only imagine Achebe's response as a young man, reading Basden's accounts of his adventures into the surrounding area, replete with their sensationalist claims that 'cannibalism, human sacrifices and other savage customs were real facts, and flourished within five miles of the outskirts of Onitsha'.[64] As an anthropologist but also a missionary, Basden's work oscillates interestingly between a tone of paternalist conservationism in relation to traditional culture, and outright celebration of its progressive erasure by colonialism. He applauds the progress made by Lugard's administration towards the 'complete upheaval of the political, economical and social affairs of the country. Every native institution has been shaken to its foundations.'[65] No other people, he argues, has been 'shrouded in so much mystery, or held in thrall by such powers of darkness',[66] and clearly, on one level, it is this occult fantasy that appeals to his evangelising consciousness. As a missionary, his own role is clear: that of leading the Igbo 'out of darkness and into light, and from the power of Satan unto God'.[67]

There can be little doubt, then, that Achebe's encounter with Basden's work while he was a student at University College Ibadan must have been difficult. At that time, however ignorant and misplaced in its judgements and assumptions, Basden's representation of the Igbo had come to be regarded as authoritative. To any reader without independent knowledge of the region or of Africa, his portraits of a people whose members included Achebe's own parents and grandparents might easily have been assumed to be faithful ones. In this sense, for the young Achebe, the impulse to expose and debunk his work must have been a powerful one. Although the figure of Basden may have informed his drawing of such characters as Mr Brown and/or the District Commissioner (an amateur anthropologist) in *Things Fall Apart*, Achebe's comments in interview suggest, however, that he provided just one of a range of sources and inspirations for the author's early fiction.

Among previous critics of Achebe's work, there has been considerable useful discussion of the importance of such colonial fictions as Joyce Cary's *Mister Johnson* (1939), with its caricatured portrayal of the African-as-buffoon. C. L. Innes' *Chinua Achebe* is a particularly notable study in this respect.[68] Joseph Conrad's 1899 novella *Heart of Darkness* is also a frequently cited intertext. Achebe's own commentary in the essay 'An Image of Africa' highlights what he succinctly calls the 'bloody racist' tendencies of Conrad's narrative, in which Africans are unrelentingly represented in crude and animalistic ways.[69] Probably an equal or greater influence which is seldom acknowledged, however, can be found in the upsurge of historical and archaeological research among Nigerians themselves, while Achebe was a young man, aimed at capturing the traces of vanished and vanishing indigenous traditions. If such colonial works as Sylvia Leith-Ross's *African Women* claimed of the Igbo that 'starting at scratch, they have nothing to unload ... no traditions',[70] formal and informal research by many of Achebe's contemporaries was in the process of building a raft of evidence to the contrary. In important ways, I would argue, Achebe's work needs to be seen not just in terms of, but as a contribution to, that collective effort.

Within academic institutions including University College Ibadan, the discipline of History was undergoing a process of radical re-evaluation. As early as 1951, while Achebe was still studying for his degree, one of Ibadan's most influential historians , Kenneth Onwuka Dike, had embarked on a comprehensive survey of documents in the possession of the colonial government, with the aim of establishing a state archive to support scholarly work on the cultural heritage of Nigeria's regions.[71] His recommendations provided the key impetus for the founding of the Nigerian Records Office in 1954 and the National Archive itself in 1958. Dike's seminal *Trade and Politics in the Niger Delta, 1830–1885*,[72] completed in 1950 and published in 1956, offered a powerful riposte to colonial historiography which tended, firstly, to focus exclusively on European expansion in Africa and, secondly, to perpetuate the myth that Africans themselves had no history worth exploring. As Toyin Falola says in *Nationalism and African Intellectuals*:

> If the Europeans had presented Taubman Goldie as 'the maker of Nigeria,' Dike would present him as the 'maker' only of the Royal Niger Company ... If Europeans had presented Jaja of Opobo as a Nigerian chief who stood in the way of free trade, Dike and others would present him as a resistance hero, a patriot who did not want the British to cheat him in trade and deny him power.[73]

For Falola, the work of Dike and his contemporaries was instrumental in challenging the orthodoxies that had informed history teaching in Nigeria throughout the period of high colonialism.

One of the more disquieting conclusions presented by Dike's survey of colonial records, conducted between 1951 and 1953, was that the British administration in Nigeria had been far from responsible in their approach to preserving historical documents. In the late 1930s, the colonial governor had ordered a mass destruction of records on at least one occasion and incredibly, as Falola and Aderinto write in their study *Nigeria, Nationalism, and Writing History*, the Director of the Geological Survey Department had destroyed all documents apart from a core of financial records:

> Certainly, the poor state of government records is explicable in terms of lax administrative procedure and administrators' poor historical consciousness; the majority of these officials did not see such documents as integral components of the historical and cultural heritage of the colonial state ... Documents of great historical value were consistently destroyed or kept in conditions that allowed them to be highly susceptible to damage ... It was Dike's Records Survey that opened the eyes of the British colonial government to the extent and degree of ruin that had befallen the nation's valuable historical documents.[74]

Researchers working in the archives, whether amateur or professional, were forced to cope with these huge gaps and deficiencies as a matter of course, and it is unsurprising that alternative methods of documenting cultural heritage, especially from oral history, became very popular. As a student and, later, as a broadcaster working for the NBC, Achebe would have been highly aware of these developments in the historical excavation of Nigeria's indigenous cultures. Indeed in 1956, as we saw earlier, the Talks Department produced an entire radio series with Dike, exploring the history of British rule in Nigeria.

Other reclamation projects which attracted significant public interest and support included the archaeological investigations made by Thurston Shaw for the Nigerian Department of Antiquities at the site of the ancient Igbo civilisation at Nri, from the late 1950s. Artefacts of remarkable artistry and sophistication of manufacture were dated to around the ninth century, using radiocarbon dating techniques.[75] Among Achebe's contemporaries, then, many had developing interests in questions of heritage and the representation of 'native' culture. Among these, a significant influence on Achebe was Adielo Afigbo who, having studied at Ibadan alongside him, went on to write a PhD there on the infamous policy of 'indirect rule' in Eastern Nigeria under Lord Lugard. As Robert Wren suggests, Afigbo's scholarship undoubtedly provides one of the most important intertexts for understanding *Arrow of God* in particular. His PhD was presented in 1964, the same year that Achebe published the novel, and as chapter 3 will show, it is interesting to compare the two books, written in the very different idioms of historical exposition and imaginative fiction respectively. Both explore, in revealing detail, the consequences of Lugard's mis-applied policy of indirect rule on Igbo communities. Afigbo's later work, much of it published after Achebe's, went on to illuminate the contexts of Igbo history in provocative and revealing ways. One notable study lays out extensive evidence of British tolerance towards the slave system, which continued to operate in a number of enclaves throughout the South East, as late as the 1940s.[76]

As Wren notes, the development of academic historiography associated with such figures as Dike and Afigbo comprises only a part of the surge of interest in questions of heritage and reclamation at the time Achebe was emerging as a novelist, however. The 1950s and 1960s also saw an exponential growth of interest in amateur history throughout Nigeria. Much of this work employed ethnographic research methods, including interviews with village elders, aimed at capturing detail about 'traditional' culture in the environs of the author's home village. The thriving culture of pamphlet production in regional centres like Onitsha ensured a life and readership for such work. By 1970, as Wren confirms from his own research, oral historiography of this type had re-crossed back to the academic domain, becoming a feature of the university curriculum, with undergraduates asked to compile histories of their own ancestral communities.

Arinze Ernest Agbogu's researches on the history of Ogidi at the end of the nineteenth century provide one key source for Wren's own work on the historical and cultural contexts to Achebe's writing.

Publishing: the making of Chinua Achebe

As Stephanie Newell says in her study *West African Literatures*,[77] by the time of Achebe's appearance on the literary scene there was already a well-established tradition of fiction publishing in West Africa, albeit not necessarily in a form amenable to large-scale commercial distribution. Among the most celebrated centres for indigenous writing was Onitsha, a city on the Niger about six miles from Achebe's home village of Ogidi. For the author as a child, Onitsha was 'a magical place'.[78] Walking there from home at the age of ten was, as he writes, something 'looked forward to so eagerly and which I cherished'.[79] Popular authors of Onitsha market literature, writing to a predominantly young male readership, often included titillating sexual material in their works, whether or not combined with some form of moral exhortation. As Newell notes, female (as opposed to male) sexual predators are a recurring presence, and much room is given to airing the anxieties of the new class of literate, educated young men who inhabited Nigeria's urban centres. In the 1940s and 1950s, this literature was supplemented by Indian romance fictions written in English, which also enjoyed a wide readership. 'As early as 1937', Newell reports, 'adverts on the front pages of West African newspapers read, "This book offers *Sex Secrets* to men and women married or unmarried! No such book has ever been offered to the public! Secrets hitherto known only by doctors now laid bare to all!" (*African Morning Post*, 3 Dec 1937).'[80] Fiction published in Igbo, including Pita Nwana's *Omenuko* (1932)[81] and D. N. Achara's *Ala Bingo*,[82] had also built up an established readership by the 1950s. After independence *Omenuko* was to become, like *Things Fall Apart*, a staple of the school curriculum. Other writers, notably Cyprian Ekwensi, found themselves able to bridge the gap between local and international publishing some years before the appearance of *Things Fall Apart*. Having established a strong reputation with such fictions as *When Love Whispers*,[83] published in Yaba, Nigeria in 1948, Ekwensi went on to garner international attention with his *People of the City* (1954),[84] partly thanks to the distribution opportunities made available by the London firm Andrew Dakers.

For Newell, the canonical status accorded to Achebe's *Things Fall Apart* by Western critics as the 'founding' or 'original' African novel tends to obscure the complexity and variety of the literary scene in this period. In particular, the rush to identify Achebe's text as the seminal expression of 'writing back' to the colonial centre has had a significant, distorting effect on critics' perception of the cultural field from which his work emerges:

> Critics have tended to condense the decades before Achebe's emergence into an expectant, Achebe-shaped pause. Indeed, in some cases, commentators have used *Things Fall Apart* to dismiss Achebe's predecessors as irrelevant, flawed, or half-fledged as writers ... If elite authors in the empire were 'writing back' to the colonial centre at this time, as Ashcroft, Griffiths and Tiffin claim for 'first generation' authors such as Achebe, many other West African writers were also writing novels, poems and plays for their own local communities, not primarily for metropolitan markets ... The Yoruba novelist, D. O. Fagunwa, who gained fame among Yoruba Nigerians for his work in the 1930s and 1940s, exemplifies the localism of this literature. Fagunwa's style of writing in the 1930s and 1940s inspired later international novelists, including Amos Tutuola, whose *The Palm-Wine Drinkard* drew many themes from Yoruba-language texts and tales ... Published six years before Achebe's anti-colonial *Things Fall Apart*, Tutuola's novel breaks all the rules set in place by the theory of 'writing back,' and for that reason it has failed to achieve recognition from critics until recently. Yet Tutuola was of the same literary generation as Achebe and his work offers a fascinating counterpart – or counterpoint – to the 'postcolonial' themes of his better-known compatriot ... Unfortunately, however, the 'starter' status conferred on

> *Things Fall Apart* tends to obscure the literary contexts in which Achebe was situated when he started to write.[85]

For Newell, what is remarkable about *Things Fall Apart* from a cultural point of view is how it seemed to be able to speak to an international readership in a way it could 'hear and relate to'.[86] Its project of cultural reclamation and defiance of engrained colonial assumptions about Africa are framed, for her, in a form which accords with, rather than disturbing, European literary expectations. As she argues, '*Things Fall Apart* directly addresses the "unspoken", or "written upon" condition of Africa in relation to Europe. Other West African writers have no such interest in Europe or colonial history. Precisely these writers are hidden by the long shadow of Achebe's short novel over postcolonial literary studies.'[87]

The relationship of Tutuola's work to the colonial, anthropologising gaze does seem to me to be quite different from that of Achebe's, but not entirely in the way Newell suggests here. Indeed, in Nigeria itself, *The Palm Wine Drinkard* was denounced by critics for the way it seemed to pander to the very stereotypes of Africans they wanted to see challenged. In Europe and America, on the other hand, it was widely celebrated for its African 'primitiveness' and 'authenticity'. For Tutuola's London publisher Faber and Faber, as the critic Gail Low observes, the key concern with Tutuola's writing was establishing whether it was 'genuine' in its apparent naïveté.[88] Instead of sending his manuscript to critical readers, as would have been standard practice with literary manuscripts, Faber sought the advice of a professional anthropologist, Daryll Forde. As Geoffrey Faber wrote to Forde on 15 March 1951:

> We have had submitted to us a highly unusual MS about which we are anxious to get a line from an anthropologist familiar with the workings of the West African imagination. [...] It is a long rambling ghost, spook and juju story by a West African native. [...] We think it possible that it might conceivably have something of a success if published here. But we should like to know whether it has its roots in *the common West African mind*.[89]

As Low reports, correspondence from the Faber archive indicates clearly that Tutuola's novel was considered by the publisher primarily as an anthropological curiosity, rather than as a serious work of literature. In a negotiation with the US publisher Norton, Director Peter du Sautoy characterised the novel as the 'unsophisticated product of a West African mind'.[90] Revealingly, when Tutuola requested that Faber proof his work to weed out irregularities in spelling and grammar, they were resistant, preferring to leave the text in an unpolished condition that, for any of their European writers, would have been regarded as amateurish. As Low's research shows moreover, even the title of Tutuola's book was altered by Faber – from *The Palm Wine Drinker* in his original manuscript to the irregular *The Palm Wine Drinkard*, which, it was felt by du Sautoy, would appear 'more colourful' to the reader.[91]

From the evidence provided by Alan Hill, the publishing entrepreneur who founded the African Writers Series, the relationship between Achebe and Heinemann was very different from that between Tutuola and Faber:

> We published Chinua Achebe's *Things Fall Apart* on 17 June 1958, in a modest edition of 2,000 copies. It achieved instant acclaim in the British national press, with enthusiastic reviews by such critics as Walter Allen and Angus Wilson. The book came as a revelation to many of my colleagues in Britain, whose opinion of Africans as writers had been influenced by the works of Amos Tutuola – particularly his quaintly-told allegorical fantasies of Yoruba folk tales. I remember Fred Warburg telling me that Tutuola's *The Palm Wine Drinkard* (published in 1952 by Faber) was the only sort of African book that he would want on the Secker & Warburg list, as 'it represented the real Africa'. For this very reason, Tutuola's work was anathema to many educated Nigerians – to whom his linguistic virtuosity seemed plain illiteracy. In *Things Fall Apart* we now had something entirely new from Africa: a novel which affirmed permanent human and social values in the context of a traditional tribal society in crisis, and which expressed those values in terms which the Western-educated reader could understand.[92]

In fact, Hill's account of *Things Fall Apart*'s critical reception in Britain is somewhat selective – prominent critics were by no means unanimous in their assessments. Writing in *The Listener*, for example, Honor Tracy congratulates Achebe for avoiding 'the dandyism often affected by Negro authors' but describes his critique of colonialism as ultimately 'facile'.[93] For her, Achebe's 'nostalgia for what was swept away' is 'mere sentimentality. It would be pleasant to know how many of the bright negro barristers of our acquaintance, with their devotion to African culture, really wish they were back in those serviceable raffia skirts, tending the yams and keeping a sharp look-out for a demon or a witch. Would Mr Chinua himself, for that matter, prefer it ...?'[94] Even the *Times Literary Supplement* reviewer, who Hill quotes selectively, suspected the novel of some kind of hypocrisy, arguing that the novel's 'fascinating' representation of tribal society was weakened by its 'confusion of attitude' towards the arrival of missionaries in Africa.[95]

For Heinemann, too, Achebe's novel was initially the subject of some doubt. As the author recalls in a 2009 interview with David Chioni Moore and Analee Heath, initially the publisher 'seemed to me very quiet about the book. They were actually thinking of ending the title after the first print run of 2,000.'[96] Under Alan Hill's influence, however, it soon began to appear to them in a very different light. What Achebe came to represent for them – very differently from either Tutuola or Ekwensi – was a model of writing which could cater effectively to the tastes and assumptions of the European literary establishment, while *simultaneously* conveying a distinctively African sensibility capable of gaining credibility in the eyes of African readers. At that point, as Hill makes clear, if Achebe was recognised by Heinemann as a serious literary talent, he also began to be recognised as an outstanding business opportunity. In the late 1950s and 1960s, as a succession of nations gained independence for their former colonisers, the book market – especially in the educational field – was changing rapidly. As Hill saw, homegrown talent would be needed to reshape the content of school and college curricula, and there was money to be made by the publisher who could both attract these writers to its list and offer the necessary infrastructure for mass production and distribution of their work. Even before *Things Fall Apart* had established itself as a success in the African market, Hill began planning the enterprise that would take form as the African Writers Series, and secure both Achebe's and his own place in the history of publishing:

> It was now clear to me that I should visit Africa, in particular West Africa – and for more than one reason. Achebe was not an isolated phenomenon. He was a product of the newly-established University of Ibadan which – soon to be followed by other universities – was creating a new intellectual dimension in the life of West Africa. Then again, our new school books, particularly in science, were selling in large quantities in Nigeria ... At that time, Ghana under Nkrumah (whom I was later to publish) was in the first flush of independence – a country full of excitement and hope for the future. Nigeria similarly was in its run-up to independence the following year. Oil had not yet been discovered; Nigeria was still a traditional society, predominantly rural. The book trade in both countries had been for many years dominated by the two British publishing houses of Oxford University Press and Longman, with a few other publishers – particularly Nelson, Evans and Macmillan – claiming a share. The trade had grown up on the back of the imported European educational system – initially the mission schools, one of which my grandfather founded in the Cameroons. After the First World War the Colonial Office set up government secondary schools in Ghana and Nigeria. By the time I reached West Africa there was a flourishing school system, leading to British O and A Level examinations, and culminating in the new Universities of Accra and Ibadan. As I now discovered, the big British publishers regarded West Africa only as a place where you sold books, not where you published them ... [This] seemed to be commercially short-sighted. I determined to make an entirely new start – to show that on the basis of our African schoolbook business we could provide a publishing service for African authors. The time was

ripe. There must be other writers comparable to Achebe, awaiting a publisher with the confidence and resources to launch them on a world-wide market ... The plan was to start a paperback series, confined to black African authors; the books were to be attractively designed with high quality production, and sold at a very cheap price – as low as 25p at the outset. This price was achieved by giving small educational discounts. Since the African bookshops sold nothing but educational books, the mass market outlets were already there on these terms. Outside Africa, the books would sell at normal trade paperback terms. Secondly I needed a general editor 'on the ground'. There was one obvious choice. I sent Tony Beal out to Nigeria to offer the job to Chinua Achebe. He accepted, and we were in business. His role was crucial. Not only did he read every MS, in some cases undertaking editorial work, but he would identify good new authors for the Series.[97]

As Clive Barnett argues in a revealing account of the development of the African Writers Series,[98] literary writers in Africa typically found themselves battling on two fronts in the late 1950s. On the one hand, they faced the patronising and exclusionary attitudes of the colonial literary establishment, and on the other hand, they had to negotiate the popular association of 'high' literary forms in general with elitism and cultural imperialism. For Barnett, the African Writers Series was particularly radical in its address to this twin challenge. By making a wide variety of high quality African writing available to metropolitan readerships, it reversed the cultural model that had defined colonial publishers' practices until that time. At the same time, it explicitly aimed to supplant the canon of older, colonial writing that had formed the core of the education agenda before independence.

In important ways, I would suggest, Achebe's involvement with Heinemann was to have a fundamental shaping effect on the reception of his own work and that of other authors. Undoubtedly, the African Writers Series gave him immense status, as the gatekeeper to international recognition for a generation of African writing. Through the highly successful efforts of Heinemann Educational Books to establish relationships with ministries of education and associated examination boards, the series also gave him access to book sales which dwarfed the experience of previous writers. However, Achebe's intimate relationship with the publishing agenda of Heinemann Educational Books can also be said to have shaped and constrained his relationship to African writing in other ways. Crucially, Heinemann Educational Books (as its name suggests) was an *educational* publisher. Its entire commissioning and marketing strategy in Africa was defined by the imperative of offering works by African authors to national and regional education systems in a form amenable for use in the post-independence classroom.

Much has been made by critics of the 1962 conference at Makerere University College, Uganda, at which Achebe and other writers were challenged by the critic Obi Wali on their use and promotion of English as the privileged means of expression for African writing.[99] Wali's central contention was that a literature which, in its every utterance, worked to entrench the hegemony of the colonial tongue, must be seen as an aesthetic and political dead end. As the evidence of the Heinemann archive shows, however, from an international publishing standpoint this entire debate was a non-starter. From the point of view of establishing the African Writers Series as a successful venture, the view of the company was that English was the only commercially viable medium to publish in. Even as late as the mid-1970s, proposals to publish in vernacular African languages were seen as 'very risky ... because it was impossible to keep costs down in the absence of a realistic expectation that books would be adopted on examination curricula', when most African states had opted to 'construct a version of nationalist education in which English [or another colonial language] was privileged as the medium of instruction'.[100]

At the 1962 conference, Achebe set out the first of two basic positions that have dominated critical assessments of his work since:

> [T]he national literature of Nigeria and of many other countries of Africa is, or will be, written in English. This

may sound like a controversial statement, but it isn't. All I have done has been to look at the reality of present-day Africa. This 'reality' may change as a result of deliberate, e.g. political, action. If it does an entirely new situation will arise, and there will be plenty of time to examine it. At present it may be more profitable to look at the scene as it is.[101]

In 1964, at the first Commonwealth Literature conference at the University of Leeds in England, he set out the other position. His address 'The Novelist as Teacher', to which I referred earlier, explicitly identifies school and college students as his primary readership, and goes on to characterise his own role as that of an educator:

> The writer cannot expect to be excused from the task of re-education and regeneration that must be done. In fact, he should march right in front ... I for one would not wish to be excused. I would be quite happy if my novels (especially the ones I set in the past) did no more than teach my readers that their past – with all its imperfections – was not one long night of savagery from which the first Europeans acting on God's behalf delivered them. Perhaps what I write is applied art as distinct from pure. But who cares? Art is important, but so is education of the kind I have in mind.[102]

From Barnett's researches in the Heinemann archives, it is not difficult to see that the critical positions taken up by Achebe at these two, defining public events are inextricable from his commitment to Heinemann Educational Books and the African Writers Series as a publishing venture. Contrary to Obi Wali's contention, it was not subservience to colonial culture that ensured the series' commitment to English as the privileged language of expression for Nigerian writers after independence, but the commercial logic of school and college markets whose curricula were designed along national and regional rather than along ethnic lines. Similarly, if in statements such as 'The Novelist as Teacher' Achebe was willing to present his work in (unfashionably) didactic, pedagogic terms, this must be viewed in the context of his enormous and growing stake in Heinemann's ambitious project, to supplant the European and American canon which had hitherto dominated the educational agenda, with works produced by Africans themselves.

For the avoidance of doubt, I am far from suggesting that this was not, in its own terms, a laudable aim. As a strategy, it was certainly a successful one for Heinemann Educational books, which under Alan Hill's direction was to become the largest educational publisher in the Commonwealth. As the publisher James Currey illustrates in his own account of involvement with the series, moreover, the project was by no means solely concerned with commissioning new writing. A key aim was also to acquire the rights to highly recognised existing work, for direct incorporation into the new canon that the series was designed to embody. In Currey's eyes, indeed, a key achievement of Achebe and his colleague Aigboje Higo, Director of Heinemann Educational Books in Nigeria, was not so much that they spotted and nurtured new talent, but that they 'captured, against several longer-established publishing rivals, many of the outstanding authors'.[103]

There is plenty of evidence that Achebe used his influence as General Editor of the African Writers Series to publish and promote a range and diversity of new writing by Africans that would not have been considered by Currey and his London colleagues without his influence. In this, the strength of sales of his own books on the education market – frequently accounting for half the series' profits – undoubtedly provided the 'moral' foundation for his insistence on keeping the series experimental and inclusive. James Curry, who at the time of the series' launch was working for one of Heinemann's rivals, recalls the incredulity of London publishers towards the idea that this approach could be combined with commercial success. 'When the Series was started', he writes, 'it could not be foreseen that the secondary-school examination boards would prescribe books by young living Africans. The exam boards were still based in Cambridge, London and Durham. Like Oxford University Press, they preferred their authors dead.'[104] However, as he goes on to say:

> [I]n the heady years of independence, new examination boards were set up in Africa. WAEC – 'Wayec' as everybody came to call it – was the West African Examinations Council for Nigeria, Ghana, Gambia and Sierra Leone. EAEC was the East African Examinations Council for Kenya, Uganda and Tanzania. We did not know that the examiners would so delight in raiding the African Writers Series to prescribe texts. In this they were far more adventurous than the English boards, where Gerard Manley Hopkins was as close as they got to a modern poet. Chinua Achebe's encouragement of Heinemann to experiment paid off in a way that we London publishers, who had grown up among the dead poets of the English educational system, had never imagined it could.[105]

As Clive Barnett argues, the importance of the African Writers Series for Heinemann Educational Books went considerably beyond the book sales it accumulated. Under Achebe's editorial influence it also came to stand as a guarantee of Heinemann's long-term credibility with post-independence regimes in Africa. As late as 1994, the corporate view from Heinemann on the commercial significance of the series was that 'the *AWS* is a backlist-led list. Chinua Achebe is perceived as the most important author on our list by the outside world. As publishers of this list we have entry to African educational markets and a kudos that other multinational do not have.'[106] Similarly in 1996, it was the view of executives that:

> As the publisher of the African Writers Series we have entry into Ministries and a reputation and esteem in Africa which far exceeds our current market position. To stop publishing the series would have a huge negative effect and make entry into local publishing agreements much harder. We would be viewed as just another multinational but without the infrastructure and contacts that companies like Macmillan and Longman have.[107]

Certainly, there were concerted efforts by Africans to wrest control of publishing from large internationals during the 1960s, and Achebe himself was involved with many of these.

Well before the establishment of the African Writers Series, as we have seen, there was an active publishing scene in several cultural centres, including Onitsha. During Achebe's time at University College Ibadan, as Bernth Lindfors has shown, there was a vigorous culture of small-scale, collaborative publishing, which functioned as a proving ground for many subsequently influential writers.[108] From before Achebe was born, nationalist newspapers had given space to literary contributions by Nigerian writers alongside current affairs and, after the Second World War, the tradition of juxtaposing literature, critical commentary and journalistic features continued in such periodicals as *The West Africa Review*. In the late 1950s, the appearance of the major literary magazine *Black Orpheus* provided an important new focus point for promoting the production and discussion of black writing.

In July 1961, however, perhaps the most significant development in independent literary publishing in Nigeria occurred with the foundation of the Mbari Artists and Writers Club in Ibadan. Convened by Ulli Beier and Wole Soyinka, with other influential figures including Achebe closely involved, the Mbari Club aimed to provide a platform for dialogue and creativity, on a basis categorically different from the conception of international promoters such as Alan Hill. As Toyin Adepoju writes, the club 'drew on the aesthetics of organic dissolution and regeneration represented by the Mbari art of the Ibo of Southern Nigeria, who created works of art only to let them decay and decompose, awaiting another season of creation. Coming to birth in the flux of the preindependence and immediate postindependence period in Nigeria, it brought together a constellation of artists whose work embodied the quality of transformation ... evoked by the Mbari tradition.'[109] As Abdul Yesufu suggests, the presence of the Mbari Club and its associated publishing arm Mbari Publications was that it offered Nigerians and other writers a platform for presenting their work to a wide audience, without being tied to the agendas and priorities of the large international firms based in London and Paris.[110] In practice, however, the initiative was to remain productive for only four years. Rights to works by key writers such as Alex la Guma, Wole Soyinka and Christopher Okigbo were bought up by Heinemann, Oxford University Press and others, and the contrast between the long-term fortunes of Mbari Publications and the African Writers Series was a sharp one. In the eyes of James Currey, this could be attributed principally to one factor: Heinemann's strategic dominance of the education market. Without a lucrative education list and agreements guaranteeing regular adoption of titles as required reading for school and college students, Mbari lacked the financial muscle to rival the London firm's machinery for marketing and distribution. In one sense, of course, Currey's commentary here misses the obvious: that the relationship between creativity, transience and organicity that Mbari celebrated is almost antithetical to the imperative of 'market dominance' within which he sees the achievements of the African Writers Series. On another level, however, it usefully underscores the extent to which Achebe's own success in this period – including his efforts to promote a variety of new writing through the series itself – was entangled with commercial imperatives in international educational publishing towards which he must have felt a great deal of ambivalence.

As this book will argue, the terms within which his early work has too often been framed, marketed and taught – usually alongside essays like 'English and the African Writer' and 'The Novelist as Teacher' – tends to entirely miss that complexity. As a public intellectual whose emergence at the end of the 1950s became closely associated with ideas of resistance and independence, ironically Achebe himself was far from being a free agent. He was a broadcaster paid to produce programming that celebrated the One-Nigeria ideal favoured by his employer, the Nigerian Broadcasting Corporation, and its colonial founders. He was a writer and editor working with the international firm Heinemann, which offered him unprecedented cultural opportunities, but also further constraints. As we will see in the following chapters, Achebe did find a means of escape from these pressures and demands – ideological, commercial and pragmatic. That was, of course, through his fictional works themselves. Far from proselytising for one-nation Nigeria or producing formulaic models of liberation struggle for convenient use in schools, these are troubled and disturbing texts that are the opposite of programmatic. Perhaps now, after his death, we can begin to see the totality of his work in all its boldness and non-conformity.

2

Things Fall Apart and *No Longer at Ease*

At the time that *Things Fall Apart* appeared in 1958, Achebe was already a major figure in the Nigerian media. The organisation he worked for, the Nigerian Broadcasting Corporation, was a highly political one, focused on promoting a particular model of independence – the One-Nigeria model – that favoured the interests of its British expatriate management. Rapidly elevated to a senior executive position, Achebe's assigned role was to produce programming that would represent Nigeria in an attractive and harmonious way to its divided and sceptical public. In his early fiction, however, we are offered a very different view. The Nigeria we glimpse there, under construction in *Things Fall Apart* and approaching self-government in *No Longer at Ease*, appears as the weak, bastard offspring of traditional culture and British colonialism, displaying none of the youthful vigour or endless promise projected by the NBC. If the nation has inherited a distinctive characteristic from its unhappy parentage, we learn in these novels, it is corrosive and in-growing corruption. Far from offering a nationalist testimonial for his country, as many have too-quickly assumed, these fictional writings represent a scandalously bleak and uncompromising assessment of the outlook for the Nigerian national project. Written and published at the very moment when his country's push towards independence was reaching fruition, they are an extraordinary, disquieting response to their times.

According to many critics who have written on his work, nationalism is the key that unlocks Achebe fiction. In *Reading Chinua Achebe*, for example, what Simon Gikandi finds at the core of Achebe's novels is a grand 'master narrative' of Nigeria's self-becoming as a nation.[1] Achebe is, Gikandi claims, 'the first of our writers to recognise the function of the novel not solely as a mode of representing reality, but one which had limitless possibilities of inventing a new national community'.[2] For Nahem Yousaf, similarly, 'Achebe is a cultural nationalist whose fiction rests on a Fanonian belief that writing is a cornerstone of national culture.'[3] According to Francis Ngaboh-Smart, going further, '[a]ny discussion of nationalist reconstruction of identity should take *Things Fall Apart* as its starting point'.[4] In actuality, as we saw in chapter 1, there is little evidence to suggest that by temperament or conviction Achebe was ever a nationalist of any kind, even during his youth and young adulthood. Moreover, there is nothing odd or surprising in this. When we consider Nigeria's journey through independence in the late 1950s and early 1960s, it is clear that by far the strongest and most consistent voice for the one-nation agenda was not the general population of Nigeria or even their representatives in the regions, but the departing British themselves. When at the age of twenty-three Achebe was offered the role of Talks Producer for the state broadcaster – a position that placed him at the centre of the cultural and media scene in Lagos – it is hardly surprising that he grasped the opportunity with both hands. Yes, employment with the NBC implied conforming to a particular editorial line in political and ideological terms. In the face of growing ethnic and regionalist sentiment throughout Nigeria, the broadcaster's key role as perceived by government was to wave a flag for the one-nation politics to which its British management were committed. In the world of his fiction, however, it is clear that Achebe did not see the same rules as applying and in *Things Fall Apart* and *No Longer at Ease*, there is no sign at all of subservience to the NBC's nationalist and integrationist agenda. As we will see, the work certainly does imply a scathing critique of colonialism and, in certain respects, of course this suggests a commonality with themes in the nationalist campaign for independence spearheaded by Nnamdi Azikiwe and others. The novels are also clearly concerned with reclamation, another emphasis of nationalist campaigns across the colonised world. To therefore hitch Achebe's *oeuvre* to a nationalist agenda, however, is to look for a form of ideological commitment that the novels simply do not support. As I will suggest in this chapter, as soon as Achebe's relationship to the Nigerian national project is properly examined, the 'cultural nationalist' approach to his *oeuvre* that has become a *de facto* orthodoxy over the past few decades loses much of its explanatory power. It becomes necessary to find a different way of reading Achebe's early novels and the ways they fit into his larger project.

'In my hometown, Ogidi, we have a saying', Achebe writes in *The Education of a British-Protected Child*. '*Ikpe Ogidi adi-ama ofu onye:* The judgement of Ogidi does not go against one side. We are social managers rather than legal draftsmen. Our workplace is not a neat tabletop but a messy workshop.'[5] The inference of this, if taken as a guide to reading Achebe's fictional works, might seem to be that in historical matters, he regarded himself as taking a detached and non-judgemental approach. In relation to his refusal to toe any orthodox political line, I would certainly agree that this is true in *Things Fall Apart* and *No Longer at Ease*. With regard to the colonial occupation of Igboland and the costs of Britain's Nigerian project, he is certainly not afraid to lay out damaging evidence for inspection. As he writes, unambiguously, 'it is a gross crime for anyone to impose himself on another, to seize his land and his history, and then to compound this by making out that the victim is some kind of ward or minor requiring protection'.[6] Recognising Achebe's effectiveness in stripping bare the iniquities of colonialism, however, does not therefore entitle us to align him with an opposing (that is, nationalist) ideological programme. Indeed, to do so is to ignore Achebe's fundamental approach to fiction writing which, in attempting to reflect the dialogic ethic of Igbo culture itself, resists that kind of ideological closure as a matter of course.

In the essay 'Named for Victoria, Queen of England', he describes the experience of being raised in the orbit of the Church Missionary Society, who regarded the society around them as primitive and worthless. As a boy, he grew up in a condition of estrangement from traditional culture, reading works of European literature and regarding Western inventions, such as the motor car, as the height of sophistication. Later, when he came to re-evaluate that legacy, he describes the writing of his first novel *Things Fall Apart* as 'an act of atonement with my past'.[7] As I will show, however, the form of this 'atonement' through fiction is by no means that of evangelising either for Nigeria or (for that matter) Igbo nationhood. The focus of these works, rather, is bearing witness to the damage wrought by colonialism, in the past and in the present, and the ways it wrecked the possibility for organic cultural development.

Achebe's Okonkwo saga

Achebe made his first attempt at a full-length novel while living in Lagos and working for the NBC. It was a weighty and ambitious narrative tracing three generations of an Igbo family, and their struggles to negotiate the successive challenges of colonial rule. Historically, the saga spans the entire period of Nigerian nation-building, from around the time of the 1884–85 Berlin conference, when European powers resolved to formalise their control of Africa, to the eve of independence at the beginning of the 1960s. Within Achebe's narrative – which was later split into two novels, as we will see – a central parallel is drawn between two main protagonists, grandfather Ogbuefi Okonkwo and his grandson Obi.

In the opening section, we see Okonkwo in a pre-colonial setting with his son Nwoye, at a moment when the practices and value-system of the Igbo clan system have yet to be disrupted by the European invasion. In Achebe's portrayal, the clan is not isolated, but lives in a state of equilibrium and relative harmony that, it is suggested, has been sustained through generations going back beyond the reach of human memory. In its way, the village of Umuofia presents quite a pugnacious image, and is feared by its neighbours. 'It was powerful in war and in magic, and its priests and medicine men were feared in all the surrounding country'.[8] Conflicts with neighbouring clans, however, are small-scale, the occasion for proving one's masculinity, as Okonkwo has done.

Although he has taken several human heads in his career, and even drinks from one of them on festive occasions, Okonkwo's own, notably aggressive instincts are held in check by moderating voices among his fellows. Within the community itself, there is room for diversity: while Okonkwo himself is a strong man, with a barn full of yams and a large compound that he rules through fear, his father Unoka was a lover of music and palm wine, who took matters of social status less seriously. Okonkwo's reputation as a fighter has 'grown like a bush-fire in the harmattan' (*TFA*, 3), but he also has a stammer and struggles to express himself when angry. Through Unoka, we learn that great skill with words is equally prized. As the narrator is careful to explain: '[a]mong the Igbo the art of conversation is regarded very highly, and proverbs are the palm-oil with which words are eaten' (*TFA*, 5). Importantly, Achebe is also keen to make clear that in its founding ethos, Umuofia is strongly egalitarian and meritocratic. It is no blight on Okonkwo that Unoka died a debtor, having taken none of the titles of his people. 'Fortunately, among these people a man was judged according to his worth and not according to the worth of his father' (*TFA*, 6). Okonkwo has shown prowess in wrestling and in war, is a skilled and industrious farmer and has taken three wives. 'As the elders said, if a child washed his hands he could eat with kings. Okonkwo had clearly washed his hands and so he ate with kings and elders' (*TFA*, 6).

In *Things Fall Apart* and all of the novels that followed it, gender is frequently the prism through which Achebe chooses to mediate his protagonists and their stories. As we have already seen, the prime way in which Okonkwo assesses his own worth is through a comparison between his own masculinity and that of his father, who a childhood playmate has told him was '*agbala* ... another name for a woman' (*TFA*, 10). For Okonkwo, as Rhonda Cobham observes, prestige and manliness are synonymous with 'the ability to do difficult, even distasteful, jobs without flinching'.⁹ In part one of the novel, a key instance of this is when he kills his step-son Ikemefuna. 'Dazed with [the] fear ... of being thought weak', we see him cut the boy down, even as he runs to him crying 'father' (*TFA*, 43). Here and elsewhere, Achebe uses Okonkwo's hyper-masculinism as an index of foolishness and fallibility rather than strength, signalling his disconnection with the values of harmony and balance prized by the clan. In chapter 4, Okonkwo has already caused scandal and offended the priestess of *Ani*, the earth goddess, by beating his wife in the Week of Peace. Almost from the beginning of the narrative, we are also invited to witness how his violence sows the seeds of rebellion in his gentle son Nwoye, who will eventually make his escape into the arms of the missionaries.

In *Arrow of God*, as I will suggest in chapter 3, Achebe seems to normalise male competitiveness and aggression as a defining feature of clan culture, but in *Things Fall Apart*, that is much less the case. By no means are Okonkwo's chauvinism and violence presented by the novel as a model that Igbo society simply welcomes and endorses. On the contrary, Achebe is careful to show how aberrant Okonkwo's style is through his friend Obierika, who repeatedly counsels him to take a more balanced and thoughtful approach. As Cobham argues:

> When the Oracle demands the life of his ward, Ikemefuna, Okonkwo finds himself without access to a system of values that would allow him to distance himself from the killing of the child who 'calls [him] father' and remain a man. He strikes the blow that kills the child, offending the earth goddess ... and setting in motion a chain of events that ultimately leads to his downfall. Okonkwo's limited understanding of physical ascendancy as courage and his equation of courage with masculinity are set against the richer and more complex values available to his clan as a whole. In the novel, Okonkwo's friend Obierika advocates this greater tradition. The narrative structurally reinforces Obierika's words by juxtaposing Okonkwo's actions and those of other members of the society in a way that invites us to consider the complexity of the clan's values.¹⁰

As Achebe introduces us to more of that complexity, we are introduced to Chielo, a powerful female figure. In everyday life Chielo is a widow who shares a shed in the market with Okonkwo's wife Ekwefi, but under the influence of the Oracle, as the Priestess of *Agbala*, she becomes a fearsome presence whose prophesies hold the whole community in awe. We also bear witness to the clan's seriousness and commitment to balance in matters of marriage and in law. When a case of domestic violence is to be decided, justice is not dispensed in European fashion by a cadre of lawgivers. Instead, it is mediated though a ceremonial performance symbolically involving the whole community, both past and present, including 'dead fathers of the clan' and figures representing other presences such as 'Evil forest' (*TFA*, 64). We see here how Uzowulu – a wife-beater like Okonkwo – is reigned in and ordered to cease his unmanly violence. Despite the fact that Okonkwo himself participates in this ceremony as one of the *egwugwu* or masked spirits, its import seems to be lost on him, however. At the end of part one, it is again his untempered violence that sets him apart from the rest of the community, as he is forced into exile for the crime of killing a clansman. For a third time, he has offended the earth goddess, and as Obierika meditates, 'if the clan did not exact punishment for an offence against the great goddess, her wrath was loosed on all the land and not just on the offender' (*TFA*, 88). Within the tragic idiom of *Things Fall Apart*, the omens have been cast for his eventual demise.

In part two, we see Okonkwo in exile. In his motherland of Mbanta, Okonkwo's uncle counsels him against self-destructive anger and resentment, pointing to the example of his daughter, who had given birth to many sets of twins and – in accordance with ancient Igbo custom – had watched them being thrown away to die in the bush. Uchendu tries to help Okonkwo understand the paradox of his culture which, while seeming to prize manliness above all things, nevertheless holds to the idea of *Nneka* or 'Mother is Supreme':

> 'It's true that a child belongs to its father. But when a father beats his child, it seeks sympathy in its mother's

hut. A man belongs to his fatherland when things are good and life is sweet. But when there is sorrow and bitterness he finds refuge in his motherland ... Is it right that you, Okonkwo, should bring your mother a heavy face and refuse to be comforted? Be careful or you may displease the dead. Your duty is to comfort your wives and children and take them back to your fatherland after seven years. But if you allow sorrow to weigh you down and kill you, they will all die in exile.' (TFA, 94–5)

His words are prophetic, but not in the literal way he intends. Sorrow, bitterness and loss are on their way, from a direction none of the clan expects. In chapter 8, Obierika relates a tale he has heard of men 'who, they say, are white like this piece of chalk' (TFA, 51). In Okonkwo's second year in exile, confirmation arrives with the news that Abame, a distant clan with whom Umuofia has traded in the past, has been destroyed. When one white man had appeared in their midst, the people of Abame had been warned by their oracle: 'They are locusts, it said, and that the first man was their harbinger sent to explore the terrain. And so they killed him' (TFA, 98). Three more white men then appeared with a large native force, ambushing the marketplace and shooting indiscriminately. 'Everybody was killed', Obierika says, 'except the old and the sick who were at home and a handful of men and women whose *chi* were wide awake and brought them out of that market' (TFA, 98). Okonkwo is dismissive and characteristically aggressive in response, but his friend is again more circumspect. 'I am greatly afraid. We have heard stories about white men who made the powerful guns and the strong drinks and took slaves away across the seas, but no one thought the stories were true' (TFA, 99).

Soon, rapid and far-reaching changes begin to happen back in Umuofia including the invasion of missionary Christianity and, in association with it, the gradual establishment of colonial government under the District Commissioner. Once again, Okonkwo is initially dismissive. The converts are *'elulefu,* worthless, empty men' (TFA, 101). One of them, however, is his son Nwoye. The latter's reasons for deserting his people and joining the alien band of Christians are, again, ominous for the future of the clan:

> It was not the mad logic of the Trinity that captivated him. He did not understand it. It was the poetry of the new religion, something felt in the marrow. The hymn about brothers who sat in darkness and in fear seemed to answer a vague and persistent question that haunted his young soul – the question of the twins crying in the bush and the question of Ikemefuna who was killed. He felt a relief within as the hymn poured into his parched soul. The words of the hymn were like the drops of frozen rain melting on the dry plate of the panting earth. (*TFA*, 104)

Despite the challenge it poses, the response of the clan to the new church is surprisingly reasonable and accommodating. 'There was no question of killing a missionary here, for Mr Kiaga, despite his madness, was quite harmless. As for his converts, no one could kill them without having to flee from the clan, for in spite of their worthlessness they still belonged to the clan. And so nobody gave serious thought to the stories about the white man's government' (*TFA*, 110–11). The real dangers for the clan, the novel begins to suggest, lie in its own inherent weaknesses. Where the clan is blind to the needs of its people, there the Christians reap a harvest – they welcome the *osu*, a caste of untouchables who are forbidden from community gatherings or entering the houses of free men, rescue twins from the bush and comfort their mothers. For their part, however, while the gods of Umuofia are 'still able to fight their own battles' – as they show by taking the life of one convert who kills a sacred python – the clan 'saw no reason ... for molesting the Christians' (*TFA*, 114). As one of the elders of Mbanta says, prophetically, at Okonkwo's farewell feast, the weakness of the Umuofians is that 'you no longer understand how strong is the bond of kinship. You do not know what it is to speak with one voice' (*TFA*, 118).

At the end of part one of *Things Fall Apart*, Okonkwo left a clan that was as-yet untouched by outside influence. By the time he returns, the work of divide-and-rule has already gone so far that his calls for resistance find few willing ears. After a period of only seven years, Umuofia 'had undergone such profound change during his exile that it was barely recognisable' (*TFA*, 129). The new religion, government and trading stores brought by the white man are now 'very much in the people's eyes and minds ... they talked and thought about little else' (*TFA*, 129). Our geographic sense of the area begins to expand, as we hear for the first time of a town 'on the bank of the Great River' where the white men have built 'the centre of their religion and trade and government' (*TFA*, 123). Plainly recalling the establishment of European trading posts at Onitsha on the Niger in the nineteenth century, together with the Church Missionary Society of which his father was a prominent member, Achebe also begins to allow a sense of historicity to seep into the narrative. A new class of native officials, the *kotma* or court messengers have appeared who, as we soon hear, have already learnt how to enrich themselves in the course of their duties. Non-converts who molest Christians or observe traditional practices such as the abandonment of twins are now taken to a prison where 'they were beaten ... and made to work every morning clearing the compound and fetching wood for the white commissioner and the court messengers. Some of these prisoners were men of title who should be above such mean occupation. They were grieved by the indignity and mourned for their neglected farms' (*TFA*, 123). Aneto, who has killed a clansman in a fight over land, is hanged.

Okonkwo, characteristically, counsels violent resistance against the white man, but as Obierika points out, the real obstacle is not the foreigners themselves but the many who have gone over to them: 'Our own men and our sons have joined the ranks of the stranger' (*TFA*, 124). Once again, Okonkwo's pugilistic tendencies are presented as exceptional and anomalous rather than representative, and as a formerly respected warrior, notably little is made of his return. As the narrator informs us, many in Umuofia feel very differently from him about 'the new dispensation. The white men had indeed brought a lunatic religion, but he had also built a trading store and for the first time palm-oil and kernel became things of great price, and much money flowed into Umuofia' (*TFA*, 126). Soon, Christianity too is being regarded as having 'something in it after all' (*TFA*, 126). The white missionary, Mr Brown, is honoured with the gift of a 'carved elephant tusk, which was a sign of dignity and rank' (*TFA*, 126) and engages in deep conversation with Akunna, a great man in the clan. Although the two men do not quite have a meeting of minds, they discover much that seems similar between Christianity and the traditional religion, including the idea of a single, all powerful male deity, who created the world.

When a more doctrinaire pastor, the Reverend James Smith, takes over, however, relations soon begin to sour. He encourages some of the converts to openly challenge the clan, and at an important ceremony in honour of the earth goddess, one of them scandalously unmasks an *egwugwu*. Again the response of the clan is balanced. Through the voice of Ajofia, the leading *egwugwu*, Mr Smith is told that he may remain among the clanspeople, but only on the basis of respect. 'You can stay with us if you like our ways. You can worship your own god. It is good that a man should worship the gods and the spirits of his fathers. Go back to your house so that you may not be hurt. Our anger is great but we have held it down so that we can talk to you' (*TFA*, 134). Mr Smith is not harmed, but at Okonkwo's instigation, his church is burnt to the ground. Soon the clan elders find themselves in the courthouse. Tricked by the District Commissioner, they are handcuffed and locked in the guardroom. One of the *kotma*, on his own malicious initiative, shaves the men's heads, and they are beaten. While the elders 'just sat and moped', Okonkwo alone is shown as being 'choked with hate' (*TFA*, 138).

After the clan has paid a fine of 200 cowries ordered by the District Commissioner, and have had fifty more extorted from them by the *kotma*, the men are finally released. A meeting is held to discuss whether war is an option against the white man's regime, but this is interrupted by the arrival of court messengers. While the other men of Umuofia draw back, so that they 'merged into the mute backcloth of trees and giant creepers' (*TFA*, 144), physical force is again Okonkwo's instinctive reaction. He beheads the court messenger, but sees in the same moment that none of the others will join him in resistance. A little later his own hanged body is found dangling from a tree behind his compound. Since suicide is a crime against the earth goddess, Okonkwo has consigned himself to the ultimate abjection: as Obierika says in an impotent expression of rage to the District Commissioner, 'now he will be buried like a dog' (*TFA*, 147). In the masterful concluding paragraph of part three, the final voice is that of the Commissioner, who as well as being judge and jury over this part of the Niger territories is also to be their historian, with Okonkwo's story as a 'good paragraph' in his book *The Pacification of the Primitive Tribes of the Lower Niger*.

In the way it was eventually published, *Things Fall Apart* ended there. In the Okonkwo saga as originally conceived by Achebe, however, what followed was the opening of Obi's story. The narrative moves directly to another trial, in which another white colonial official, Mr Justice William Galloway is passing judgement on Ogbuefi Okonkwo's grandson Michael Obi Okonkwo. We are in contemporary (1950s) Lagos and learn that Obi, too, has been in exile, getting his university education in England. Like his grandfather, Obi has proved himself energetic and ambitious, and his education has been sponsored by the Umuofia clan with the expectation that, as a colonial civil servant, he'll be able to siphon some of the new national wealth their way. Unlike his grandfather, Obi is an anglophile and a nationalist. Like him, however, he is a dissident by temperament, naïvely dismissive of social conventions.

Colonialism of a rather later vintage provides the backdrop to this part of Achebe's narrative, and we are soon introduced to Obi's boss, William Green, airing an almost parodic version of imperialist ideology:

> 'I'm all for equality and all that ... But equality won't alter facts ... over countless centuries the African has been the victim of the worst climate in the world and of every imaginable disease. Hardly his fault. But he has been sapped mentally and physically. We have brought him Western education. But what use is it to him?'[11]

When we meet the latter-day Umuofians, represented by the Lagos branch of the Umuofia Progressive Union, Achebe stresses, precisely, their clannishness. If clansmen are often forced to leave home in search of work in the urban centres, we are told, 'they regard themselves as sojourners. They return to Umuofia every two years to spend their annual leave. When they have saved up enough money they ask their relations at home to find them a wife, or they build a "zinc" house on their family land. No matter where they are in Nigeria, they start a local branch of the Umuofia Progressive Union' (*NLE*, 4). Obi has been sentenced to prison for accepting a bribe of twenty pounds, and Achebe uses this early opportunity to establish that, in fact, the Umuofians are far from antipathetic to corruption. The president of the Lagos union expresses their disgust, not at Obi's crime, but at him having been caught for such a measly sum. 'He repeated twenty pounds, spitting it out ... "we have a saying that if you want to eat a toad you should look for a fat and juicy one"' (*NLE*, 6).

Obi's family in Umuofia itself, headed by his father Isaac (who since we saw him in part two has changed his name from the pagan Nwoye), are Christians. Much of the communal ritual we have seen in Achebe's portrait of pre-colonial times, however, is still in evidence. In a way that takes something from Okonkwo and something from his grandfather Unoka, Isaac is 'famous for his open-handedness which sometimes bordered on improvidence. Whenever his wife remonstrated against his thriftlessness he replied that a man who lived on the banks of the Niger should not wash his hands with spittle – a favourite saying of his father's' (*NLE*, 10). A continuity is also suggested between Okonkwo's fearlessness in battle and Obi's boldness of ambition in going to England. '"In times past," he told him, "Umuofia would have required of you to fight in her wars and bring home human heads. But those were days of darkness from which we have been delivered by the blood of the Lamb of God. Today we send you to bring knowledge"' (*NLE*, 10). While Obi's sense of his own destiny is quite an adventuristic one, it is clear that he is expected to return the investment his community has made in him.

In Lagos, to which he returns as a privileged member of the new middle class, sexual mores are liberal, as we discover when Obi's friend Joseph discusses his various conquests. Unlike the privileged European enclave of Ikoyi, where Obi lives, Lagos is by no means all given over to pleasure and thoughtless consumption, however. On the side of a road, a small boy scrapes a living selling beans, while a night-soil-man trails 'clouds of putrefaction' (*NLE*, 17). During his stay in England, Obi has written a nostalgic poem about Nigeria, but now realises its naïvety. Surveying his nation's capital, he adapts T. S. Eliot, musing 'I have tasted putrid flesh in the spoon' (*NLE*, 17).

From the very opening of Obi's narrative, as I have suggested, Achebe has indicated that the question of corruption, and especially bribery, will be central to the second part of the Okonkwo saga. In part three of (what became) *Things Fall Apart*, we saw how readily the native *kotma* appointed by the colonial authority had begun to abuse their powers, and in modern Lagos, we are soon given to believe that corruption is the norm. Speaking of the typical senior Nigerian, Obi's assumption is that he must necessarily have 'worked steadily to the top through bribery – an ordeal by bribery. To him the bribe is natural. He gave it and he expects it' (*NLE*, 21). Initially, Obi is strongly opposed, and makes himself immediately unpopular with the Umuofia Progressive Union by preaching a lesson of service and integrity at his welcome home dinner. '"Education for service, not for white-collar jobs and comfortable salaries. With our great country on the threshold of independence, we need men who are prepared to serve her well and truly"' (*NLE*, 32–3). In different forms, this is a message which will echo through much of Achebe's subsequent writing, notably *The Trouble with Nigeria* and *Anthills of the Savannah*. For Obi at least, however, it proves an impossible doctrine to sustain.

As in his grandfather's narrative, gender is again a key terrain on which Achebe chooses to dramatise the choices and dilemmas faced by Obi. While in London, he has met a Nigerian girl who is, herself, studying for a degree. Back in Lagos, his desire is piqued by seeing her in the car of a well-known politician, with a reputation for philandering. As Obi and Clara's relationship develops, and despite the fact that both of them have a Christian, educated background, the problem arises that by descent, she is *osu*, traditionally untouchable, and certainly unmarriageable to a free man of the clan. Although Obi is inclined to see the prohibition as nothing but out-dated superstition, it gathers importance in a paradoxical way through the interjection of his mother, Hannah Okonkwo. Her husband Isaac is a church catechist and she is even more zealous than him in promoting the Christian message. However, both co-exist in easy dialogue with those around them, including adherents of the old religion. If Obi married Clara, as his father says, who would marry their children, who would themselves be considered outcasts? Hannah is old and ill, and when she threatens to commit suicide if Obi goes ahead with the wedding, he is thrown into a serious dilemma. In his theory of the 'Old Africans', dreamt up at University, what Nigeria needs is to sweep away the tired old ways of the past, as represented by those of the older generation, and create a new elite based on the young, educated class emerging from the universities. As the *osu* narrative illustrates, however, things are not so simple. In the lives of his parents, and in his own life, modernity and tradition turn out to be more inextricably entwined than he had thought.

Obi has already begun to experience some financial pressures. In his new job as Secretary to the Scholarship Board he is expected (not least by the Umuofians) to swank around a little, and has jumped at the chance of an advance to buy a brand new motorcar. He is obliged to repay regular instalments of the £400 loan the Umuofia Progressive Union have provided for his education. In Umuofia, he feels compelled to help his parents out financially, at least a little, and to pay school fees for his brother John. As he soon discovers, his salary, extremely generous as it is by the standards of most Lagosians, is not enough to cover his outgoings. At first, his strategy is to buy some breathing space by requesting more time to pay back his loan. When they question him about his relationship with an *osu* girl, however, that possibility soon evaporates. An opportunity arises in the form of a visit, at work, from the brother of a scholarship candidate, which Obi terminates before bribery can be explicitly offered. The girl also makes a private visit to his home, but it is interrupted by Clara before anything untoward can happen. Financial pressures are building, however. An unexpected bill arrives for the insurance premium on his car, closely followed by an electricity bill. Unexpectedly, Clara offers to lend him £50, but this small ray of sunshine is extinguished when it is stolen from the glove box of their friend's car.

In a further dramatic twist, Clara discovers that she is pregnant. She herself is adamant that she cannot marry Obi, and in a move that brings the theme of thrown-away infants full circle, he arranges a visit to an abortionist. The operation has a bad effect on Clara and she does not want to see him afterwards. When he finally sees her at the hospital, she turns her back and faces the wall. Obi's financial crisis deepens further as he discovers that a travel allowance he had claimed to go to Umuofia was not a free bonus but only an advance that he must now repay. When his mother dies, it is partly through a want of petrol money that he scandalously fails to attend her funeral.

When the season for scholarships comes around again, Obi has reached an impossible impasse. A man visits him at home and offers £50 in return for recommending his son for an award, and he allows the man to leave the wad of notes on the table. Immediately after, we see him accepting a sexual bribe from a schoolgirl with the same ambition. Soon, his overdraft and other pressing debts are cleared. Tolerance of corruption does not entirely define the system, however, as we discover when he is caught in a sting operation by a plainclothes officer. As at the end of *Things Fall Apart*, Achebe brings us sharply back to the colonial context:

> He began to say some things, invoking the name of the Queen, like a District Office in the bush reading the riot Act to an uncomprehending and delirious mob. (*NLE*, 170)

In lots of ways, then, Achebe's Okonkwo saga is a narrative about cultural loss of different kinds: the loss of the pre-colonial way of life at the turn of the twentieth century, the fragmentation of family and clan loyalties, the deracinating effects of colonialism on successive generations of Nigerians, and the inability of even the most idealistic to weather the cultural maelstrom it engendered. If both men begin as the protagonists of their own stories – Ogbuefi Okonkwo representing a tragic model of anti-colonial resistance and Obi a more bathetic one of the ambitious 'New Nigerian' – the final, bitter irony of Achebe's narrative is that both end as incidentals. Both will be marginal inscriptions in a vast narrative of empire writing, penned by countless District Commissioners, missionary anthropologists, expatriate administrators, colonial judges and their like – a narrative whose power and scope seem to lie far beyond the resistive capacities of literature.

By 1956 Achebe had worked his novel up to manuscript stage and, as biographer Ezenwa-Ohaeto says, in that year he was sent to London with some young NBC colleagues, to attend a radio production course run by the BBC, followed by a period working in one of the company's departments.[12] For the NBC's British expatriate Director Tom Chalmers, as we saw in chapter 1, one of the corporation's key objectives in arranging this international posting was to build key members of their broadcasting staff as 'Nigerian national figures'[13] who would be capable of injecting a new credibility into the corporation's programming. The training course included editorial skills, programme research, studio techniques and speech training. Undoubtedly, however, the trip was also designed to allow Achebe and others to interact with elements of the British media and cultural establishment in ways which would not have been possible in the normal circumstances of work at the NBC.

Achebe was encouraged by a Nigerian colleague to show his manuscript to one of the tutors on the course, the English novelist Gilbert Phelps (1915–93). Phelps' reaction was very positive, according to Ezenwa-Ohaeto, but Achebe himself still had misgivings about the form and shape of what he had written. Instead of sending the novel out to London publishers as Phelps suggested, he went back to Nigeria and cut it back to something very different, representing less than half of the original manuscript. In 1957, it was only the historical sections of the Okonkwo saga, set at an indeterminate date in the late nineteenth century, that were sent out for typing and which eventually found their way to Heinemann.

In an interview with Kirsten Holst Petersen published in 1991, the publishing entrepreneur Alan Hill describes *Things Fall Apart*'s reception at the firm's London offices:

> Heinemann's normal fiction reader read it and did a long report but the firm was still hesitating whether to accept it. Would anyone possibly buy a novel by an African? There are no precedents. So the rather doubting bunch at the top of Heinemann's thought of the educational department, who after all sold books to Africa and were supposed to know about Africans. So they showed it to one of our educational advisers, Professor Donald MacRae, who was just back from West Africa. He read it in the office and ended the debate with an eleven word report: 'This is the best novel I have read since the war.'[14]

What significance can be drawn from Achebe's decision to separate the narratives of Ogbuefi and Obi Okonkwo? Undoubtedly, his choice was to have a defining and, arguably, unhelpful effect on the critical interpretation of (what then became) his first two novels. Despite the obvious family link between Okonkwo in *Things Fall Apart* and his grandson Obi in *No Longer at Ease*, they have rarely been read as complementary halves of a single narrative, and seldom even considered in direct relation to each other. Indeed, in many influential studies (Gikandi, Innes, Ogede, Yousaf) the historical novel *Arrow of God* is treated as the *de facto* sequel to *Things Fall Apart*, while *No Longer at Ease* and *A Man of the People* are grouped together as a rather different species of writing, in which the author changed style and approach in order to address more contemporary questions. When the two halves of the saga are considered together as originally conceived, however, much light is shed on Achebe's narrative strategies and the cultural politics that inform them. As *No Longer at Ease* echoes and elaborates on the themes of

Things Fall Apart, our reading of both texts is illuminated in significant ways.

In the first part of *Things Fall Apart*, as we have seen, Achebe presents the Igbo community of Umuofia in an almost a-historical state, untouched by outside influences. When, early in the novel, Okonkwo's father Unoka is castigated by the priestess of Agbala for the laziness of his farming methods, for example, Achebe conjures a world in which men may still 'go out with their axe to cut down virgin forests' (*TFA*, 13) for cultivation. Twenty years later, when Okonkwo reaches his prime, interaction with white men is still completely outside the clan's experience, and even in part two it is the stuff of stories that 'no one thought ... were true' (*TFA*, 99). It is important to recognise that, from a historical point of view, this would really have been a scene of centuries ago, before Igbo–European commerce in the slave and palm-oil trades was firmly established and before yam cultivation had expanded to its limits throughout the region. All available historical evidence would suggest that this world had, in fact, long disappeared by the late nineteenth century. As Robert Wren shows in his study *Achebe's World*, the people of the area Achebe describes had, by that time, 'absorbed the available land long ago'.[15] In Achebe's own home village Ogidi, on which Umuofia is largely based, this was certainly the case. Arinze Agbogu's 'Ogidi Before 1891' (1976) provides a variety of evidence that ecological depletion and arable land shortage were serious problems faced by Achebe's forebears in this period.[16] Communities of the kind Umuofia is modelled on, in other words, by no means enjoyed the limitless 'virgin forests' conjured by *Things Fall Apart*. Interestingly, moreover, it is clear from the texts themselves that Achebe is well aware of this history, because it forms an important element of the back story to Obi's rise in *No Longer at Ease*. Where in *Things Fall Apart* Okonkwo is able to overcome adversity and amass wealth and security through yam cultivation, the people of his children and grandchildren's generation must toil 'from year to year to wrest a meagre living from an unwilling and exhausted soil' (*NLE*, 12). Land disputes are so prevalent in these later times of shortage that Umuofians have 'taxed themselves mercilessly' (*NLE*, 7) to fund a law degree for Obi Okonkwo, so that he will be able to represent them in the courts. In constructing his narrative, however, Achebe chooses to wait until the second half of the Okonkwo saga to introduce these ideas. The effect of his strategy is clear: it enables Umuofia's development to be represented much more dramatically in terms of a transition from the timeless, almost Edenic scene of *Things Fall Apart*'s early scenes to the dis-eased modernity of *No Longer at Ease*.

In the second novel, the changing modes and strategies of British colonial rule are brought out in plenty of revealing detail, from the high-handed arrogance of Schools Inspector Jones, scandalously floored by Headmaster Simeon Nduka in the 1930s, when 'to throw a white man was like unmasking an ancestral spirit' (*NLE*, 65), to Mr Green, senior civil servant in the late 1950s, forced unwillingly to accommodate the rights of the new black middle class. By stark contrast, as I have suggested however, the Umuofia of the first part of *Things Fall Apart* is styled very deliberately as a pre-lapserian space, before the work of cultural hybridisation has begun. While a succession of historians from Flora Shaw to Adielo Afigbo would describe the different phases of entrepreneurial and more formal colonialism, including the Atlantic slave trade, as an enormous shaping influence on the life of Igboland from the seventeenth century right up until the 1950s,[17] Achebe chooses at the beginning of his portrayal to represent the Umuofians as a people who are themselves, in a sense, 'virgin', uncorrupted by foreign incursion. From the beginning of the second part of *Things Fall Apart*, he then takes us through a chain of narrative development in which the clan must respond to more and more intrusive foreign intervention into its lands and way of life. As the story proceeds, the negative effects of this process of cultural hybridisation become progressively more central, working systematically towards the final question posed by Judge Galloway at the end of *No Longer at Ease*: why a young man of Obi Okonkwo's promise would succumb to corruption. None of Achebe's characters know the answer to his question. 'The British Council man, even the men of Umuofia, did not know' (*NLE*, 170). Having followed the Okonkwo saga from beginning to end, however, the answer is abundantly clear to the reader: Obi, once regarded as 'Okonkwo *kpom kwen*' (*NLE*, 53), the re-incarnation of his fiercely independent grandfather, has become his polar opposite. He has succumbed to corruption because he embodies the snarl-up of cultural contradictions that is the new Nigeria. He is the authentic fruit of Britain's nation-building endeavours.

As I have already suggested, in order to arrange his narrative this way Achebe is forced to shape and select his historical referents very self-consciously. In part two of *Things Fall Apart* when Okonkwo is in exile from the clan, for example, the arrival of colonialism is heralded by the news of a massacre at far away Abame. A white man who we presume to be a missionary, travelling alone on an 'iron horse' (*TFA*, 97), which we infer to be a bicycle, had arrived and beckoned to the people. When the clan decided to kill him on the advice of their oracle, they provoke a revenge attack that does, indeed, serve as a potent warning to surrounding clans, as we see in the case of Mbanta and Umuofia. In Robert Wren's study, it is argued in convincing detail that in his presentation of this pivotal scene, Achebe drew on actual Colonial Office records of 1905, detailing the collective punishment of Obezi and Eziudo, settlements which lie some fifty miles south west of Achebe's home village of Ogidi. Historically, this event constituted a small incident within a much larger British campaign of 'pacification' in Igboland just after the turn of the twentieth century. The historical parallel identified by Wren is striking in its closeness:

> The story corresponds to but one actual incident – though many Igbo towns were 'punished' (to use the colonial term), often with loss of life. The one case is that of Dr. J. F. Stewart, who at 1:00 p.m. November 16, 1905, set off on his bicycle from Owerri (today the capital of Imo State) intending to ride to Calabar via Bende. At a branch in the 'road' (really a track), he turned toward Obizi – a serious error, according to a letter to the Colonial Office from H. M. Douglas. 'Natives', he said, who reported the matter to

Owerri, reported that Stewart was stripped, bound, and beaten, and afterwards 'his body was cut up and shared. His bicycle also was broken up and shared.' [...] On December 13 – nearly a month later – a Captain Fox, commanding two groups of black soldiers (if each had a white officer this would meet Obierika's 'three white men'), came, intending a surprise attack. He found few people and concluded his surprise had failed. (Perhaps the scarcity of people merely indicated that there was no market that day.) Fox removed 'cooked' leg bones which he took to be Stewart's. On December 16, a force 'managed to kill 19 Obezis and Eziudos' – that is, people of villages where Stewart was thought to have been captured. Probably – the records do not say – the towns were destroyed.[18]

In *Arrow of God*, as we will see in chapter 3, the destruction of Abame takes on a whole new resonance, in that the Abam people are presented there as having been looters and slave-dealers whose destruction by the colonial authority comes as a blessing to the surrounding clans. Since the event comprises the main incidence of colonial violence presented by *Things Fall Apart*, this obviously has a major, retrospective influence on the way colonialism is perceived in the novel. Even leaving this knowledge aside, however, the way Achebe presents the punishment of Abame raises some difficult and interesting questions. As historians of this period such as A. E. Afigbo have attested, a very much larger colonial incursion into the area of Igboland described by Achebe had in fact occurred a few years before the incident at Obezi and Eziudo, with the Aro-Chukwu expedition of 1901–2. Destroying one of the most renowned and culturally significant oracles in Igboland and forcibly subordinating a vast area measuring some 6,000 square miles, this intervention was regarded by Sir Ralph Moor, High Commissioner for the Protectorate of Southern Nigeria, as the crucial event of its time in Britain's 'pacification' of the Igbo and other peoples of the Lower Niger. The expedition was, as Afigbo writes in *The Abolition of the Slave Trade in Southeastern Nigeria 1885–1950*, the decisive early push that defined the tenor of Britain's campaign in the Igbo hinterland in the first decade of the twentieth century. Aro-Chukwu was not only perceived by the British as the symbol and centre of the dominant Aro people, who spearheaded much of the coordinated resistance to colonialism among the Igbo in this period. It was also the site of *Ibim Ukpabi*, the 'Long Juju', an oracle which operated as the regional seat of judgement, linked to a network of 'lesser' oracles throughout the surrounding country. From the seventeenth century onwards, Aro-Chukwu had become established as a major coordinate in the transatlantic slave trade. Defendants brought before the shrine and found guilty were sent as sacrifices to Chukwu (the Umuofians' supreme deity, referred to by Akunna in his conversation with Mr Brown) before being covertly sold to slave merchants, first from Europe and later from the Islamic states north of Igboland. Having spent '[u]pwards of two centuries developing the slave trade',[19] as Flora Shaw candidly puts it in her 1905 study *A Tropical Dependency*, the suppression of slaving infrastructure provided Britain with one of the key political pretexts for its aggressive subordination of the South East in the period depicted by Achebe.

If *Things Fall Apart* were read in strict adherence to the history of the period, Moor's (successful) campaign to subordinate the lands of the Umuofians and all of their neighbours would have taken place a couple of years before Okonkwo's banishment to Mbanta. As far as the clan are concerned in part one of Achebe's novel, however, it is as if the Aro-Chukwu expedition simply has not happened. His depiction of Umuofia does not suggest that it exists in a state of special isolation – on the contrary, the affairs he describes work to suggest a network of relationships with the surrounding clans. Ikemefuna's arrival in Okonkwo's compound follows the killing of a daughter of Umuofia in Mbaino's market, near Abame, for example. Okonkwo's motherland is Mbanta, and it is there that he must take refuge when he accidentally kills a Umuofia clansman. Although Okonkwo's uncle Uchendu bemoans the insularity of the younger generation, it is clear that an entire fabric of inter-clan relationships, established over the course of many generations, continues to structure and define Igbo social life. Within the world of Achebe's narrative in part one of *Things Fall Apart*, then, Sir Ralph Moor's campaign of 'pacification' in Igboland, beginning with the Aro-Chukwu expedition, has not yet begun.

Why does Achebe strategically choose to omit one of the crucial military-historical developments of the period and instead to use the collective punishment of Obezi/Eziudo in his framing of the colonial encounter? The reason, I would suggest, is that any attempt to deal with the Aro-Chukwu conflict would have the effect of taking Achebe's narrative into a very different space than the one he chooses. In Afigbo's estimation, 'there can be no doubt that [this] military conquest was by far the severest single blow the colonial administration dealt against the slave trade in the hinterland of the Bight of Biafra. For one thing, it was with the successful capture of Aro Chukwu on Christmas Day 1901 that the government felt able to make Proclamation No. 5 of that year, abolishing slave trading and slave keeping'[20] throughout the Protectorate of Southern Nigeria. His assessment connotes a whole colourful and extended history of cultural, commercial and entrepreneurial interaction, colonial incursion and resistance in Igboland which, for the purposes of *Things Fall Apart*'s thematic development, Achebe clearly prefers to elide.

This is historical *fiction*, and it is of course Achebe's prerogative to shape the material as he sees fit, simplifying the picture so we encounter his Igbo first in an 'originary' state prior to colonial intrusion, and later in a state of adaptation and change, as they respond to its influence. Within this narrative framework the Abame incident – in which indigenous people encounter a white man for the first time, and kill him without understanding the likely consequences – fits neatly. It is easy to see that the Aro-Chukwu expedition, by contrast, would have taken Achebe's narrative into much more complex territory. It would necessitate acknowledgement of the centuries-long interaction between Europeans and the Igbo, around a series of trades including the slave trade, with complex associated ethical and political questions. It would place Britain's aggressive policy of 'pacification' far more to the fore. Perhaps most importantly, moreover, it would also necessitate a much fuller examination of Igbo *resistance* to British colonialism than Achebe apparently wants to make space for.

Anti-colonial resistance?

In *The Education of a British-Protected Child*, the author is unhesitating in acknowledging his people's grim, sustained campaign to repulse and frustrate Britain's imperialist ambitions in this period. 'Colonial rule was stronger than any marriage. The Igbo fought it in the battlefield and lost. They put every roadblock in its way and lost again.'[21] As F. K. Ekechi's 1971 study *Missionary Enterprise & Rivalry in Igboland 1857–1914* attests, there was plenty of historical material on which Achebe could have drawn to conjure a sense of those struggles.[22] Some of this, he does draw on. For example, in his depiction of the District Commissioner in *Things Fall Apart* it is possible to see clear echoes of the duplicitous tactics employed by Moor at the turn of the century, in his attempts to disguise his aggressive intentions from the Igbo:

> The expedition against the Aros and to control 'the country of the producers' was planned for December 1900. But owing to a number of factors, it was postponed until 1901–1902 … While preparations were under way, Moor became a little apprehensive that the Igbo chiefs and their neighbours might attack the administration on the suspicion that the Government was making elaborate plans to invade them. To forestall such precipitate action, Moor informed the Colonial Office that 'steps of a friendly and unofficial nature' would be taken not only to quiet the people but to 'disabuse them of the idea that any active measures are being taken against them by the Government.'[23]

What is notably absent from Achebe's narrative, however, is a sense of the determined and coordinated manner in which the Igbo both anticipated and resisted Moor's campaign to 'pacify' them. When set against such historical accounts as Afigbo's and Ekechi's, indeed, it becomes clear that Achebe's approach to representing both the British colonial incursion into Igboland

and Igbo resistance to it in *Things Fall Apart* is, in fact, extremely light and sparing. The narrative is arranged so that protagonist Okonkwo is in exile when the missionaries arrive and when the white man sets up his administration in Umuofia, for example. Although we hear that the village of Abame has been destroyed in part two, the scene is placed at a distance, rendering it as a subject for discussion and debate rather than as an immediate part of the novel's action. When six elders are tricked and humiliated by the District Commissioner and we see them handcuffed, taunted and with heads shaved in the guardroom, as we have seen, they are represented as having 'just sat and moped' (*TFA*, 138). By contrast to Ekechi's account of alliance building and organised defence, in the final part of *Things Fall Apart* 'Umuofia was like a startled animal with ears erect, sniffing the silent, ominous air and not knowing which way to run' (*TFA*, 139).

Okonkwo himself is, of course, far from embodying this tendency towards fear and defeatism. Even when imprisoned by the District Commissioner his counsel is for killing the white man. At the climactic clan meeting in the penultimate chapter of *Things Fall Apart*, he is resolved to fight alone if his kinsmen decide against war. For critics who want to see the novel as a prime exemplar of anti-colonial resistance, such as Herbert Ekwe-Ekwe, Okonkwo exemplifies the principle of struggle-against-all-odds that characterised Africa's heroic attempts to repulse the European colonialists in the late nineteenth and early twentieth centuries. According to Ekwe-Ekwe:

> As history has shown, each and every invader of some other person's lands is potentially militarily superior to their would-be victims. But the latter's response to the event is the defence of the homeland under attack despite the odds and even when these are known by the defenders as overwhelming. As the European invasion got underway in Africa during the period, African armed resistance, expectedly, was the most featured element of Africa's initial or first phase of the defence of its homeland. It is this fact of African history that Chinua Achebe captures so dramatically in Okonkwo's steadfast response to the British invasion of Umuofia ... It should be stressed that

> the African historical landscape is extensively and indelibly marked by the people's heroism during this defence, a heroism made more pronounced considering the very obvious superiority of the military forces deployed by the invaders as was evident in some of the most outstanding military confrontations of the era ... African resistance was victorious in a number of Epic battles fought during the course of these conflicts.[24]

In his account of the history of anti-colonial struggle in Africa, Ekwe-Ekwe rightly emphasises the scale and violence of the genocide visited on the Igbo, the Yoruba and other ethnic groups in the era of slavery and, later, state colonialism. With justification, he emphasises the historical importance of narrative as a means for Africans to reclaim control of their historiography and to supplant the legacy of distortions which, at the time Achebe is writing, continue to dominate the representation of their continent's past. As he argues, '[t]he African story must be told unequivocally with confidence, commitment and courage'.[25] Does Achebe's narrative fulfil that charge, however? Certainly, the story of Nigerian nation-building he tells through the experiences of the Okonkwo family can be seen as courageous, but not, I would argue, in the sense that Ekwe-Ekwe describes. In fact in *Things Fall Apart*, as we have seen, Achebe gives very little space indeed to the history of organised resistance among the Igbo. There is no attempt to engage seriously with the real campaigns of 'steadfast response' against the British, the coordinated, large-scale and sustained struggles against colonial domination at Aro-Chukwu and elsewhere, discussed by historians who are direct contemporaries with Achebe. In *No Longer at Ease* – published in the very year that Nigerians finally ousted the colonial British – some kind of heroic Independence narrative might have seemed the perfect complement to Okonkwo's tragedy. Again, however, Achebe turns decisively away from those thematics. At the conclusion of Obi's story, we certainly aren't heading into a bright future of postcolonial freedom, where the ignorance of Mr Green and the other expatriate administrators will be forced to make way for young and idealistic, or even wise and seasoned, Nigerians.

Against Ekwe-Ekwe, then, I would argue that when *Things Fall Apart* and *No Longer at Ease* are read as complementary halves of a single narrative – spanning the whole seventy-five year period of Britain's experiment in state colonialism, through the era of nationalist campaigning for self-government to the eve of self-government – what is really striking is Achebe's *lack* of interest in developing the oppression–resistance–independence narrative that so many critics are looking to find.

Things fall apart, in the historical part of the Okonkwo saga, because people are tempted and coerced, in a variety of ways, to let go of their values. Indeed, this is exactly what Okonkwo's wiser, more far-sighted friend, explains to him when the former argues for violent resistance:

> 'It is already too late,' said Obierika sadly. 'Our own men and our sons have joined the ranks of the stranger. They have joined his religion and they help to uphold his government. If we should try to drive out the white men in Umuofia we should find it easy. There are only two of them. But what of our own people who are following their way and have been given power?' (*TFA*, 124)

In the chapter immediately following, the analysis advanced by Obierika is confirmed, as Achebe depicts division in Umuofia over the problems and opportunities brought by the new dispensation. While on the negative side the white man had attempted to install a 'lunatic religion' (*TFA*, 126), his approach (in the person of Mr Brown) was sensitive and respectful. On the positive side, meanwhile, a new trading store had also been established 'and for the first time palm-oil and kernel became things of great price' (*TFA*, 126). In Achebe's narrative, the economic opportunities that colonialism has brought with it are among the key reasons why people are tempted to accept the new dispensation. Once again, however, it is clear that this is by no means the only historical interpretation Achebe could have chosen. According to material presented by Gloria Chuku in her study *Igbo Women and Economic Transformation in Southeastern Nigeria 1900–1960*, for example, the response of many communities to the economic opportunities brought by the upsurge in demand for palm products in this period was to make the most of the situation, but in ways that reinforced rather than eroding their values. A form of regulation known as *imachi nkwu* was instituted, equalising access to the fruit-bearing trees so as to prevent unfair or monopolistic exploitation of the trade. In these communities, Chuku reports, 'money realized from *imachi nkwu* was usually used for community development projects such as road construction, building of schools, hospitals or even for scholarship awards'.[26] In *No Longer at Ease*, we do indeed see how Umuofia has come together to forward its collective advancement, through a scholarship scheme for bright young sons and daughters. In Achebe's portrayal, as we have seen however, this idea is entirely yoked to themes of corruption and civil irresponsibility, rather than (for example) to ideas of ethical community or the strength of Igbo egalitarianism. In the face of the challenges and the temptations brought by colonialism, Achebe's narrative suggests, such values were simply not strong enough to hold the community together.

This is certainly a disquieting message, and it is interesting to note how flawed and disappointed some early critics, including some very notable ones such as Arthur Ravenscroft and David Carroll, found themselves when encountering *No Longer at Ease* as a sequel to *Things Fall Apart*. Their reaction, when turned on its head, indicates the effectiveness with which Achebe works to confound reader expectations in the second part of his saga. In the third part of *Things Fall Apart*, he has concentrated an intense ethical force against the arrogance of those who had dispossessed the Igbo and sought to represent them as a lesser form of humanity. The hero has hanged himself, and we have learned with disgust of the District Commissioner's ambitions as a historian of Igboland's 'primitive tribes' (*TFA*, 148). As we enter the second half of the saga, then, it initially appears that Achebe is laying the groundwork for a reciprocal narrative manoeuvre. In the privacy of their club, we see senior civil servant Green – in many ways a contemporary avatar of the District Commissioner – discussing Obi's conviction for corrupt practices with a British Council representative:

'I cannot understand why he did it,' said the British Council man thoughtfully. He was drawing lines of water with his finger on the back of his mist-covered glass of ice-cold beer.

'I can,' said Green simply. 'What I can't understand is why people like you refuse to face facts.' Mr Green was famous for speaking his mind. He wiped his red face with the white towel on his neck. 'The African is corrupt through and through.' ... 'They are all corrupt.' (*NLE*, 3)

Placed as it is within the Okonkwo saga, less than four pages from the Commissioner's meditation as a 'student of primitive customs' (*TFA*, 147), the clear inference readers are invited to draw here is that the remainder of Obi Okonkwo's narrative will work to debunk Green's patronising, colonialist thesis. As a result, when we do reach the end of the novel and the conclusion of the saga, it comes as a deeply unpleasant surprise to find that the reverse has actually been accomplished. Obi has, indeed, wasted his expensive education. He has, indeed, comprehensively betrayed the trust placed in him, and these developments have been set against a backdrop where they do not seem odd or anomalous, but as an inevitable reflection of Nigeria's modernity. This is a tale, it is worth remembering again, published at the very moment when that nation was gaining its freedom. Where every readerly instinct tells us that the heroic narrative of resistance should find its climax in freedom and independence, the themes Achebe instead chooses to leave us with are those of deracination, alienation and corruption.

Kola

Just like *Things Fall Apart*, *No Longer at Ease* ends on a note of bitter irony, as the coloniser once again has the final word, and in Obi's conviction the devastating force of this in Achebe's narrative makes itself felt. Reflecting back on the whole of the Okonkwo saga we now see the centrality of 'kola' as the emblem that truly links the past with the present. On the third page of *Things Fall Apart*, we are first introduced to the idea when

Okoye comes to visit Unoka. 'I have kola' (*TFA*, 5), he ceremoniously announces, and the disc is passed between the two men before he accepts the 'honour' of breaking it, praying to the ancestors as he does so. When the nut has been consumed, the serious business of the day is then addressed: Unoka is a debtor with obligations to fellow clan members, including Okoye. In *No Longer at Ease* his gestures and words – 'he who brings kola brings life' (*TFA*, 5) – are repeated as, in our first view of the Umuofians in Lagos, Obi Okonkwo's financial obligations to the clan are also opened for debate. We remember that, early in the first novel Okonkwo, too, has enacted the kola ritual when he visits the wealthy elder Nwakibie to ask for a loan of seed yams. As Kalu Ogbaa explains in *Gods Oracles and Divination: Folkways in Chinua Achebe's Novels*,[27] the bringing of kola here is much more than a respectful contribution of food, in the sense that a European might bring a bottle of wine to dinner at a friend's house. It signifies an acknowledgement of and tribute to Nwakibie's success and experience, before which Okonkwo demeans himself. The act of partaking in the kola by the senior man, his neighbours, wives and sons also, moreover, fulfils a further function, signifying that a space of negotiation between the two men is being opened up. Even as he humbles himself by paying tribute to his host, custom then allows Okonkwo to state his own expectations and ambitions: 'Let the kite perch and let the eagle perch too. If one says no to the other, let his wing break ... As our people say, a man who pays respect to the great paves the way for his own greatness' (*TFA*, 14). His language is coloured with proverbs. By bringing kola and breaking it before Nwakibie and the assembled company, he opens the formal dialogue that is necessary to his request for sponsorship. Claims he might make for himself in more everyday exchanges are here put as public undertakings:

> I know what it is to ask a man to trust another with his yams, especially these days when young men are afraid of hard work. I am not afraid of work. The lizard that jumped from the high iroko tree to the ground said he would praise himself if no one else did. I began to fend

for myself at an age when most people still suck at their mothers' breasts. If you give me some yam seeds I shall not fail you. (*TFA*, 15–16)

Reciprocating Okonkwo's display of purpose and moral seriousness, Nwakibie must also respond before the gathered company, justifying why, when he has refused the same favour to other young men, he will now give preferment to Okonkwo:

> When I say no to them they think I am being hardhearted. But it is not so. Eneke the bird says that since men have learnt to shoot without missing, he has learnt to fly without perching. I have learnt to be stingy with my yams. But I can trust you. I know it as I look at you. As our fathers said, you can tell a ripe corn by its look. I shall give you twice four hundred yams. Go ahead and prepare your farm. (*TFA*, 16)

In *No Longer at Ease*, both Unoka's and Okonkwo's narratives echo in careful and deliberate ways. From the outset, like them, Achebe places Obi in the debtor's position of one with material and ethical liabilities. How he will handle these liabilities is a test of character. In *Things Fall Apart*, Unoka refuses his obligations and dies shamefully, without title or status. By contrast, his son Okonkwo overcomes adversity to repay his debts, amassing wealth and respect within the clan. In Obi's narrative, however, the social order and hierarchies of esteem that both Unoka and Okonkwo take for granted have metamorphosed, almost beyond recognition. As a callow youth, instead of bringing kola to clan elders as a mark of respect, and as a preamble to requesting their patronage, 'kola' has now become a backhand payment offered by rich citizens to secure unfair preferment for their children. Like Nwakibie, Obi has the power to favour one young man or woman over many others, by providing them with the seeds (in this case, a place on the shortlist for overseas scholarships) from which a successful future can be cultivated. However, the social dividend he stands to derive is not, as for Nwakibie, acknowledgement of his wisdom and generosity of spirit, but egoistic sex with young girls and cash to cover his financial improvidence. While in the Umuofia of *Things Fall Apart*, we see the ritualistic meaning of kola as a token of respect and of dialogue conducted in good faith, in the Lagos of *No Longer at Ease* it has become almost the opposite: a symbol of corruption, inequity and civil irresponsibility. The young people for whom Obi can decide to exercise or withhold his influence will not be assessed on their merits or seriousness of purpose, as Okonkwo is before Nwakibie. They are to be preferred or not depending on their ability and willingness to secure advantage through monetary or sexual bribery.

The intervening event that has occasioned this cultural metamorphosis, between Okonkwo's offer of a kola nut to Nwakibie and Elsie Mark's offer of her body to Obi is, of course, the establishment of Britain's colonial hegemony over Nigeria. As the checks and balances that guaranteed the integrity and stability of pre-colonial culture break down in Umuofia, so we have seen how new hierarchies and mechanisms for the exercise of power have proliferated. In *Things Fall Apart*, Okonkwo and the other titled men are tricked and imprisoned by the District Commissioner when they attempt to open a respectful dialogue with him. When they have their heads shaved and are beaten and forced to soil themselves (*TFA*, 138), however, these humiliations are inflicted by his Igbo subordinates, a new class of intermediaries that, from the start, Achebe shows as born in corruption. Umuofia is fined two hundred bags of cowries by the Commissioner for burning down the missionaries' church: while sympathising with the clan's actions the reader is not prevented from perceiving the colonialist's logic in imposing such a punishment. When native court messengers compound the fine by extorting a further fifty bags for their own profit, however, there is no ambivalence of view. By the time we enter the world of *No Longer at Ease*, both bribery and extortion are depicted as commonplace and practiced by blacks and whites alike. As the president of the Umuofia Progressive Union remarks when the question of Obi's application to the senior civil service is discussed, '[y]ou think white men don't eat bribe? Come to our department. They eat more than black men nowadays' (*NLE*, 33). Once in post, Obi's belief is that when 'the old Africans at the top were replaced' (*NLE*, 38) by younger, educated men such as himself and his friends, corruption would be a thing of the past. His theory, which flagrantly compartmentalises corruption as an African and traditional practice while equating integrity and civil responsibility with Western values and with modernity, is soon put to the test, however. We know from the outset, after all, that he himself will ultimately be unable to resist the culture of bribery. Even at his trial, we have heard that fellow civil servants have 'paid as much as ten shillings and sixpence to obtain a doctor's certificate of illness for the day' (*NLE*, 2). Small-scale fraud, we are encouraged to conclude from the start, is endemic among Nigerian professionals generally. Certainly, the idea that Obi's position on the Scholarship Board would include the perk of personal payments has always been an assumption, rather than a hypothesis:

> 'What department he de work?'
> 'Secretary to the Scholarship Board.'
> "E go make plenty money there. Every student who wan' go England go de see am for house.'
> "E no be like dat,' said Joseph. 'Him na gentleman. No fit take bribe.'
> 'Na, so,' said the other in disbelief. (*NLE*, 77)

While Obi himself has presented himself, for a while, as more high-minded than his fellows, we have never seen much evidence of his attitude being a widespread one. On arrival from England, he has been offered a reduction of the import duty on his radio-gram in exchange for a cash-in-hand payment (*NLE*, 30). When travelling to Umuofia, police have extorted an inflated tariff of ten shillings when he challenged their demand for two shillings. As Mr Mark observes when he approaches Obi to offer a bribe on his sister's behalf, '[i]t is all very well sending in forms, but you know what our country is. Unless you see people …' (*NLE*, 86). Even the minister of state, the Honourable Sam Okoli, is reported as saying 'albeit in an unguarded, alcoholic moment, that the trouble was not in receiving bribes, but in failing to do the thing for which the bribe was given' (*NLE*, 88).

In the senior service, Obi has discovered the extent of the perks and privileges that expatriate officers, on secondment from the UK, have awarded themselves at the expense of the impoverished masses. While in Britain itself in the 1950s, car ownership, golf club membership and residency in the most prestigious districts of the capital would have been restricted to the rich alone, such emoluments are taken by Mr Green and his colleagues as of right. When Obi takes local leave (in colonial Nigeria, senior civil servants may take up to four months, compared to two weeks for their counterparts in England) he can claim an additional special allowance of £25. To put this in the perspective of contemporary readers, Nigeria's National Accounts for 1956 show that the country's Gross Domestic Product amounted to £54 per capita, in that year.[28] In the novel, Achebe is not slow to inform us that Isaac Okonkwo's monthly pension from the Church Missionary Society amounts to only £2, while clansmen working in Lagos must manage on £5. When he thinks about buying himself a fashionable, new model Morris Oxford motorcar, nothing more is required than walking into a dealership and showing that he is a 'senior civil servant entitled to a car advance' (*NLE*, 66). The same day, he receives an 'outfit allowance' (*NLE*, 67) of £60. Every month, as Obi reflects, even before perks and benefits he 'earned nearly fifty' (*NLE*, 98). In this context, the pecuniary outlook Achebe ascribes to the Umuofia Progressive Union is not difficult to understand:

> 'Have they given you a job yet?' the Chairman asked Obi … In Nigeria the government was 'they'. It had nothing to do with you or me. It was an alien institution and people's business was to get as much from it as they could without getting into trouble. (*NLE*, 33)

Far from working to refute the attitude of colonial administrator Green, who sees 'no single Nigerian who is prepared to forego a little privilege in the interests of his country' (*NLE*, 153), in other words, Achebe's depiction of the contemporary scene consistently seems to reinforce it. While Green fantasises about an Old Africa of 'tribal head-hunters' and 'weird ceremonies' (*NLE*, 106), the colonial enterprise for which he strives has been busy ensuring the breakdown of all of the values and social structures that guaranteed the health and cohesion of the community in traditional culture. As the missionary anthropologist George Basden wrote approvingly in 1921, 'every native institution [had] been shaken to its foundations'.[29] The modernity bequeathed to Obi and his generation in the form of the Nigerian nation-state is nothing more nor less than the product of that effort. 'Colonial rule was stronger than any marriage', Achebe tells us in *The Education of a British-Protected Child*.[30] If so, what *No Longer at Ease* does is to show us its offspring – a nation thoughtlessly and pragmatically cobbled between highly divergent cultural systems, whose forced union seems to have propagated the worst characteristics of each.

Although *No Longer at Ease*, standing on its own, does not take the outward form of a tragedy, its narrative does form the completion of *Things Fall Apart*. As Achebe repeatedly stresses in works such as *The Education of a British-Protected Child*, one of the unquantifiable costs of British colonialism was that it eroded and destroyed many of the most distinctive and, in many ways, admirable characteristics of the pre-colonial culture of the Igbo. Chief among these were its radical egalitarianism and commitment to meritocracy. Indeed, as we will see in the next chapter, the struggles of the colonising British to control a people so resistant to imposed hierarchies once again provided Achebe with one of the central themes in *Arrow of God*. In *Things Fall Apart*, as C. L. Innes argues, Umuofia is shown as regulated by the wisdom and experience of elders, who contrast sharply with the 'despotic and greedy native rulers' imagined by Joyce Cary and other white ventriloquists of African culture.[31] Achebe's elders, she suggests, 'share decision making' rather than arrogating power to themselves, earning the trust of the clan by demonstrating concern for 'the maintenance of a peaceful prosperous and respected community for all'.[32]

In that world, the very mechanism for rising to elder status, by acquiring progressively higher 'titles', itself worked as a democratising force. As Robert Wren says in *Achebe's World*, when *ozo* title holders spoke, they were expected to do so not on their own account but as spokesmen for the 'collective will of the clan itself'.³³ The requirements of *ozo* were such that they worked to prevent rather than to encourage the concentration of wealth and power, and in the communal interactions of traditional culture, the expectations engendered by the taking of the *ozo* title also worked to discourage abuse. Wren quotes Achebe's own account of the *ozo* institution to a group of students at the University of Washington in 1976:

> [Y]ou were not allowed ... to become too powerful, either politically or even economically ... the way they insure this was to say to you, 'you must take titles.' ... Now the [first] title taking will insure that you spend all your money ... after that, you ... take the second ... And the third, at greater cost, and even (rarely) a fourth ... they used to have the fifth title, the title of king ... and the reason this title went out of use was that you were required to pay the debt of every member of your community before you could become their king.³⁴

In this way, *ozo* helped to sustain the democratic equilibrium of communities like Umuofia at the same time as it provided a means of encouraging and recognising achievement. At one and the same time, it registered status and curtailed individual power. In *Things Fall Apart* even Okonkwo, who is depicted as strongly autocratic by temperament, is seen as conforming to the principle Wren describes. In both Umuofia and Mbanta, we see how he earns respect from clan members for the openhandedness with which he displays – but thereby expends – his wealth. In the inverted world of *No Longer at Ease*, Achebe shows how a similar set of expectations fall on Obi when he is elevated through foreign education. Within the very different dynamics of Nigeria's modernity, however, we soon learn that the show of wealth carries quite another set of connotations. Rather than working as a democratising force, it now functions to reinforce *separations* of power, access and status. The rewards that accrue to position – the club, residency in the sedate enclave of Ikoyi, car ownership – are privileges that isolate and insulate the elite from the rest of the people. Fraud, the acceptance of sexual bribes and the corrupt use of position for financial gain

– rather than the demonstration of open-handedness and generosity – now define the framework of social advancement. In other words, the forces governing status, wealth and power are no longer centrifugal but strongly centripetal. Just as we see in Achebe's depiction of the changing meaning of 'kola', here his narrative describes a movement from harmony and stability towards social division and unresolved conflict.

As we saw earlier, Achebe is frequently identified as a cultural nationalist, a mode in which colonial discourse is debunked in order to be supplanted by celebratory representations of a colonised people and their aspirations towards independent statehood. When *Things Fall Apart* and *No Longer at Ease* are viewed as originally conceived by Achebe, as a single family saga spanning the entire period of Britain's nation-building project in Nigeria, from the time of the Berlin conference to the eve of Britain's departure in 1960, the narrative decisions he takes, as well as those he chooses not to take, come to stark visibility. From a political and historical point of view, as we have seen, one of the most notable features of the Okonkwo saga is the self-conscious way it *avoids* programmatic opportunities for 'narrating the (Nigerian) nation' in an affirmative or aspirational way. There is, as we have seen, very little of the anti-colonial resistance narrative that histories of Igboland around the turn of the twentieth century would have supported. As we approach the moment of independence half a century later, indeed, the picture Achebe presents of Nigeria's final transition to self-government in the late 1950s is one seemingly calculated to extinguish hope and belief in patriotic sentiments. If pre-colonial culture in Igboland is seen as having its problems – domestic violence and infanticide being notable among them – Achebe's portrait of a modernity dominated by corruption, in which young women must prostitute themselves for advancement or undergo botched, backstreet abortions as Clara does, works to suggest that these have not disappeared, but merely taken new forms. In this sense, if Achebe's narrative does present a 'Nigerian master narrative, the organizing story of a nation'[35] as critics have been wont to claim, then it is certainly not a story told by a believer.

3
Arrow of God

Arrow of God was written in 1962 and 1963, during the heady years of independence. In his broadcasting career, Achebe had risen to Head of External Broadcasting for the Nigerian Broadcasting Corporation, directing its international service the Voice of Nigeria. Against an array of technical, financial and political constraints, his professional role was to project a strong and affirmative national image to surrounding African countries and the wider world. As we have already seen with *Things Fall Apart* and *No Longer at Ease*, however, the image of Nigeria-in-the-making offered by Achebe's first two novels by no means reflects that flag-waving brief. Despite the celebratory mood in Nigeria in the early 1960s, the tone of *Arrow of God* is also far from nationalistic. Continuing Achebe's archaeology of the processes that formed his nation, it exposes the destructive legacies of Britain's West African colonial project.

The historical focus of *Arrow of God* is on the 1920s, a decade in which Britain attempted to consolidate the gains made in its military campaign of 'pacification' against the Igbo, by imposing the indirect rule system favoured by the first Governor General of Nigeria, Lord Lugard. From the turn of the century, as High Commissioner in Northern Nigeria, Lugard had enjoyed comparative success with indirect rule. In the largely Islamic states of the north, political power had been centralised in the hands of Emirs for a hundred years prior to colonisation by the UK. Once colonial domination of the region had been established through a mixture of military force and negotiation, British rule then worked through these established authorities. Governing through local rulers who retained their former hierarchies and apparatuses of power presented much less of a challenge for the colonial administration in the North, it soon became clear, than did the more radically egalitarian 'stateless' societies in the South East. Igbo historian Adielo Afigbo's study *The Warrant Chiefs: Indirect Rule in Southeastern Nigeria, 1891–1929* records, for example, that colonial instructions issued to the Emirs of the North were officially known as 'advice',[1] with all the term's implications of consent and civility. The contrast between these polite codifications of control and relations in the South East during the same period could hardly have been starker. As Afigbo says of colonial methods in Igboland:

> The traditions of various villages as well as the official reports of the military patrols are full of stories of burnings of towns and seizures of traditional village headmen as a means of overawing the people ... During the Aro Expedition the policy was to demand guns from a village at the rate of one gun for every four houses. If the villagers failed to surrender guns to the satisfaction of the political officer accompanying the column, the soldiers either burnt the town or lived off it until the demands of the government were fully met ... It was also official policy to seize local leaders and keep them as hostages to be released only if government demands were met by their people.[2]

In the early years of the century, stories of the capture and maltreatment of elders were so widespread in Igboland that clans would frequently hand over individuals who 'were either courageous young men or rascals' in place of the real chiefs.[3] By comparison to the situation in Northern Nigeria, the refusal of Igbo communities to co-operate with their own colonisation made the policy of indirect rule very hard to implement. Indeed, by the time that *Arrow of God* is set in the 1920s, Britain had still not managed to establish a satisfactory template for government throughout the region. British District Officers had been stationed in each locality, overseeing the appointment of numerous native Warrant Chiefs who, it was thought, should have been able to mediate British authority successfully to their own people. As Achebe's novel accurately reflects, however, these arrangements met with strong passive resistance across the region. Since indigenous 'kings' were not forthcoming as the British had ignorantly expected, and because respected clan elders seem to have regarded the entire policy with scepticism and distrust, little help was forthcoming from the people to assist the British in establishing control of Igboland through a native 'governing class', as Lugard envisaged.

In *Arrow of God* Achebe illustrates this impasse in dramatic fashion through the story of Ezeulu, a priest who is offered, and declines, the chance of authority over his people as colonial Warrant Chief. As in his earlier fiction, Achebe's approach in the novel is fundamentally dialogic, allowing different and contradictory perspectives to complement and balance each other, including those of British colonialists as well as Igbo clanspeople. An interesting aspect of the narrative in this respect is that it takes care to depict the anxieties among some colonial officers over the inappropriateness of the policy pushed by the administration, whose effect was frequently to elevate 'libertines' and 'nonentities',[4] who 'all manage to turn themselves into little tyrants over their own people' (*AG*, 107).

When Achebe set out to write the novel, his intention was to create the missing part of a trilogy whose action would span a hundred years of history in South East Nigeria. Interviewed for the journal *Afrique* in 1962, he described his then work-in-progress as being 'about my father's generation, those who were Christianised'.[5] Already at that stage, he had fixed on the theme of conflict between a head priest and his village. Although the author's method at that time was not to conduct formal research, it is possible to identify certain key influences. Perhaps most importantly, Adielo Afigbo, a contemporary of Achebe's at University College Ibadan, was conducting his PhD research into the Warrant Chief system at the same time that Achebe was planning *Arrow of God*. Afigbo's work contains an extraordinary detailed analysis (for its time) of the origin and workings of the indirect rule system in Igboland. Afigbo was becoming one of the rising stars of new Nigerian

Historiography, and Achebe took an interest in his developing reputation while working as a features producer for the Nigerian Broadcasting Corporation. In *Arrow of God*, the subtlety and detail with which he represents British colonialism suggests that, although *The Warrant Chiefs* was not published until 1972, Achebe was privy to much of Afigbo's work. Indeed, as Robert Wren remarks, although 'Achebe denies that he researched the novel ... he was well aware of details of the Warrant Chieftaincy dispute that only a successful worker in colonial archives could discover.'[6] One of the effects of this is seen in the way he approaches the portrayal of white colonial officers. While in *Things Fall Apart* his portrait of District Commissioner George Allen in swift and scathing, in *Arrow of God* he invests much more space and time in evoking the distinctive sensibility of colonialists such as Winterbottom and Wright. The novel communicates a sophisticated understanding of the way such men seemed to understand their role in Nigeria, combining unshakeable racism with affection and concern for 'the African'. This in turn allows Achebe to create a split focus in the novel that throws the colonial encounter into vivid perspective. Familiarity with both the political disputes within the colonial administration, and the ways these were mediated to officers on the ground, makes it possible for him to present colonialism as a force that was, in reality, far from monolithic, often incoherent and lacking clear policy direction.

In the 1970s, the reputation of *Arrow of God* and of Achebe himself were thrown into crisis by the accusation that he had lifted the bulk of the novel, without any kind of acknowledgement, from the work of another writer. The work in question was amateur historian Simon Nnolim's *The History of Umuchu*.[7] In 1957, during his time in the Talks Department at the NBC, Achebe and a media team had visited the village of Umuchu, about twenty five miles from his home town of Ogidi, to research the performance of its Night Masks. During that visit he had interviewed Nnolim about the history and traditional customs of the area, many of which were (apparently) adapted for use in *Arrow of God*. Among other things, Nnolim's pamphlet describes a series of historical events in 1913, when the High Priest Ezeagu was called to Akwa by District Commissioner J. G. Lotain, who offered him the position of Warrant Chief, with jurisdiction and authority over his entire clan. When Ezeagu refused, arguing that the role was incompatible with tradition and with his priestly function, he was imprisoned for two months. Like Achebe's fictional Ezeulu, it was part of Ezeagu's ceremonial role to roast and eat one sacred yam each month and to initiate the Feast of the Seed Yams at the appointed time each year. While incarcerated by the colonial authorities, he was unable to fulfil this role and on his return, like Ezeulu, he refused to eat two yams in one month. The symbolic feast, which represented the conclusion of one harvest year and the beginning of the next, was delayed as a result, and its changed position in the calendar remains to this day.

In a 1977 article in the respected journal *Research in African Literatures*, the author's nephew Charles Nnolim publically attacked Achebe for his use of this source, claiming that the writer had 'lifted everything in *The History of Umuchu* and simply transferred it to *Arrow of God* without embellishment'.[8] Going further, he asserted that '*Arrow of God* is little more than a fictional expansion of *The History of Umuchu* by Simon A. Nnolim.'[9] In common with other critics such as C. L. Innes, who published a riposte in the following issue of the same journal,[10] I would argue that Nnolim's claims that Achebe essentially 'copied' the whole of his third novel from Nnolim's uncle's pamphlet are, in fact, wildly overstated. Although Achebe does draw some key narrative elements from Umuchu's local history, in common with other sources of information such as Afigbo's research on the Warrant Chief system, the impact and meaning of his work arises from the bold way he assigns significance to the events recorded by Simon Nnolim, patterning them into a larger analysis of the Igbo experience in the 1920s. In the latter's account, a feast is postponed, but no one suffers as a result. In *Arrow of God*, on the other hand, a clan is brought to the point of self-destruction. This is because, in the climactic final part of the novel, Ezeulu's refusal to abandon tradition by eating two yams has the effect of delaying the start of the harvest, so that Umuaro's vital yam crop is left rotting in the ground. The on-going implications of his refusal are disastrous: if the clan follow him and adhere to tradition, both planting and harvest will not only be delayed for one year but for every year following. What is in Nnolim's account an episode illustrating the adaptability and resilience of traditional culture therefore becomes, in Achebe's version, almost the reverse – a narrative of perverse inflexibility and self-destructiveness. Where Nnolim's pamphlet illustrates minor disruptive effects wrought by the colonial administration, Achebe's novel shifts the focus on to the unwitting role of Igbo communities in facilitating their own subjugation.

With *Things Fall Apart*, we have already explored this to some extent. There, colonial violence is represented through the destruction of Abame, but as I argued in chapter 2, only obliquely and at some distance from Umuofia and its dealings. In this sense, *Things Fall Apart* works to circumvent the large scale campaign of military suppression against the people of Igboland led by Sir Ralph Moor at the turn of the century, including the destruction of the Igbo's pre-eminent shrine at Aro-Chukwu. As a work that is often read as an effort at reclaiming the historical experience of the Igbo immediately prior to and during the colonial phase, this elision is of some significance for the way we read Achebe's first novel. In *Arrow of God*, we see a similar ambivalence. Umuaro is presented in the novel as the most resistant of all the clans within the District Officer's jurisdiction. The punishment it suffers at the hands of the colonialists is, however, really a pale shadow of Britain's actual campaign of pacification, as described by Afigbo and others. We see a seizure of guns – and the effect of this is that wars between the villages are suppressed. We see the forced co-option of some young men to assist with road building in their area, and the whipping of Ezeulu's son Obika. Here too, however, we see some measure of mitigation. Obika is drunk when he turns up for work, mocks the white overseer and then tries to attack him. Resistance, too, is underplayed: although the young men later arrange a meeting to discuss their response, Achebe prefaces his account of the exchange with the simple summary: 'Nothing came of it' (*AG*, 83). They agree not to contest the demand for their labour, and decide instead to ask for payment in line with that of other co-opted workers.

As the work of numerous historians illustrates, Achebe's portrayal here once again has the effect of drawing a veil over many reports of abuses perpetrated by the British against Igbo communities. According to the well-respected historian Don Ohadike, for example, 'in 1906 when some clans in the Agbo district protested against the incessant use of forced labour, several hundreds of them were shot by colonial troops'.[11] Reinforcing Ohadike's analysis, Adielo Afigbo reports similarly in his study *The Abolition of the Slave Trade in Southeastern Nigeria 1885–1950* that 'during one of the expeditions against the Qua Iboe (Annang), nineteen towns were burnt to the ground. Before executions took place, the government would usually invite observers from within a radius of 15 to 20 miles and later enjoin them to spread the story of what they had seen.'[12] The reputation of individual District Commissioners and their officers – often much less sympathetic as characters than Achebe's Winterbottom – preceded them to the communities who had to deal with them. In Nssuka district, for example, Afigbo cites a Mr Heron, who was known to the locals as *Otikpo Obodo* or 'wrecker of villages'. The ruthless approach adopted by the British was specifically designed to induce 'shock and fear' in the local population, he argues, as 'harsh punishments taught all and sundry that the new masters were not to be toyed with'.[13]

In the specific region of Igboland described by *Arrow of God*, which includes Ogidi, the ancestral village of Achebe's family, colonial muscle was flexed particularly strongly between 1904 and 1908, during the Bende–Onitsha expedition. This was an enterprise designed to forcibly subdue an area of around 3,500 square miles extending (north–south) from ten miles north of Onitsha to Owerri and (east–west) from the Niger river to Afikpo. An illuminating eye-witness account of participation in this expedition was published by British Royal Artilleryman

Lieutenant Edward Steel in *The Geographical Journal* in 1908. In his narrative, Steel describes the tactics used to subdue the peoples of the area, as well as providing first-hand testimony of Igbo responses to the British incursion. As he remarks, 'that they [the Igbo] are full of self-assurance is evident from the insolent messages and presents of guns and gunpowder which often arrive by emissaries for the nearest political officer, expressing the hope that the "white man" will *now* not fear to come, for "we are ready to fight him."'[14] Columns of British soldiers typically proceeded by trapping unwary locals and subjecting them to interrogation about the surrounding country and population centres. According to Steel, however, when an individual was caught, he typically 'professed to know nothing about the next town, either its name or the way to it, saying he had never been out of his own compound'.[15]

Steel's description, like those of many subsequent, historical accounts of the colonial encounter in Igboland in the early decades of the twentieth century, evidences both the aggressiveness of the tactics deployed by the British in the region, and the extent of active and passive resistance to their campaign of control. As Afigbo argues, the fundamental tools of colonial subjugation for the first two decades of the century were military patrols and incursions, with political negotiation and cultural rapprochement playing a distinctly secondary role. Summing up the events of the period, he concludes that '[m]ilitary conquest was the ultimate basis of the *pax Britannica* in colonial Southeastern Nigeria ... clear[ing] the way for the traders and missionaries who had been hovering around the estuaries of the major rivers and creeks ... to surge into the interior'.[16]

In *Arrow of God*, we see a little, but not much of this violent struggle between the British colonialists and the Igbo who resisted them. Indeed, just as we saw with *Things Fall Apart*, Achebe shows very little interest at all in developing the nationalist narrative of invasion, resistance and confrontation that many critics have sought in his work. If the Igbo were ultimately subjugated by British colonialism in this period, that tragedy offers little in the way of catharsis, as Achebe presents it. If anything, it is more of the kind described by Obi in *No Longer at Ease*, one that 'takes place in a corner, in an untidy spot', without the 'purging of the emotions' (*NLE*, 39) that a grand, heroic tale of conflict and loss might engender. Subverting formulaic expectations once again, what he portrays instead in *Arrow of God* is a community, lacking clear direction, which falls apart largely as a function of its own internal squabbles.

Early in the narrative, this story begins when we learn the reason why Umuaro exists at all. It is a union of six villages which, in earlier times, were often at war with each other, but which were eventually forced to come together to defend against the attacks of Abam warriors:

> Then the hired soldiers of Abam used to strike in the dead of night, set fire to the houses and carry men, women and children into slavery. Things were so bad for the six villages that their leaders came together to save themselves. They hired a strong team of medicine-men to install a common deity for them. This deity which the fathers of the six villages made was called Ulu. Half of the medicine was buried at a place which became the Nkwo market and the other half was thrown into the stream which became Mili Ulu. The six villages then took the name of Umuaro, and the priest of Ulu became their chief priest. From that day they were never again beaten by an enemy. How could such a people disregard the god who founded their town and protected it? (*AG*, 14–15)

Achebe's portrayal here stays close to historical evidence. As John Oriji argues in an essay on the history of slavery in Igboland, the Abam were a feared mercenary force used by the dominant Aro people in Igboland during the eighteenth and nineteenth centuries to conduct slave raids on weak and poorly defended communities. During this period, Igbo villages frequently linked together for mutual defence. One historical example cited by Oriji is that of Umuchu, formed from the union of Ihite, Ogwugwu and Okpu-na-Achla peoples, 'autonomous communities that are said to have collectively hired the services of a native doctor, not only to cement their unity but to prevent Abam incursions with his medicine'.[17]

In *Things Fall Apart*, as we have seen, the destruction of Abame by the British appears as a pure example of colonial aggression. In *Arrow of God*, however, it acquires a completely different resonance. By destroying the Abam, we now find, the British have successfully rid all the surrounding peoples of the most serious threat to their safety and livelihoods. By the same token, and before the main action of *Arrow of God* has even commenced, the founding reason for Umuaro's existence has also been eliminated.

Protagonist Ezeulu's position as high priest of a deity created to guard against a now-obsolete threat is, at the outset, ripe for challenge. Even as, in chapter 1, Ezeulu considers 'the immensity of his power over the year and the crops and, therefore, over the people' (*AG*, 3), Achebe begins to set him up for a fall. From the first, we are privy to his anxieties about the resilience of his power:

> It was true he named the day for the feast of the Pumpkin Leaves and for the New Yam Feast; but he did not choose it. He was merely a watchman. His power was no more than the power of a child over a goat that was said to be his. As long as the goat was alive it could be his; he would find it food and take care of it. But the day it was slaughtered he would know soon enough who the real owner was. (*AG*, 3)

At the same time, we see Ezeulu fantasising about the drama he might create if he were to refuse his duty to announce the symbolic annual feasts. Even as he does so, the intuition of his real impotence fills him with self-disgust. No man in Umuaro can question his will, he tells himself, as he worries simultaneously about the meaning of a power that could never be used. 'Better to say that it was not there, that it was no more than the power of the anus of the proud dog who sought to put out a furnace with his puny fart' (*AG*, 4). As the narrative proceeds, it is in the space between these warring impulses that Achebe begins to build Ezeulu's character.

When we see dissenting opinions voiced within the clan, Achebe makes Ezeulu the mouthpiece for custom and tradition, but also inserts a note of lamentation in his voice: 'the world is spoilt, and there is no longer head or tail in anything that is done' (*AG*, 27). As the drama steadily builds, he then uses the figure of Nwaka to suggest the increasingly precarious nature of Ezeulu's power. Nwaka himself is drawn as an exemplar of other revered principles, including those of meritocratic achievement and the traditional Igbo refusal of autocracy. As Nwaka is not slow to point out to the clan's titled men, the god Ezeulu serves, Ulu, was nothing but a pragmatic creation, made years ago as a forced response to a threat at that time. In such circumstances, he points out, the people of Aninta destroyed an obsolete god by carrying him to the boundary of their lands, burning him and driving out his priest. His suggestion is brazenly blasphemous, and Nwaka's friends and kinsmen tremble for him, anticipating Ulu's displeasure. As Achebe tells us, however, their fears are misplaced. 'His head did not ache, nor his belly; and he did not groan in the middle of the night' (*AG*, 39). What is the status of Ulu's power, we are encouraged to ask, in these changing times?

As *Arrow of God* unfolds, the schematic opposition between Ezeulu and Nwaka, as representatives of opposing strands of Igbo culture, provides one of the central structures of Achebe's narrative. On the one hand, Ezeulu's power derives directly from his relationship to Ulu, but his position as high priest is also a hereditary one, passing from father to son rather than earned like other titles through merit and application. Without it, as a son of the weakest of the six villages, he would have no influence at all. On the other hand, Nwaka's own status as a man who commands respect for the eloquence of his voice and for the success of his enterprises is repeatedly emphasised. Sketching his imposing figure in chapter 2, Achebe foregrounds the bronze anklet and red cap with its eagle feather that mark him as an achiever of the high *Eru* title. When Nwaka meets with his mentor Ezidemili, priest of the water deity, however, we begin to see that the growing rivalry within the clan encompasses more than the difference between earned *versus* inherited status. On a different level, it also revolves around key, unanswered questions about the changing status of traditional deities, as colonialism strengthens its grip. As Ezidemili is keen to remind Nwaka, before the creation of Ulu as an expediency against Abam attacks, 'the leaders of each village had been men of high title like Nwaka' (*AG*, 41). Ezeulu, too, is aware of this underlying struggle for precedence. 'He knew that the priests of Idemili and Ogwugwu and Eru and Udo had never been happy with their secondary role since the villages got together and made Ulu and put him over the other deities' (*AG*, 40).

Having built his narrative largely in terms of these tensions and oppositions within Umuaro, Achebe brings matters to a head in the sequence in which Ezeulu is summoned to Okperi by the white man. Until this point, Ezeulu has been painted as a man who, while uncertain and equivocal in his own thinking, presents a face of pride and arrogance within the public setting of the clan. We hear early in the novel that he has gone against the will of other elders in his testimony to the white man in a land dispute, and that he has courted criticism by sending his son to learn the white man's knowledge in the mission school. As we learn in chapter 8, he regards possession of the English language as an 'honour' (*AG*, 77). Among Umuaro people he has garnered prestige from the belief that he and Winterbottom are friends. As readers, we know that the District Officer has chosen Ezeulu for the position of Warrant Chief and can anticipate that the priest is worldly enough to understand the implications of the messenger's summons. With the offer of unassailable authority in the white man's name, it would seem as if all of Ezeulu's plans are coming to fruition.

Instead, in a dramatic reverse, we see Ezeulu first insult Winterbottom by refusing to attend him in Okperi, before compromising with the empty gesture of sending his son. Sensing advantage, Nwaka likens the white man's invitation to that of a leper who, having shaken hands with Ezeulu now 'want[s] an embrace' (*AG*, 143). His assumption is that a trap has been set for Ezeulu, and that he has no one to blame but himself. 'You passed the shit that is smelling; you should carry it way' (*AG*, 144). Over the following two chapters, Achebe then dramatically and unexpectedly resolves this narrative uncertainty, crystallising the foregoing action not in terms of a campaign of resistance to colonialism, but instead in terms of a self-destructive internecine struggle over Umuaro. As we follow the direction of Ezeulu's thoughts in chapter 14, we now see that the real struggle was never with the British administration, but always between the warring personalities of the clan.

> Now he looked at it again more closely and one thing stood out. His quarrel with the white man was insignificant beside the matter he must settle with his own people. For years he had been warning Umuaro not to allow a few jealous men to lead them into the bush. But they had stopped both ears with fingers. They had gone on taking one dangerous step after another and now they had gone too far. They had taken away too much for the owner not to notice. Now the fight must take place, for until a man wrestles with one of those who make a path across his homestead the others will not stop. Ezeulu's muscles tingled for the fight. (AG, 160)

Speaking to the clan elders, Ezeulu is provocative and infantilising, deliberately setting aside the Igbo ethos of dialogue and mutual respect. Gone is the man who exercised power with moderation, advising his friend Akuebue to soften his authority with conciliatory words. His refusal of the Warrant Chieftaincy, we now see clearly, was motivated simply by the determination to strengthen his power in a different way. As he reflects, 'his real struggle was with his own people and the white man was, without knowing it, his ally' (AG, 176).

Achebe's portrayal of Ezeulu's interactions with the acting District Officer Clarke, here, are illuminating. While Clarke, with predictable colonial arrogance, offers the chieftaincy with the complacent feeling of a 'benefactor' (AG, 174), Ezeulu's response is 'proud inattention' and 'instead of gratitude ... scorn' (AG, 174). Both men are aware of the daring and insubordination implicit in his stance as a 'witch-doctor making a fool of the British Administration' (AG, 175). For his part, although Clarke vents his annoyance by having Ezeulu locked in the guardhouse following their confrontation, however, Achebe also shows him as being disturbed by the 'silly' situation of having 'clap[ped] an old man ... into jail without reasonable explanation' (AG, 178).

After a month Ezeulu is released without charge or further molestation.

For the priest, the only important question is how to wield the power he has acquired over the clan. Sitting back in his Obi as a procession of visitors come to congratulate or commiserate, the dilemma once again is not how to fend off the white man but how far to punish Umuaro for their failure to follow him unquestioningly. In his account of the ensuing days Achebe represents his protagonist as a man engrossed with scheming and the weighing of his own advantage; '[b]ehind his thinking was of course the knowledge that the fight would not begin until the time of harvest, after three moons more. So there was plenty of time. Perhaps it was this knowledge that there was no hurry which gave him confidence to play with alternatives' (*AG*, 191). As the narrative enters its last phase, Achebe is careful to make the reader aware of the costs Umuaro is likely to suffer for the struggle between its leaders. By this stage, it is also clear that Ezeulu's perverse adherence to tradition (reflecting the perversity of Ulu himself) needs little help from colonialism to mortally wound the clan.

In affective terms, Achebe's arrangement of this final part of the novel works strongly to throw our sympathies as readers into question. As the protagonist with whom we have been encouraged to sympathise becomes increasingly withdrawn and destructive, the narrative works to diminish him in other ways too. In one episode, for example, Ezeulu calls his son Oduche into his hut to impress on him the importance of gathering knowledge from the white man. Speaking of Clarke, he tells his son, 'I could see that he had very little sense. But he had power; he could shout in my face; he could do what he liked. Why? Because he could write with his left hand' (*AG*, 189). Achebe's reader of course understands the priest's error, and the narrative, in effect, mocks at his ignorance in equating left-handedness with mastery. On an emotional level, Ezeulu is shown as deriving comfort only from thoughts of revenge and from such accomplishments as humiliating Oduche and reducing him to tears. When he is visited by the god Ulu and ordered not to stand in the way of his will,

Achebe plays skilfully on the ambiguity of the scene. Is the reader to understand Ulu here as an authentic manifestation of Igbo ontology – in other words to consider this as a genuine, divine visitation? Alternatively, is the reader to interpret the encounter as a product of Ezeulu's fantasy? In the preceding chapter, Achebe has already raised the question of his precarious grasp on sanity through a taunt from Nwaka about the priest's mother who, as the narrator has confirmed, 'suffered from severe but spasmodic attacks of madness' (*AG*, 176). Earlier, when Obika attacks Mr Wright, we have also heard the rumour from Moses Unachukwu that 'not one person in your father's house has a right head' (*AG*, 82). As the reader will soon discover, Ezeulu's ultimate trajectory is precisely in this direction, towards the image of a broken man destined 'in his last days, to live in the haughty splendour of a demented high priest' (*AG*, 229) who understands none of the consequences of his actions. Both possibilities – that Ulu is an active deity, controlling his priest, or alternatively that Ezeulu, as the priest of an obsolete god and verging on insanity, is engaging in a private war of his own – are kept alive by the novel. On the level of affect, however, I would argue that the way Achebe chooses to frame his narrative here seems calculated to erode and undermine the reader's sympathies with the priest and his god. In a detached way, we are invited to observe how Umuaro's resilience and self-determination are undone by those who should fight hardest to defend it.

At the beginning of the novel, it is worth pointing out, this outcome is far from clear. In the opening chapters, we were given to understand that the Ulu and his associated priesthood were created by the fathers of the clan in a wise and far-sighted way intended to assure mutual defence and at the same time to 'ensure that none in the alliance became too powerful' (*AG*, 15). Like Obierika in *Things Fall Apart*, Akuebue airs the celebrated philosophy of the Igbo when he urges his friend to be tolerant and to accommodate differing voices and views. When the crisis arises over Ezeulu's invitation from Winterbottom, we have again seen the dialogic ethos of Umuaro in action. After Nwaka has spoken against Ezeulu, other dissenting voices are raised, presenting alternative perspectives. Despite Nwaka's wealth and position, Nwokeke Nnabenyi feels entitled to chastise him when he attempts to interrupt: 'Ogbuefi Nwaka, please do not speak into my words. You stood up here and spoke to your fill and no one answered you back' (*AG*, 144). Much later in the novel, when the elders come to Ezeulu to beg him to seek appeasement from Ulu, the flexible and accommodating nature of the clan's culture is foregrounded once again:

> Nnanyelugo deftly steered the conversation to the subject of change. He gave numerous examples of customs that had been altered in the past when they began to work hardship on the people. They talked at length about these customs which had either died in full bloom or had been stillborn. Nnanyelugo reminded them that even in the matter of taking titles there had been a change. Long, long ago there had been a fifth title in Umuaro – the title of king. But the conditions for its attainment had been so severe that no man had ever taken it, one of the conditions being that the man aspiring to be king must first pay the debts of every man and every woman in Umuaro. (*AG*, 209)

As we saw in chapter 2 and will see repeatedly throughout this book, this is of a piece with Achebe's writing as a whole, in which the theme of Igbo culture's egalitarianism and commitment to dialogue is referred to again and again. In *Arrow of God*, we see this culture under threat from two directions. Externally, it is put under pressure by the ever increasing encroachment of colonialism. Internally, it is set the challenge of dealing with the ambitions and rivalry of powerful individuals who are prepared to sacrifice much to see their own ideas prevail.

Beginning with the external dimension, how much of a threat is colonialism shown as posing, in *Arrow of God*, to the integrity of traditional Igbo culture? As we have already seen, colonial aggression certainly figures as a backdrop to Ezeulu's tragedy, in that it is the destruction of Abame and its warriors that has precipitated Ulu's crisis of legitimacy. In chapter 8, when Obika arrives drunk and late for a road-building detail, Achebe shows the white overseer Wright, 'unable to control his anger any longer' (*AG*, 81), lash out with his whip. Obika responds by charging at him, and we see Wright viciously dealing out 'half a dozen more lashes on his bare back' (*AG*, 82). Ezeulu too, of course, experiences the authoritarian side of the administration when he humiliates Assistant District Officer Clarke by refusing to accept the Warrant Chieftaincy. Throughout the novel, Achebe also shows the racism that predefines the thinking of the colonial officers. We witness Captain Winterbottom theorising, for example, about the 'elemental cruelty in the psychological make-up of the native' (*AG*, 58) and his belief that tyranny is a 'trait in the character of the negro' (*AG*, 107). With Wright, Achebe presents the image of a colonial functionary who oscillates between affection for the co-opted workers who he imagines to be 'loyal as pet dogs' (*AG*, 76) and anger with them as lazy, workshy 'black monkeys' (*AG*, 82). In this sense, *Arrow of God* is not afraid to show some aspects of the physical and ideological violence that characterised Britain's attempts to subjugate Igboland in the 1920s.

At the same time, however, it is important to recognise that Achebe's overall portrait of colonialism itself in this novel is also that of a fundamentally self-divided and incoherent enterprise. This is something of which the District Officer is acutely aware:

> 'What I find so heart-rending,' said Winterbottom, 'is not so much the wrong policies of our administration as our lack of consistency. Take this question of Paramount Chiefs. When Sir Hugh Macdermot first arrived as Governor he sent his Secretary for Native Affairs to investigate the whole business. The fellow came over here and spent a long time discovering the absurdities of the system which I had pointed out all along. Anyhow, from what he said in private conversation it was clear that he agreed with us that it had been an unqualified disaster. That was in 1919 ... More than two years and we still have heard nothing about the man's report. On the contrary the Lieutenant-Governor now asks us to proceed with the previous policy. Where does anyone stand?' (*AG*, 108–9)

At first hand we see Wright's disregard of the rights of his Igbo workers, as he crumples Winterbottom's written advice that '[t]he natives cannot be an exception to the aphorism that the labourer is worthy of his hire' (AG, 76). By the same token, however, we also see his superior's concern at his methods, to the extent that Winterbottom asks his assistant Clarke to investigate. In the world of *Arrow of God*, Wright's abuses are presented as the exception to the rule rather than as representative of British behaviour in general. Similarly, while Ezeulu is subjected to false imprisonment at the hands of the colonial regime, we also see Clarke's discomfiture over this, when he recognises the lack of defensible principle in his actions.

Repeatedly, in his portrait of the colonial enterprise, Achebe takes trouble to portray a sense of idealism, uneasily rubbing shoulders with exploitation and abuse. In chapter 5, for example, we see Winterbottom receive a memorandum from the Lieutenant-Governor stressing that the objective of colonialism is not to establish 'government by white men' but to 'build a higher civilisation upon the soundly rooted native stock that had its foundation in the hearts and minds and thoughts of the people ... enlisting the real force of the spirit of the people' (AG, 55–6). His sentiments, juxtaposed with Winterbottom's emotional response to them – 'couldn't someone tell the bloody man that the whole damn thing was stupid and futile' (AG, 56) – perfectly illustrate the divided colonial mind-set evoked by the novel. In *Arrow of God*'s later scenes, we see Winterbottom's physical as well as political diminishment, and Achebe uses this to bring a sense of division and disquiet to the fore. When Winterbottom is finally vindicated by the instruction that all plans to extend the Warrant Chief system are to be suspended, we are told only that he 'muttered under his breath something like: *Shit on the Lieutenant Governor!*' (AG, 181).

In Achebe's portrayal, the overall impression we are offered of British colonialism is of an inconsistent and somewhat unhappy endeavour. If these qualities tend to hamper its efforts to win the hearts and minds of the Igbo, the ignorance and arrogance of its officers do little to help. Winterbottom, for all his seriousness, is painted as something of a buffoon. In his own mind, he is 'the man on the spot who knew his African', unlike the 'starry-eyed fellows at headquarters' (AG, 56). Like the District Commissioner George Allen in *Things Fall Apart*, he is a collector of native customs who approaches his governmental role partly with the eye of an anthropologist. As the narrator says, 'Captain Winterbottom enjoyed mystifying other Europeans with words from the Ibo language which he claimed to speak fluently' (AG, 149). On such fundamental political questions as the place of kingship and the structure of authority within the region he is attempting to govern, however, Achebe shows the ways in which his pomposity is grounded in ignorance. Justifying his choice of Ezeulu for the Warrant Chieftaincy, he explains to Clarke that 'the man's title is Eze Ulu. The prefix *eze* in Ibo means king. So the man is a kind of priest king' (AG, 107). As the reader knows, Winterbottom is quite wrong in this context to interpret 'Eze' – Ezeulu's priestly title – also as 'king'. Through Nwaka, Achebe has stressed in chapter 2 that Umuaro has no king. As Achebe himself explained to Michel Fabre in a 1973 interview, in speaking to the Umuaro elders the term 'king' is used 'to talk about an individual who sets himself apart and against society by wanting to set himself above it. Such behaviour would run against the social cohesion and group integration so dear to traditional Ibo communities.'[18]

Ignorance, pomposity, incoherence and sporadic abuse of authority are all included in Achebe's portrait of the British administration in *Arrow of God*. For all this, however, and in common with *Things Fall Apart*, his representation of colonial violence is ultimately very restrained. While we are reminded of the destruction of a village (Abame) two decades before, we now also learn that its people were slave-raiders, terrorising nearby clans. While we see a village elder (Ezeulu) imprisoned, we also see that he anticipates and exploits this treatment, hoping to gain advantage in an internal struggle for power over his clan. We do not see villages burnt to the ground, like the ones documented by Afigbo in *The Warrant Chiefs*. We are not asked to witness the implementation of Lugard's *Collective Punishment Ordinance* of 1912, which in the hands of District Officers throughout Igboland, as Romanus Okey Muoneke writes, 'became one of the most obnoxious means of pacification'.[19] In practice, communities who resisted the British advance through the Igbo hinterland in this period were met with far greater brutality than *Arrow of God* suggests. In such cases, according to Robert Wren, the typical pattern of response was that '[n]o effort would be made to identify guilty individuals ... the soldiers came to shoot people and to destroy dwellings'.[20] In the novel, Achebe does suggest something of the unease with colonial policy felt by officers on the ground, especially through the character of Winterbottom. He shows little, however, of the actuality experienced by Igbo people in this period, which as Wren argues was that 'the white man could not rule these independent stateless societies save by terror'.[21]

If Achebe's representation of colonialism as an external threat to Umuaro tends to underplay the levels of brutality and violence reported by historians, then what of his portrayal of *internal* tensions that threaten the clan? Here, I would suggest, we find the reverse to be the case. It is not Achebe's District Officer, or even the catechist, who forbids the harvesting of the crucial subsistence crop, precipitating a fatal division of loyalties, but the clan's chief priest himself. It is not the abusive overseer Wright who sews dissention among the elders, so that they are left fatally dis-unified in their response to invaders, but key figures among the priests and elders themselves. In this sense, what we see in *Arrow of God* is a clan brought to the point of falling apart less because it is proactively subordinated by the machinery of colonialism, than because it is unable to regulate the internal tensions and rivalries that the colonial presence has lifted to the surface.

In such episodes as Oduche's attack on the sacred python, we see how Achebe's narrative works to propel us towards this narrative conclusion. On the side of the Christians, he uses the episode to vividly dramatise the moral dilemmas of the Igbo converts, who were urged by their missionary teachers not merely to abandon the traditional religion but to desecrate its sacred symbols. As Ifi Amadiume records in an influential study of Igbo traditional culture, in this period Christian converts and upholders of the traditional religion did frequently clash over the issue of respect for religious symbols such as the python of Idemili.[22] For their part, as Achebe shows in *Things Fall Apart*, communities typically responded to abominations committed by Christians by ostracising their missions and denying them access to key shared resources like waterways. At times, as in one particular incident in Nnobi, described by Amadiume, they responded more violently, pursuing offenders and setting fire to their houses. As she says, the practice, among zealous converts, of killing and even eating the python was the focus of particular controversy.[23] In *Arrow of God*, however, we hear voices of moderation among the Christians, with even ardent converts such as Moses Unachukwu counselling caution. When catechist Goodcountry denounces veneration of the python as idolatry and associates it with original sin, Unachukwu's advice is that 'if you want to do your work in peace you will heed what I have said, but if you want to be the lizard that ruined his own mother's funeral you may carry on as you are doing' (*AG*, 50). Umuaro people, he foresees, will want to exact a terrible price for interference with one of their most sacred symbols. In Ezeulu's compound, soon afterwards, we see Oduche's fear and ambivalence when he resolves to prove his faith by killing one. On the side of the clan, however, these dramas of faith and commitment are very weakly reflected. Idemili's priest, the servant of a subordinate male god, takes the opportunity not to declare war on the Christians, but instead to insult Ezeulu and question his authority. For his part, Ezeulu sends not one word of protest to the mission, so preoccupied is he to trade Ezidemili's insult and to 'hurl defiance' (*AG*, 59) at all of his other detractors. When Oduche returns, his father does not even address the subject of the abomination he has committed, and neither does he withdraw him from the mission school. Once again, what Achebe chooses to foreground is not the clan's efforts to counter the imperialist threat posed by missionary Christianity, but rather the way its own internal struggles and tensions prevent it from mounting such resistance.

Gender and resistance

In 1963, while he was working on *Arrow of God*, Achebe was interviewed by Lewis Nkosi and Wole Soyinka at the Museum of Nigeria in Lagos. Their discussion started by considering a carving of Ikenga picked out by Achebe and representing, as Soyinka says, the 'spirit of manhood'.[24] Asked by Soyinka to elaborate on its significance, Achebe cites Okonkwo in *Things Fall Apart* who, for him 'symbolises strength and aggressiveness'. As Achebe says of the Igbo in traditional culture, these are 'qualities that his people admire, and I wanted a character who could be called representative of this particular group of people'.[25] Questioned, then, on his own attitude to this society which, in Soyinka's words, 'places so much premium on ... a kind of exhibitionist side of the masculine ego',[26] Achebe is startlingly unambiguous:

> The weakness of this particular society, I think, is a lack of adaptation, not being able to bend ... the strong men were those who did not bend, and I think this was a fault in the culture itself ... This is what I was saying to Wole earlier on, that this particular society has believed too much in manliness and perhaps this is part of the reason why it crashed in the end.[27]

At the time when he was working on *Arrow of God*, it seems, Achebe's perception was that traditional Igbo culture had a fatal flaw. Colonialism may have provided the catalyst for change at the turn of the twentieth century, but it was also Igbo culture's inbuilt, self-destructive competitiveness and masculinist bias that caused things to fall apart.

When we look at *Things Fall Apart*, as I argued in chapter 1, it is actually quite difficult to see Okonkwo as simply representative of the values of Umuofia. By contrast to most of the other male figures we meet, including Nwoye, Unoka, Uchendu and Obierika, his violence and masculinism are clearly presented as an aberration. Several times he brings opprobrium upon himself by offending the earth goddess, to the extent of being excluded from the community for seven years during part two. At the end of the novel, he is provoked to suicide by precisely the realisation that his instinct for aggressive resistance is *not* shared by the rest of the clan. In *Arrow of God*, then, how does Achebe seem to address the same theme? Certainly, from the outset, the theme of overweening masculinity is again a central one. Like Okonkwo's in Achebe's first novel, Ezeulu's outlook as chief priest in Umuaro is portrayed very much in terms of patriarchal dominance, with little recognition given to female agency or autonomy. Here, though, such a masculinist attitude is presented much more as the norm than in *Things Fall Apart*. In the first chapter, Achebe efficiently represents the gendered economy of Umuaro through the case of Akueke, Ezeulu's daughter, who has been repeatedly beaten by her husband. For Obika, the attacks on his sister provide a welcome opportunity to prove his manliness by beating up Akueke's husband, taking him from his village and depositing him in Ezeulu's compound. For the male elders of that village, in their turn, this then provides an opportunity to assert their own claims to respect. The key question for them is not that of wife battery, but 'why a man with a penis between his legs should be carried away from his house and his village. It is as if to say: You are nothing and your kinsmen can do nothing' (*AG*, 12). At the conclusion of the episode, with Akueke's own view yet to be heard, it is resolved that she will stay in her father's compound. Palm wine has not been carried to Ezeulu in acknowledgement of *his* entitlement to respect. Nor have there been any assurances (as the reader observes) that Akueke will not be beaten in future, but this is not shown as the principal concern. In Achebe's Umuaro, we are given to understand, the prevention of domestic violence is seen less as a matter concerning men's respect for women, than as one concerning their mutual respect for each other.

Later, advising his friend Akuebue on the appropriate way to handle a domestic dispute, Ezeulu stresses the fundamental inequality between the sexes. 'My wife's cock belongs to me because the owner of a person is also owner of whatever that person has' (*AG*, 173). If circumstances arise in which that inequality is challenged, because a man has to beg a favour from his wife or to ask forgiveness for having wronged her, he must do so in secret. '*When such a thing happens nobody else must know it, and that woman if she has any sense will never boast about it or even open her mouth and speak of it. If she does it the earth on which the man has brought himself low will destroy her entirely*' (*AG*, 172–3; italics in original). A woman's reason for being, in Achebe's Umuaro, is to please her husband. When Ezeulu's younger wife Ugoye prepares a meal for him and watches him eat everything on his plate, we are told by the narrator that this spectacle 'should have made any woman very happy' (*AG*, 190). The consequences of a woman breaking with decorum, on the other hand, are implied by the story of the priest's mother, whose 'feet were put in stocks, at the new moon' (*AG*, 223) because of her eccentric singing. In spiritual and ceremonial matters, as we learn from Edogo, the gaze of women, like that of children, is regarded as 'profane' (*AG*, 51). In material terms, while the power and wealth of men like Nwaka may be publically displayed through the ornamentation of his wives with ivory and velvets, women are never seen as powerful or wealthy in their own right. Aside from squabbles between themselves over domestic responsibilities, women are largely passive and ancillary. As the central drama plays out, male rivalry is unchecked by balancing influences and there is nothing to stop it from bringing the clan to destruction.

In gender terms, then, the culture of Umuaro is certainly a profoundly unequal one, and this is a characteristic that Achebe is at much greater pains to show than he was with Umuofia in *Things Fall Apart*. How fair or reasonable is this representation of Igbo culture in this period? Achebe's novel was published in 1964, and so in one sense it might seem unreasonable to judge it by the standards of commentators working many decades later. Historical perspectives change, and new information becomes available. Nevertheless, if in the interests of gauging the authenticity of Achebe's portrayal, we compare it to the subsequent work of gender historians such as Ifi Amadiume, Gloria Chuku and Nina Mba, it is difficult to resist the conclusion that in gender terms, *Arrow of God* presents a very partial view of Igbo gender relations indeed.

In the area of domestic violence, for example, evidence presented by Chuku suggests that in traditional culture, Igbo women were often far from passive in relation to their rights and interests, in the way the novel seems to suggest. Men who had committed crimes such as wife battery or stealing women's goods, she reports, risked being 'sat on' by the women of the village:

> To sit-on the offender entailed forceful occupation of his compound by women. During this time, women usually danced and sang scurrilous songs (composed on the instant) against the offender. In such songs, women outlined their grievances and at times called the manhood of the offender into question. In most cases, the dancing was sexually loaded with obscene fashions. At times, green leaves and sticks as well as mud were piled in the offender's compound. His farm crops and livestock might be confiscated allegedly to appease the ancestors, gods and goddesses of the land. Women could rough-handle the offender or force him naked in public.[28]

In *Arrow of God*, men are seen as the sole guardians of traditional values and as exclusive deliberators on matters of justice and order, while women are confined to subservient roles. Again, Chuku's historical account contrasts sharply with this picture. Her study draws on hundreds of contemporary records and ethnographic accounts to suggest, for example, that in cases where the women of traditional villages felt that compounds were ill-managed or, for example, that sanitation was not being adequately maintained, matters would be taken into their own hands. Parties of sweepers would force entry to offending compounds: their incursion, carried out in a way that was highly visible to the community, conveyed moral as well as practical authority:

> The women's sweeping and ritual cleansing of some compounds implied that some segments of the population had failed ... in performing their duties. The youth who through their age-grades engaged in sweeping and organising occasional clean-ups of the village paths, squares, streams and springs had abandoned their duties for church,

school and other related activities. No wonder, in Owerri Province, women in protest, withdrew their children from school. The chiefs who were heads of their compounds were forced to pay fine[s] of a goat or 10 shillings or both to the women for failing to live up to their responsibilities and to compensate women for their time and labor.[29]

As we can see in these cases, the actions of Igbo women in this period were often designed to condemn or discourage involvement with Christianity or the adoption of its habits and values. As contemporary reports such as that of District Officer M. Macgregor of Onitsha Province attest, displays of resistance were frequently taken to marketplaces and the compounds of chiefs. These performances, in Macgregor's view, were often 'anti-government in the sense of seditious ... the women desired to return to their native customs and native modes of living'.[30] Far from being limited to isolated incidents, the prevalence and concerted nature of such actions were such, in Chuku's view, that they can reasonably be considered as a social movement.

While the British administration continued in its efforts to implement the policy of indirect rule, the efforts of women, particularly in the older age range, to preserve and enforce traditional Igbo values illustrate the depth of their opposition. During the period in which Achebe's parents were growing up and extending into the author's own lifetime, European values, including clothing norms, were strongly resisted. While in traditional culture, for example, the innocence of unmarried girls was associated with unashamed nudity, Western dress was often seen as a moral affront. The abandonment of traditional modes of adornment featuring the elaborate use of skin dyes and beads, in favour of fashions reflecting colonial ideas and values, was seen as a symptom of decadence. Indeed, Christianised girls who paraded in the dresses prescribed by their churches risked attack by so doing, as Chuku writes: 'For example, at Umuahia market, young unmarried girls had their clothes torn off. The clothes were seen as symbols of the girls' profligacy.'[31] In a rather different action, when churchwomen in Bende District refused to join a women's protest in November 1925, their property was seized.

As such examples only begin to illustrate, Igbo women's proactive resistance against what they saw as the destructive spread of Europeanism, including the neglect of traditional responsibilities in favour of church activities, was both widespread and sustained during the period in which *Arrow of God* is set. Colonial Office records contain plenty of evidence of their activities. To the Christians who had their clothes stripped off in marketplaces, for example, the experience was felt exactly as intended, in all likelihood: as a public humiliation. 'It was therefore not surprising that girls and young women ... reported the matter to the colonial authority for its intervention.'[32] Clearly, as a novelist working in the early 1960s, it is possible that Achebe was not aware of such events and practices among the women of his parents' generation. Perhaps girls in the church mission to which his mother and father were attached escaped such humiliation, or did not talk about it afterwards. A conclusion that certainly can be drawn from Chuku's work, however, is that Igbo gender relations in the 1920s may have been far less simple, and far less one-sided, than *Arrow of God* seems to suggest.

In this respect, Ifi Amadiume's 1987 study *Male Daughters, Female Husbands: Gender and Sex in an African Society* is particularly interesting, in that it focuses on a community with which the Achebe family was directly associated, that of Nnobi, where Achebe himself was born in 1930, and where his father worked for the Church Missionary Society at St Simon's church. By that time, as we will see, resentment against the colonial presence – especially the taxes levied on local communities – was widespread in Igboland, and Igbo women's collective attempts at resistance would have been impossible to ignore. In Nnobi itself in 1925, as the historian Nina Mba reports for example, the extent of the disturbances they created had been such that a detachment of troops was deployed to quell it, when women barricaded one of the main roads, piled refuse in the courthouse and set the market on fire.[33]

Amadiume's research, which supplements written records with dozens of accounts by Nnobi people themselves, sheds useful light on the causes of their anger. In pre-colonial times, she argues, Igbo culture was by no means exclusively male-dominated, but in fact strongly matri-focal. The industriousness and achievement of older women, like that of older men, were recognised with titles. Wealthy, successful women, like men, were able to take wives. Although ownership of land was predominantly passed down through the male line, the notion of 'maleness' itself was not entirely essentialised. For example, as Amadiume writes, it was not inadmissible for women to own land as '"male daughters," where they had been accorded full male status in the absence of a son, in order to safeguard their father's *obi*, line of descent and the property associated with it'.[34] Prosperous women, whether falling into this category or not, were recognised with the *Ekwe* title.

Although religious in origin, moreover, the institution of *Ekwe* itself was strongly inflected towards material success and entrepreneurialism:

> Descriptions of the *Ekwe* phenomenon show its economic base. People were quick to notice thrift, industriousness, a money-making ability and leadership qualities in a woman. They would begin to point out such a woman as a potential candidate for the *Ekwe* title. Even a young girl could be identified as a candidate and thenceforth she would be encouraged in her economic ventures.[35]

In traditional society, *Ekwe* titled women typically had a lot of people working for them, including wives who they took through the practice of *igba ohu*, or marriage between women, Amadiume writes. 'The "female husband" might give the wife a (male) husband somewhere else and adopt the role of mother to her but claim her services. The wives might also stay with her, bearing children in her name. Potential *Ekwe* women were, therefore, wealthy women, who through control of others' services were able to create more wealth.'[36]

Under colonialism, protest and resentment among older, previously successful women can partly be attributed to the suppression of these aspects of traditional culture, in favour of a more Victorian model of gender organisation that reflected the values promoted by colonialism. Practices such as *igba ohu* were 'condemned by churches as "pagan" and anti-Christian' with the result that they were either 'abandoned or reinterpreted to the detriment of women. The *Ekwe* title, which was both a social and a political acknowledgement of female economic success ... was banned.'[37] Church schools, run by organisations like the Church Missionary Society, also worked strongly to entrench Victorian domestic ideals and a hierarchised understanding of gender relations. The intake of the schools was overwhelmingly male, and as Amadiume notes, when the need came to train native teachers, clerks and administrative officers for colonial service, women were routinely passed over. Schools were able to use their close connections to the administration to offer major social and material advancement to the boys and men who imbibed their wisdom. St Simon's church and school in Nnobi where Isaiah Achebe worked in the early 1930s, for example, enjoyed the active patronage of Eze Okoli, the local Warrant Chief with judicial and taxation powers over the whole community, as well as access to the support from the colonial government.[38] In this context, it is perhaps unsurprising that Igbo women who opposed the cultural changes these schools stood for organised boycotts against them (as happened in Nnobi) or withdrew their children.[39]

In traditional society, the distribution of power and influence was intended to reflect the meritocratic ethos of Igbo culture for women as well as men. Among gender historians such as Amadiume and Nina Mba, there is disagreement over the question of whether it was possible for women to be recognised as head of a household, lineage or clan. What is accepted, however, is that Igbo women collectively wielded a substantial share of influence within their communities. At meetings of village councils (unlike in *Arrow of God*) adults of both sexes were allowed to be present, to speak and to be judged on the persuasiveness and articulacy of their arguments. While judicial deliberations for serious offences were limited to male elders, more everyday disputes were typically settled by women's associations, to which men were not admitted. In Achebe's novel, we see nothing of these. Mba's description of their culture is, however, illuminating:

> In keeping with the democratic nature of Igbo government, leadership in the organisations was informal: a spokeswoman was usually nominated by consensus, but she saw herself only as representing, not leading, the women. The spokeswoman was usually selected for her wisdom and rhetorical skills rather than on the basis of age or wealth, although wealth was usually a sign of enterprise and intelligence and elderly women did exercise a moral authority. Each village had its own society, which was self-contained and had no formal affiliation with societies in other villages in the same village group or other groups, but there were informal ties of kinship and trade which resulted in a 'shuttle-like movement of women backwards and forwards across the country.'[40]

According to Mba, women's associations commanded clear authority in traditional culture. Decisions were democratically arrived at, but 'there was no question of a woman's right not to belong or to disobey a communal decision of the association'.[41] In marital disputes, men could be subjected to punishment or public humiliation, and if the association had a major complaint, it 'could also apply collective sanctions against the whole male community, such as threatening to leave the village en masse, refusing to cook, or refusal of intercourse'.[42] On a political level, in relations between different clans and villages, she writes, women often also played the role of negotiators or peacemakers. Unlike men, who remained in their home village after marriage, it was usual practice for a wife to come from some distance away. Thereafter, married women were always regarded as 'having a foot in two camps', promoting intra-village organisation between them as well as facilitating communal relations across Igboland.[43]

As Amadiume argues, the arrival of colonialism together with Christianity and a domestic ideology drawn from Victorianism heralded a major assault on women's power and influence in communities across the region. Among Igbo people themselves, almost without exception, the individuals to whom the administration gave power, whether court clerks or messengers or the Warrant Chiefs themselves, were men. As we see in *Arrow of God*, such appointments often lacked support from local communities and were by no means always successful. The individuals elevated were frequently unsuitable, with colonial records themselves recording the establishment of petty tyrannies, where taxation and extortion merged into one, in the name of the administration.

What we do not see in Achebe's novel, however, is any sign of the women who campaigned, ultimately successfully, against the Warrant Chief system and the abuses it produced. In the 1920s, as Amadiume argues, '[w]omen throughout Igboland were actually demanding the removal of the warrant chiefs and the closure of the native courts and European firms. Women had no place in the colonial government or law courts and were rapidly losing out in the new economic structure.'[44] For her, in common with other cultural historians including Nina Mba, Gloria Chuku and, indeed, Adielo Afigbo, this gendered dimension of struggle is crucial to understanding the colonial encounter in Igboland in the 1920s.

In *Arrow of God*, we do see the beginning of the end of the Warrant Chief system. In chapter 15, District Officer Winterbottom learns in a note from the Lieutenant Governor that a report by the Secretary for Native Affairs has given a negative assessment of the indirect rule system as practiced in Igboland. All plans to extend the system are suspended, and Winterbottom is instructed to act with a careful eye to the opinions and impressions of the natives. The historical development to which this chapter alludes was the abrupt reorientation of colonial policy, at the end of the 1920s, which heralded the demise of the Warrant Chief system. What the novel once again elides, however, is the crucial role of organised resistance by Igbo women in forcing this change of heart on the British administration.

Organised action began in 1925 when, as Nina Mba records, bands of women 'ranging from fifty to three hundred strong' fanned out across Igboland, attacking Christians and ceremonially sweeping the compounds of community chiefs.[45] Chiefs were exhorted to pass on a 'message' from *Chineke* (God) which comprised 'a demand for a return to the precolonial social system'.[46] Its stipulations included the abolition of the colonial currency, the destruction of tarred roads and the restriction of (colonial) native courts to cases involving the wealthy. The 'message' further demanded the banning of marriages between Christians and members of the traditional religion, the banning of prostitution and the return of the tradition of nudity for unmarried girls. It also called for the decriminalisation of adultery for women.

In 1928, when the British administration introduced taxtion in Igboland, women were at the forefront of resistance. At Aboh, as Mba writes, a campaign of fundraising was mounted to send representatives to Lagos, to press their concerns with Herbert Macauley, leader of the oppositional Nigerian National Democratic Party. When the local Warrant Chief reported their activities to the District Officer, by way of retaliation 'the old women of the town "kidnapped" [him] and forced him to sing all over the town'.[47] The women's rising levels of organisation and information was evident elsewhere too. In Afikpo, women publically demonstrated against the administration's tax demands, arguing for parity of treatment with Calabar, in the Niger Delta, and Lagos, in Yorubaland. The District Office there, as Mba says, recorded in his Annual Report that 'the atmosphere had an artificial air about it as if being fostered from outside'.[48] In Onitsha, a major centre only walking distance from the village where Achebe grew up, the administration attempted to introduce further taxes to pay for a new piped water supply. In response, a mass demonstration of women laid siege to the magistrate's office, stating that 'they would not use the water or help their men pay the water rate. They further threatened to stop all transactions with European firms and to stop selling to Europeans and their cooks in the markets until the government withdrew the water supply scheme or the water rates.'[49] When firms tried to lower the price they paid to women for palm-oil, similarly, women refused to supply any further produce until established rates were restored.

As Adielo Afigbo writes in his essay 'Revolution and Reaction in Eastern Nigeria 1900–1929', the resistance of Igbo women was regarded as being of the utmost importance. 'To the people, the taxing of women raised the whole question of the continued existence of society.'[50] Their demonstrations grew and multiplied, with increasing violence against symbols of colonial occupation. In the final year of the disturbances the women had burnt ten native courts to the ground and attacked numerous members of court staff, as well as the premises of Europeans companies. According to Judith van Allen in an essay on the Aba uprising:

> In November of 1929, thousands of Igbo women ... converged on the Native Administration centres – settlements that generally included the headquarters and residence of the British colonial officer for the district, a Native Court building and a jail, and a bank or white trader's store (if such existed in the district). The women chanted, sang songs of ridicule, and demanded the caps of office (the official insignia) of the Warrant Chiefs ... At a few locations the women broke into prisons and released prisoners. Sixteen Native Courts were attacked, and most of these were broken up or burned. The 'disturbed area' covered about 6,000 square miles and contained about two million people. It is not known how many women were involved, but the figure was in the tens of thousands. On two occasions, British District Officers called in police and troops, who fired on the women and left a total of fifty dead.[51]

In subsequent colonial historiography, the uprising was referred to as the 'Aba Riots'. Among the Igbo, it was remembered as the *Ogu Umunwanyi* or Women's War. In response to it, as Afigbo records, the British set up a Commission of Enquiry which, having taken evidence from 485 witnesses, made recommendations for a fundamental reorganisation of government in South East Nigeria.[52] For Toyin Falola, in his study *Colonialism and Violence in Nigeria*, 'the most important outcome of the Women's War was the government's recognition of the need to understand indigenous political institutions and create changes that people could tolerate and live with'.[53] To that end, almost 200 intelligence reports on Igbo traditional life were ordered, and leading colonial anthropologists (including Sylvia Leith-Ross) were commissioned to make detailed studies. As Afigbo concludes in *The Warrant Chiefs*:

> Truly, some of the old Native Courts continued to linger on for many years after 1929 because the problems of staff shortage and the need to make thorough investigations of the basis of the reorganisation caused delay. But in point of fact the policy and system of local rule through chiefs came to an end with the Women's Riot.[54]

In the light of all of this, how should we understand Achebe's apparent failure in *Arrow of God* to provide a balanced representation of Igbo women's experience in the 1920s? One answer to this question, certainly, is to consider the general paucity of understanding of Nigerian women's history at the time he was writing the novel. As Falola and Aderinto write in *Nigeria, Nationalism, and Writing History*, right from the beginnings of Nigerian historiography in the 1950s up until the early 1980s, the study and analysis of women's history was comprehensively side-lined. Indeed, in the case of the Nigerian Historical Society, it was not until the 1990s that it was recognised as a significant area for research. The major ethnographic study available at the time Achebe was writing the novel was Sylvia Leith-Ross's *African Women* (1939). This work, although admirable for its time in its extensiveness and detail, was as Falola says commissioned and written to 'serve the purpose of the institution of colonialism and the institution of patriarchy in general'.[55] Even such major episodes of gendered resistance as the Women's War were subsequently subjected to a 'male-centred interpretation' by mainstream historical commentators, which seriously misconstrued the women's aims and methods.[56] In the early 1980s, as we will see with *Anthills of the Savannah*, Achebe's own writing would make a major advance in terms of his exploration of the gendered axes in Igbo culture. In *Arrow of God*, however, the female dimension – balancing the competitive masculinism he represents so strongly – remains almost completely absent.

In the narrative itself, unsurprisingly, this key elision has significant consequences. At the heart of Achebe's conception for *Arrow of God*, as he made clear in the 1963 interview cited earlier, was an exploration of the changing relationship between the Igbo and their tradition deities during the colonial era. In framing this project, however, certain ideas that may have originated in the work of colonial anthropologists like George Basden and Sylvia Leith-Ross and gone uncorrected in his informal explorations of Igbo communities themselves, seem to have impelled Achebe towards a conception of traditional Igbo religion which is significantly distorted in gender terms. On a spiritual level in *Arrow of God*, as we have seen, the central battle to be waged is that between Ulu, the created god, and Idemili, who 'was there at the beginning of things' (41). When Ulu pays a visit to his priest in chapter 16, the nature of that conflict is spelt out:

> 'Ta! Nwanu!' barked Ulu in his ear, as a spirit would in the ear of an impertinent human child. 'Who told you that this was your own fight?'
> Ezeulu trembled and said nothing, his gaze lowered to the floor.
> 'I say who told you that this was your own fight to arrange the way it suits you? You want to save your friends who brought you palm wine he-he-he-he-he!' Only the insane could sometimes approach the menace and mockery in the laughter of deities – a dry, skeletal laugh. 'Beware you do not come between me and my victim or you may receive blows not meant for you! Do you not know what happens when two elephants fight? Go home and sleep and leave me to settle my quarrel with Idemili, whose envy seeks to destroy me that his python may again come to power. Now you tell me how it concerns you. I say go home and sleep. As for me and Idemili we shall fight to the finish; and whoever throws the other down will strip him of his anklet!' (*AG*, 191–2)

On the level of the human, as we have seen, the competition for control of the clan between Ezeulu and Nwaka is arranged by Achebe to directly mirror that of their gods. The latter is spurred on by Idemili's priest, who stokes his masculine competitiveness by suggesting that, if Ulu were destroyed, men like Nwaka would be leaders of the clan. When Ezeulu's son Oduche molests the sacred python, Ezidemili uses the opportunity to further fan the flames of war. Ezeulu, 'holding his rage firmly between two hands' (*AG*, 54) and threatening to kill the messenger that his rival sends to taunt him, fires back a reciprocating challenge: 'Go back and tell Ezidemili to eat shit. Do you hear me? Tell Ezidemili that Ezeulu says she should go and fill his mouth with shit' (*AG*, 54).

The image created here, of gods and their priests locked in ruinous combat, is exactly that of a society that 'believed too much in manliness' and is destined to 'crash in the end' as Achebe says in interview.[57] However, it is also an image that diverges radically from most understandings of Igbo religion in which Idemili, far from being imagined as a pugilistic male god, is a female deity representing what Madhu Krishnan calls the 'sacred feminine' in Igbo ontology.[58] 'In precolonial Igbo tradition', she writes, 'the notion of an entirely masculinised or entirely feminized society stands as alien. Instead ... the male and female were figured as halves of a whole, operating to temper and balance the other as independent discourses.'[59] Around the time when Achebe's father was working as a catechist, the cultural significance of Idemili was such that, as Amadiume writes, 'shrines dedicated to the goddess pervaded the whole of Nnobi'.[60] Her priest, who was highly venerated throughout the community, bore the signs of his dedication to the sacred feminine. According to Gloria Chuku, '[b]y this role, he became a male priestess. As a male priestess, he had to dress like a woman. He had to tie his loincloth not as men did but as women tied it. He exercised enormous power and authority, which he would not normally have had. For this role, every member of the community, including those who came from afar to consult the goddess, respected him.'[61]

In *Arrow of God*, Achebe picks up none of these symbolic markers in his portrait of Ezidemili, who is figured simply as 'very small and black as charcoal' (*AG*, 40) with skills as a wrestler and unusual powers of psychological domination. Indeed, set against historical accounts of Igbo religious culture, his portrait of both priests is questionable. As the servant of a male deity, Ulu, traditional practice would almost certainly have made Ezeulu a priestess. As Nigerian critic Tejumola Olaniyan says in an essay on *Arrow of God*, in the traditional religion 'most masculine deities are ministered to by female priests, while male priests are servants to the most central female deities'. Olaniyan's telling commentary on Achebe's novel is that its 'gender relations need some serious sorting out'.[62] In Nnobi, interestingly, it was the 'male priestess' of Idemili who had the symbolic duty of inaugurating the New Yam Festival, which Achebe gives to Ezeulu. At harvest time, s/he was responsible for performing the ritual known as *olulu* which, as Amadiume says, 'marked the day upon which the goddess ate new yam .... The priest of Idemili, who for this occasion was referred to as the king of *olulu*, would display new yam first in his compound, then in the market, to indicate that it was time for the eating of new yam.'[63] Whether dealing with male priestesses or the female priests of male gods, historiographic research since the 1980s leaves no doubt that in the traditional religion, genders were not separated but entwined.

The fact that, in his novel, Achebe masculinises the goddess Idemili, trading her well-established associations of life-giving, health and prosperity for masculine ones of ambition and the struggle for dominance, has profound implications for his representation of the culture of the clan. Where we might imagine an *Arrow of God* organised around the structural opposition between the defensive and war-like deity Ulu, on the one hand, and Idemili, representing balancing feminine principles, on the other, the actual text is framed almost exclusively around the axis of male rivalry and competition. In his fifth novel, *Anthills of the Savannah*, this is not at all the case. There, Idemili is represented in the commonly recognised female guise in which her role is, precisely, to balance and channel the masculine energies of the clan. We see how a man of wealth and success, seeking titles, must approach her with humility. Refraining from putting his claims directly, he must send a daughter ahead of him to lay down seven fragile fingers of chalk, in signification of peace and its fragility. If he can then sit so gently on these that not a single finger is broken, he begins to prove himself worthy:

> Neither at the first audience nor at the second does Idemili deign to answer him directly. He must go away and await her sign and pleasure. If she finds him unworthy to carry the authority of *ozo* she simply sends death to smite him and save her sacred hierarchy from contamination and scandal. If, however, she approves of him the only sign she condescends to give – grudgingly and by indirection – is that he will still be about after three years. Such is Idemili's contempt for man's unquenchable thirst to sit in authority on his fellows.[64]

In *Arrow of God*, the ideas suggested by this ritual, in which ambition and humility, authority and precarity exist in equilibrium, are almost entirely evacuated. As a result, resonances which might have suggested themselves, had Idemili retained the form celebrated in traditional culture, are lost. In *Anthills of the Savannah*, Idemili's myth is partly analogous to that of Jesus, sent by God 'to bear witness to the moral nature of authority by wrapping around power's rude waist a loincloth of peace and modesty' (AS, 97). In *Arrow of God*, however, Achebe's male Idemili and the clan as a whole are bereft of any such conciliatory function. At the end of the novel, therefore, it is left to Christianity to harvest the souls of the people, with its offer of the peace and protection that traditionally it would have been Idemili's role to uphold.

Within the frame of Achebe's narrative, in this sense, what we see in *Arrow of God* is an Idemili-shaped hole in the life of Umuaro, filled by the figure of Jesus. As we hear in the last lines of chapter 19, with nowhere else to turn 'many a man sent his son with a yam or two to offer to the new religion and to bring back the promised immunity. Thereafter any yam harvested in his fields was harvested in the name of the son' (AG, 230).

In chapter 2 we saw the ways in which, in his first two novels, Achebe attempts to explore the legacies and effects of British colonialism in Igboland. If *Things Fall Apart* deals with the years around the turn of the twentieth century and *No Longer at Ease* explores the scene of the 1950s, *Arrow of God* extends their joint project by examining some of the intervening period. As Robert Wren points out in his study *Achebe's World*, at the time that Achebe was working on the novel in the 1960s, much amateur and professional research was in progress exploring the cultural history of Igboland and other parts of the nation. Part of the significance of all three novels, in that context, lies in the insights they were able to offer readers of its own time into the struggles that had produced modern Nigeria.

As we have seen in this chapter, nevertheless, in the light of subsequent historical analysis it is difficult to read *Arrow of God* as a wholly authentic or balanced historical account of the colonial encounter in the 1920s. Interviewed in 1963 about the ideas behind his then work-in-progress, Achebe described *Arrow of God* as an exploration of an indigenous society which suffered from a serious internal weakness. Igbo traditional culture's obsession with manliness, and concomitant inability to adapt to changing historical conditions provided, in his view, one of the key reasons why it struggled to resist ideological colonisation. Speaking to Michel Fabre ten years later in 1973, this still seems to have been Achebe's view. Taking Ezeulu as an exemplar of the Igbo struggle, he stresses that 'the important thing was that Ezeulu was able to fight and to cope, as best he could, with the consequences. Even when he failed, he failed as a man, you see. That is very important in our culture.'[65] Just as in the Biafran war, '[t]here were leaders who showed up complete cowards and others, a few, of whom people could say, "This is a man."'[66] When Achebe's portrayal of Igbo masculinism in the novel is set against the work of subsequent analysts such as Ifi Amadiume, Gloria Chuku, Nina Mba and Adielo Afigbo, as we have seen however, it struggles to stand up to the historical evidence, at least as currently interpreted. The unbridled masculinism we see in *Arrow of God* appears, in this light, to be as much a function of Achebe's portrayal as of Igbo traditional culture itself.

If resistance to colonisation, including against the spreading influence of Christianity, was widespread and sustained in

Igboland during the period that *Arrow of God* is set, we have seen in this chapter that women were often at the forefront of efforts to resist the attack on traditional values and ways of life. For their part, evidence cited by Amadiume and others suggests that Christian missions, with the active support of the British administration, worked hard to undermine, disparage and distort traditional Igbo beliefs and practices. One aspect of this on-going campaign was the preaching of Victorian gender roles including meek domesticity for women. Another aspect was a strong stress on the maleness of God, and a denial of the principle of female divinity. In the work of George Basden, mentor to Achebe's father and an influential colonial anthropologist, for example, Idemili herself is simply re-described as a masculine deity. Amadiume quotes some of Basden's erroneous claims in his 1938 study *Niger Ibos: A Description of the Primitive Life, Customs and Animistic Beliefs of The Ibo People of Nigeria* (1938), including that 'there are five Ide-millis, each with his distinctive status and functions ... All of these five gods have but one patronal head, namely the python.'[67] Basden's hegemonic status as a 'universal reference on Igbo indigenous culture'[68] for several decades up to and including the 1960s may shed some light on the reasons why *Arrow of God* (presumably, unwittingly) reproduces this distortion. By the time of *Anthills of the Savannah*, as I have suggested, Achebe would recognise and reverse his oversight. Idemili reappears in her conventional feminine guise in that novel, and is ascribed the qualities of peace and restraint with which she is traditionally associated. In *Arrow of God*, however, Achebe's competitive, masculine Idemili helps instead to conjure an image of Igbo culture in which there is no principle of the sacred feminine at all, to balance the ambition and rivalry of male gods and men. As Amadiume's work makes clear, at the time that Achebe was writing the novel, there would have been plenty of live evidence throughout the Igbo hinterland that would have enabled him to gain a better sense of the balanced gender economy in traditional culture and religion. Such material would have had the effect of disrupting the tragic narrative of male hubris that drives *Arrow of God*.

As the author repeatedly made clear, however, his research for the novels was always interest-driven and informal. It seems most reasonable to assume that his encounters with traditional culture at this stage simply failed to dislodge the misrepresentations of Basden and the subsequent historians who unquestioningly accepted his accounts.

The history of the Warrant Chief system in Igboland, according to most commentators including Adielo Afigbo, is that it was defeated by a long campaign of organised resistance, and primarily by women. Taking this material, it is easy to imagine how narratives of Igbo men and women's long and bitter campaigns to repulse the invading British might have fed into a trilogy of novels about liberation struggle and national self-becoming. What is clear, however, is that these are not the stories that Achebe preferred to tell in *Things Fall Apart, No Longer at Ease* and *Arrow of God*. As we have seen repeatedly in this book, it was his professional role in broadcasting to find ways of affirming the Nigeria project to peoples at home and abroad, but this was evidently not an imperative to which he wanted to yoke his fiction. In the world of Achebe's novels, the glimpses we get both of colonial aggression and the Igbo response to it are, in fact, surprisingly light and fleeting. Readers who wish for the Manichean oppositions of colonialism *versus* resistance must turn to other writers to find those stories played out.

In *Arrow of God* particularly, the image Achebe actually shows of colonialism is of a sometimes aggressive, sometimes incompetent, sometimes idealistic, often muddled and self-divided enterprise, partly mired in ambivalence. The Nigeria we see under construction in these novels is not a land of freedom, wrested by its people from the grip of greedy invaders. It is the messy product of ill-designed policy, indigenous non-cooperation, the elevation of unsuitable leaders and the entrenchment of corrupt practices. They may have been written in the years immediately preceding and following decolonisation, but heroic independence narratives these are not. Two years after the publication of *Arrow of God*, Achebe would further extend his analysis of his nation's painful birth and development with a shockingly scathing portrait of Nigerian political culture in the 1960s. With *A Man of the People*, as we will see in chapter 4, however, Achebe's boldness in 'speaking the truth to power' turned out to be a strategy fraught with risk.

4
A Man of the People and the Biafran writings

Achebe's remarkable rise to prominence in the late 1950s and early 1960s was, as we saw in chapter 1, very much a story of Nigerian independence. As British colonial officials began to vacate their senior positions in key institutions and professions, a concerted process of 'Nigerianisation' was set in train to instruct, mentor and elevate the new educated elite in whose hands the future of the nation would be entrusted. The young Achebe was typical in this regard: he did not seek a position within the Nigerian Broadcasting Service, but rather was identified by its expatriate management (advised by the expatriate staff of University College Ibadan) as an appropriate candidate to be trained in its values and methods. Working under that British management, he cut his teeth in the Talks Department, producing programming in English that reflected the over-riding One-Nigeria ethos promoted by Director Tom Chalmers and his staff. A joint venture of the BBC in London and the British Colonial Office, the NBS itself had always been regarded by the British as a tool of government, educating its largely middle-class listenership against the pitfalls of communism and untempered nationalism. As the head of the Schools Broadcasting Unit, Charles Armour wrote in an account of the Nigerian media at that time that Colonial Secretary Arthur Creech Jones was firmly of the view that broadcasting in Nigeria continued to require 'close governmental supervision'.[1] Although the Talks Department provided coverage of key political events to a national audience, the service itself did not enjoy the independence enjoyed by its mother company, the BBC. While Achebe was working there, press accusations of its strong political bias were rife, even when the organisation was reformed in its entirety as the (comparatively more autonomous) Nigerian Broadcasting Corporation. In an effort to strike less of a propagandist tone, one of Chalmers' key strategies for sustaining the new NBC's political influence and reach was to train up a select group of young producers, including Achebe, who would be capable of earning the trust of a sceptical public. In the NBC, in other words, the process of 'Nigerianisation' was about much more than simply finding local replacements for departing British officials. It also implied a concerted effort to preserve and sustain, through the decolonisation process, the guiding political values of the colonial establishment. In Achebe's case in the late 1950s, rapid promotion to the position of NBC Controller for Eastern Nigeria must have seemed like an unbelievable stroke of good fortune. As we saw in chapter 1, however, what his acceptance of that position implied was an undertaking to strive in the service of the NBC's central goal – to promote the idea of One-Nigeria to a predominantly regionally minded and tribalist populace.

By 1963–64, when he began working on his fourth novel, *A Man of the People*, Achebe had been redeployed as Director of the NBC's international service, the Voice of Nigeria. Broadcasting to the outside world, however, his function was in one sense unchanged. As the NBC's new British Director Ian MacKay stated quite unambiguously, 'the purpose of external broadcasting is to secure long or short term advantages for the originating country'.[2] On the ground, what that translated to was a continual effort to project a strong and unified image of Nigeria at all times.

On the level of day-to-day coverage of political events, that brief must often have been very difficult to fulfil. As Toyin Falola and Matthew Heaton argue in *A History of Nigeria*, the political culture of Nigeria throughout the 1960s continued to be haunted by the 'national question'. '"What is Nigeria?" "Who are Nigerians?" "How does a country go about developing a meaningful national identity?"'[3] Since the establishment of the Nigerian constitution in the mid-1950s, a great deal of political power had resided with regional legislative assemblies in the East, West and North, and within those regions themselves, influence was further stratified along ethnic lines. From the point of view of the political class, as Falola and Heaton suggest, 'there seemed to be very little to gain in domestic politics from identifying on a national level. As a result, when Nigeria became an independent sovereign state in 1960, in many ways it was a state without a nation.'[4] Important efforts were certainly made at bolstering the idea of One-Nigeria through infrastructure development and through the broadcasting efforts of the NBC, whose programming stressed the common interests of Nigerians and promoted intercultural understanding between different ethnic groups. As Falola and Heaton argue, however:

> Ultimately ... these efforts failed, largely because of the overwhelming trend in the political sphere towards consolidating power at the regional level at any cost. Official corruption, rigged elections, ethnic baiting, bullying, and thuggery dominated the conduct of politics in the First Republic which existed from 1960 to 1966.[5]

At the time he was writing *A Man of the People*, as a leading media professional Achebe would have been acutely aware of this political context, in which as Falola and Heaton suggest, many educated Nigerians had already come to regard the national structure as dysfunctional and had concluded that 'Nigeria should cease to exist in its present form'.[6] In the novel, the political events that seem to have imprinted themselves most strongly are those surrounding the federal elections of 1964, in which regional political rivalries reached an even greater heat and intensity. According to the historian Max Siollun, '[m]any of the politicians were little more than ethnic champions uninterested in a national outlook. The campaign was conducted not on platforms of policy or ideology, but on the basis of personal abuse and vitriolic ethnic chauvinism.'[7] Siollun quotes classified diplomatic correspondence from the US State Department, describing a political situation in which Nigeria's Eastern Region was already threatening to secede from Nigeria, while the North responded with threats of violence 'that would make the Congo look like child's play'.⁸ The politics of oil, newly discovered in the Niger Delta, already threatened further tension. In the parliamentary elections for the Western Region, similarly, *Time* magazine reported widespread and open abuses, with ballot boxes rigged, opposition candidates 'scrubbed from the ballot' and election officials kidnapped.⁹

As Director of the Voice of Nigeria, Achebe's job was to smooth over these issues and to continue to project a larger narrative of Nigeria's progress, influence and increasing prosperity. As a writer of fiction working on the draft of his fourth novel, however, it is clear that he saw his role very differently. In its nascence in *Things Fall Apart*, and entry to modernity in *No Longer at Ease*, Achebe's fictive portrait of Nigeria's development was already, as we have seen, filled with disquiet. The world for Obi Okonkwo, already prefigured in his grandfather's story, was one in which a culture of colonial privilege and ignorance was in the process of settling into a toxic combination with nepotistic and parochial tendencies within traditional culture. In such circumstances, *No Longer at Ease* implies, even the most promising and idealistic would be unable to withstand the hegemony of corruption. In *A Man of the People* Achebe reprises and extends this analysis. Where Obi's narrative, set at the tail end of the colonial era, ends with a trial and with the application of justice, the story of Odili Samalu concludes with a much stronger note of foreboding, predicting the implosion of Nigeria's democratic state.

A Man of the People

In the context of increasing ethnic tension and political violence, then, the waters Achebe entered with this novel were dangerous ones. Whether in recognition of this, or from a desire to broaden the significance of his analysis, the nation he represents in *A Man of the People* is not quite Nigeria as it is. The place names do not fit, and coffee (an East African product) is the main crop. Furthermore, as Bernth Lindfors argues in an important early essay, 'Achebe's African Parable', the conditions of turmoil depicted by the novel reflected the circumstances of many newly independent African nations. That said, however, the parallels between the scenes depicted in this novel and those unfolding in Nigeria itself in this period are unmistakable. At the time Achebe began writing the novel around February 1953, as Lindfors says, a seven-month state of emergency in Western Nigeria (where Achebe was living) had just come to an end. Obafemi Awolowo, one of the pivotal figures in Nigeria's independence story, a former premier of the Western Region and leader of the official opposition, had been imprisoned for treasonous conspiracy to overthrow the federal government. Even as Achebe worked on his narrative, the political crisis continued to intensify. In late 1964, in preparation for fresh elections, a nationwide census had been conducted, on the basis of which a balance of power would be worked out after the votes had been counted. The results, evidencing flagrant ballot rigging in many areas, radically undermined confidence in the democratic process. In December of that year, although elections did go ahead, they were boycotted by the Eastern Region, the Mid-West and by Lagos itself. Calls for United Nations monitors to ensure fairness and due process were rejected by Prime Minister Abubakar Balewa. As Achebe worked to complete the final sections of the novel in early 1965, elections proceeded in the face of widespread international disquiet. Lindfors describes the febrile atmosphere:

> One observer reports that 'countless acts of political violence and thuggery occurred almost daily throughout the campaign, but notably increased during the last few weeks.' Electioneering irregularities were so frequent and widespread that one of the major political parties, the United Progressive Grand Alliance, announced that it would boycott the elections. This precipitated another crisis, for President Nnamdi Azikiwe, judging the elections invalid, refused to call upon victorious Prime Minister Abubakar Balewa to form a new government. For five days the country teetered on the brink of political chaos. On January 4, 1965, Azikiwe and Balewa finally reached a compromise and Azikiwe announced to the country that Balewa would

form a 'broadly-based national government.' By-elections were to be held in constituencies where elections had been totally boycotted, and allegations of fraud and intimidation were to be reviewed by the courts.[10]

In this context, Lindfors suggests, the fact that *A Man of the People* predicts (or arguably, even calls for) a military coup to resolve the deepening political impasse in Nigerian politics is perhaps not as strange as it might appear. Since independence, as he says, the effectiveness of the Nigerian military as a peace-keeping force had been well demonstrated, and there was no reason in principle why it could not fulfil that function at home.

Part of the mystique of *A Man of the People*, published as it was in January 1966, was not only that it exposed Nigeria's terminal situation to an international audience, but also that it predicted the fall of the First Republic. When he comes to narrate this event – the end of state democracy – Achebe does so in a provocatively light-hearted, throw-away manner: 'the army obliged us by staging a coup at that point and locking up every member of the government'.[11] In the novel as a whole, however, it is clear that he is concerned to place the nation's political meltdown within a clear explanatory context. His narrative centres on the figure of Odili Samalu, a member of the young educated elite who, like Achebe himself, emerged out of the colonial school system in the 1950s. Echoing the author's own early career before he became a broadcaster, we first see Odili as a schoolteacher. At a political rally at the school, Achebe begins to build up his protagonist through a schematic comparison to two other figures. Jonathan Nwege, the school's sour and cynical headmaster, is active in the local party, obsequious towards those in power, and resentful at the lack of preferment these efforts have afforded him. Chief Nanga, Minister of Culture in the national government, is a populist politician who, ironically considering his position, flaunts his anti-intellectualism. Odili, although ambitious, is scornful of both, regarding them as retrograde influences on national development. Early in the narrative he recalls Nanga's oration in a parliamentary debate:

'From today we must watch and guard our hard-won freedom jealously. Never again must we entrust our destiny and the destiny of Africa to the hybrid class of Western-educated and snobbish intellectuals who will not hesitate to sell their mothers for a mess of pottage ...' (*MP*, 6)

Odili, like Achebe, is precisely one of the university educated class whose 'death sentence' (*MP*, 6) Nanga wants to pronounce. Throughout the text, Achebe plays with the idea of a correspondence between himself and the protagonist. When Odili attends a literary exhibition, for example, Achebe has him confide an ambition 'to write a novel about the coming of the first white men to my district' (*MP*, 58). While the author's own father was a catechist for the Church Missionary Society, striving to convert the Igbo heathen to the white man's religion, Odili's father is a former District Interpreter, one of the more privileged native positions established by the British in their efforts to govern their restive colonial subjects. In an early scene recalling Odili's childhood, we see him thrown out of a friend's house for the crime of being son to a colonial stooge. In other respects, however, Odili is certainly not a carbon copy of his creator. Unlike Nanga, who has the common touch and who the people seem so complacently to regard as the true 'man of the people', he is painted from the first as effete and deracinated. As he admits in an aside that reeks of disdain, 'I don't care too much for our women's dancing' (*MP*, 1), openly admitting his contempt for the 'silly ignorant villagers' (*MP*, 2) who turn out to honour Chief Nanga, their community's most successful son. As Odili meditates, further revealing the Christianised set of his mind, 'I wished for a miracle, for a voice of thunder, to hush this ridiculous festival and tell the poor contemptible people one or two truths' (*MP*, 2).

In his vocabulary and the cadence of his speech, Odili is unmistakably anglophile. From the beginning, though he reports the words of others in pidgin, his own account is delivered in a clipped Standard English. For Nanga's part, while he freely advertises his anti-intellectualism and is himself comparatively unschooled, Achebe shows him responding instinctively to the aura that university educated Odili exudes. Singling him out from the crowd on a slight acquaintance of years ago, the minister is keen to invite him to stay in the capital, with the clear intention of turning him into his place-man in the government service. Despite his own reticence towards Nanga and his politics, Odili is not too high minded to accept and, in a move that echoes Obi's failed struggle against the temptations of 'kola' in *No Longer at Ease*, accepts Nanga's offer of friendship and hospitality. One of Odili's key motivations, as we soon discover, is that he anticipates using Nanga's luxurious publically funded residence as a place to have sex with his girlfriend Elsie, a nurse in the capital. He and Nanga spend time swapping tales of sexual conquest and, feeling 'somehow compelled to speak in derogatory terms about women in general' (*MP*, 59), he is dismissive of the girl and their relationship. Nanga's response is predictable enough, and in narrating Odili's humiliation Achebe takes the opportunity to reinforce the depth of his prissiness and anglophilia. When he discovers Elsie having sex with Nanga, his gut responses are those of a repressed upper-class colonial: 'Good Heavens' and 'My Word' (*MP*, 70). On confronting Nanga, he slips into a more demotic, but no less English idiom: 'You can't do fuck-all' (*MP*, 73).

In this sense, in his drawing of Odili in *A Man of the People* Achebe is consciously concerned to explore the double-consciousness of the young educated elite in Nigeria and other newly independent African states. On the one hand, the young man is vocal in his scorn for the culture of 'dash' and corrupt scrambling for advantage, jointly personified by Nwege and Nanga. Watching the latter at work, he meditates with seriousness on the corrosion of public life, and its implications for the nation's future:

> From the day a few years before when I had left Parliament depressed and aggrieved, I had felt, like so many other educated citizens of our country, that things were going seriously wrong without being able to say just how. We complained about our country's lack of dynamism and abdication of the leadership to which it was entitled in the

> continent, or so we thought. We listened to whispers of scandalous deals in high places – sometimes involving sums of money that I for one didn't believe existed in the country. But there was really no hard kernel of fact to get one's teeth into. But sitting at Chief Nanga's feet, I received enlightenment; many things began to crystallize out of the mist – some of the emergent forms were not nearly as ugly as I had suspected but many seemed much worse. (*MP*, 38–9)

On the other hand, however, the attitude he and his idealistic political friends show towards the nation – in its actual living reality – is squeamish and aloof. Wandering the capital at night, Odili sees the depth of inequality that Nanga's government has presided over, but is left unmoved. Sexual jealousy towards the minister, and resentment at Elsie's betrayal, are his primary concerns. Neither poverty nor deprivation in themselves, nor the obscene contrast between the condition of his own class and those of the masses, find any ethical purchase with him.

As the novel proceeds, the protagonist's vacillating, conflicted sensibility becomes one of the key dimensions of narrative development. As we have seen in the early parts of the book, although he is contemptuous of Nanga's vanity and disingenuous professions of humility, he has keenly accepted the minister's offer of preferment. When, a little later, Nanga sleeps with his girlfriend Elsie, he abruptly detaches himself from the minister, and begins to think in more political terms about the values he represents. Under the influence of his friend Max, he joins in founding a progressive new political party, the Common People's Convention (CPC). He is counselled by a leftist from the Eastern bloc, who applauds the sight of young African intellectuals 'coming out of their "tower of elephant tusk" into active politics' (*MP*, 77). Amid the revolutionary rhetoric, however, Achebe makes sure that we see the partialness and ambivalence of Odili's commitment. Recalling the masculine rivalries that dominate *Arrow of God*, the question Odili returns to again and again is not how to contest the common enemy – in this case the culture of nepotism and corruption Nanga represents – but rather how to redeem his ego after the Elsie affair. Becoming an activist for the CPC offers Odili, not the chance to effect real change, but rather 'a second string to my bow when I came to deal with Nanga' (*MP*, 78). His first priority, as we soon realise, is how to challenge the minister's masculine authority by seducing his beautiful wife-to-be Edna:

> What mattered was that a man had treated me as no other man had a right to treat another – not even if he was master and the other slave; and my manhood required that I make him pay for his insult in full measure. In flesh and blood terms I realized that I must go back, seek out Nanga's intended parlour-wife and give her the works, good and proper. (*MP*, 76)

We begin to learn of a deep disillusion among young intellectuals about the legacies of independence, which many had imagined would bring advances and freedoms that have not materialised. Max reads a poem he had written in the 'intoxicating months of high hope' (*MP*, 80) after the departure of the colonial British. 'Now he sang it like a dirge', as Odili observes. 'And believe me, tears welled up at the back of my eyes; tears for the dead, infant hope' (*MP*, 80). Between them, seemingly incredibly, it is still a point of contention whether the colonialists should have left at all. The party they have founded is not composed of non-entities. One of their number already boasts experience of power in government, as a serving junior minister. Clearly, however, his belief in the possibilities of change is fairly ambivalent:

> 'What is he doing in the Government if he is so dissatisfied with it?' I asked naively. 'Why doesn't he resign?'
> 'Resign?' laughed Max. 'Where do you think you are – Britain or something? Don't be funny, Odili.'
> 'I am not being funny,' I said hotly, perhaps more hotly than was called for.
> I knew very well and needed no reminder that we were not in Britain or something, that when a man resigned in our country it was invariably with an eye on the main chance – as when a few years ago ten newly elected

P.A.P. Members of Parliament had switched parties at the opening of the session and given the P.O.P. a comfortable majority overnight in return for ministerial appointments and – if one believed the rumours – a little cash prize each as well. (*MP*, 82)

Here Achebe makes reference to currents of corruption in Nigerian politics which were, for him, defining. Even before independence, the nationalist NCNC (National Council of Nigeria and the Cameroons) under Nnamdi Azikiwe had been prevented from forming an effective anti-colonial front by manipulations in the Western House of Representatives, with key nationalist politicians offered lucrative political positions (such as the town clerkship of Lagos) in return for foregoing a seat in the central legislature. As Richard Sklar argues in his study *Nigerian Political Parties*, such episodes perversely lent support to Britain's credibility, in its reticence towards full home rule and with its half-baked model of 'semi-responsible government'.[12] What they also set in train, however, was a culture of political manipulation and corruption that was to dog Nigeria for years after independence.

A few pages later, Achebe offers up a contrast to the CPC's elitist and ambivalent politics in an incident that shows the people in genuine self-government. Returning to Anata, the home of the grammar school where he has worked as a teacher, Odili sees a public disturbance surrounding the shop and bar owned by a well-known local figure, Josiah. A trader, Josiah has made his money, in effect, by selling the people's produce back to them, packaged as commodities in the white man's fashion, including rice and local palm wine which he decants into beer bottles. The cause of the commotion is that, seeing these activities being tolerated by the local community, he has now overstepped the line, stealing the stick of a blind man in order to make a medicine 'to turn us into blind buyers of his wares' (*MP*, 85) as one old woman explains. Boycotted by young and old, within a week Josiah is ruined, as Odili reports. He had 'taken away enough for the owner to notice ... and the owner, I discovered, is the will of the whole people' (*MP*, 86).

Against this image of open-air democracy in action, Achebe is keen to underline the extent to which Nanga and the political class have become complicit with neo-colonial interests. We are already aware that part of the minister's bid for re-election involves a road-building project between Anata and another town, an enterprise Odili initially approves of since it would pass through his home village. The ten luxury buses that will run along it are supplied on the 'never never' (MP, 43) from a multinational named British Amalgamated. Later, Odili overhears Nanga on the phone to a fellow minister, saying that he 'distrusted our young university people and would rather work with a European' (MP, 65). Now Achebe reveals that the four-story house Nanga is building next to his own government residence is 'a "dash" from the European building firm of Antonio and Sons whom Nanga had recently given the half-million-pound contract to build the National Academy of Arts and Sciences' (MP, 96). When a 20 per cent increase in textile import duties is announced, it emerges that 'someone had told the firm of British Amalgamated of the Minister's plans as long ago as October and that they had taken steps to bring in three shiploads of the textiles by mid-December' (MP, 99). Nanga, who defends the government against hostile accusations, has himself used his former position as Minister for Foreign Trade in similar corrupt ways, it transpires, 'and had built out of his gains three blocks of seven-storey luxury flats at three hundred thousand pounds each' (MP, 99). The flats are then leased by Nanga back to British Amalgamated at a rent of £1400 a month. British Amalgamated also, kindly, fund his election campaign.

As unions threaten strikes and outbreaks of looting force the closure of shops, Odili is called by Max for urgent consultations with the revolutionary CPC. Caught up in the moment, Odili's rhetoric is hotly political. 'After seven years of lethargy ... the country was ripe and impatient to shed in violent exercise the lazy folds of flabby skin and fat it had put on in the greedy years of indolence' (MP, 100). When Odili agrees to stand for the party against Nanga in the forthcoming election, however, Achebe again ensures that the reader is primed to question his motives. His first act is to acquire a brand new automobile and £100 for campaign expenses. He then goes immediately in pursuit of Edna, Nanga's wife-to-be. As his campaign of seduction with Edna begins to show signs of bearing fruit, so Odili's concern with battling Nanga in the political field begins to dwindle. As he examines his motives, Achebe makes plain that the contest of masculinities – rather than that of ideology or democratic principle – remains Odili's primary, and perhaps only, motivation:

> How important was my political activity in its own right? It was difficult to say; things seemed so mixed up; my revenge, my new political ambition and the girl. And perhaps it was just as well that my motives should entangle and reinforce one another. For I was not being so naive as to imagine that loving was enough to wrench her from a minister. True, I had other advantages like youth and education but those were nothing beside wealth and position and the authority of a greedy father. No. I needed all the reinforcement I could get. Although I had little hope of winning Chief Nanga's seat, it was necessary nonetheless to fight and expose him as much as possible so that even if he won, the Prime Minister would find it impossible to re-appoint him to his Cabinet. (*MP*, 108)

Even if it does not prove possible to mount an effective challenge for Nanga's seat, at least it may be possible to stir up enough filth to discredit him and prevent his reappointment as a minister, Odili reasons. What he regards as his 'high-minded thinking' (*MP*, 115) is, the reader has been left in no doubt, inextricably intermixed with more questionable motives. Odili's pursuit of personal advantage may take a different form than Nanga's, but the question that hovers over the novel's final chapters is clear. How distinct is the new educated class of Odili and Max from the corrupt elite they are seeking to supplant?

The bedrock of Odili's electoral support is his home village of Urua, and we soon learn the basis on which that support is offered: 'that our son should go and bring our share ... The village of Anata has already eaten, now they must make way for us to reach the plate' (*MP*, 125). As far as the community is concerned, if elected to parliament his first duty will be to syphon as much of the national wealth as he can to his own people. Odili is not quite so brazen in the pursuit of his self-interest, and we see him refusing a bribe from Nanga to give up his campaign. The value of this gesture is soon placed in question, however, by 'high-minded' (*MP*, 115) Max's choice to take a similar payment in bad faith. When Odili's father then refuses a tax break promised by the minister in return for disassociating himself from his son and the party, the young man is scathing. 'I thought to myself: You do not belong to this age, old man. Men of worth nowadays simply forget what they said yesterday' (*MP*, 135). Once again, Achebe makes us aware here of the inconsistency and blinkeredness of Odili's perspective. His negative perception of his father has been of an old colonial servant 'who made a fortune out of the ignorance of poor, illiterate villagers and squandered it on drink and wives' (*MP*, 135). Now he sees the possibility that 'I had got everything terribly, lopsidedly wrong' (*MP*, 135). If Achebe's portrait of Nanga faithfully reflects the clannishness and complacency of his people, therefore, his representation of Odili provides the negative complement to that image. Naïve, deracinated and self-serving, the young man's democratic rhetoric is never much more than a ruse.

To Odili, from the beginning of the novel to the end, the common people remain fundamentally 'contemptible' (*MP*, 138). In that sense, it does not altogether come as a surprise that, at the point where he narrates the story's final conflagration, his account amounts to an apologia for military dictatorship. In his unsettling, fairy-tale ending, young army officers seize power to save the nation from itself, while 'overnight, everyone began to shake their heads at the excesses of the last regime' (*MP*, 148). What remains unaltered, however, are Odili's elitist and undemocratic sentiments. Guardianship of the nation, he wants us to conclude, should never be entrusted to the people, of whom the cynicism and corruption of Nanga are simply the organic extension:

No, the people had nothing to do with the fall of our Government. What happened was simply that unruly mobs and private armies having tasted blood and power during the election had got out of hand and ruined their masters and employers. And they had no public reason whatever for doing it. Let's make no mistake about that. (*MP*, 144)

Framing his fourth novel in this bold, uncompromising way, Achebe departs a very long way indeed from the affirmative rhetoric associated with the Voice of Nigeria, as well as some of his own public statements in the period. In a famous address delivered in 1964, at a time when he was deep into the writing of *A Man of the People*, he described his role as a writer in terms of the need to teach his own people self-worth, in the wake of their decades-long colonial subjugation. Published soon after as a 'position piece' situating Achebe and his goals in fiction writing, the address calls explicitly for a 'revolution' in African consciousness. This is a liberal revolution, however, in which scholars, writers and educators join forces to raise the consciousness of their communities. Far from enjoining intellectuals to challenge the governing *status quo*, he stresses the need to focus on 'the question of education, in the best sense of that word'.[13] Approvingly, he quotes the Ghanaian philosopher William Abraham:

> Just as African scientists undertake to solve some of the scientific problems of Africa, African political scientists concern themselves with the politics of Africa; why should African literary creators be exempted from the services that they themselves recognize as genuine?[14]

Did something happen between the first publication of this address in the *New Statesman* on 29 January 1965 and the completion of his novel the following month, to shake Achebe's belief in the possibility of liberal democratic development? According to Bernth Lindfors' account of Nigerian politics in this period, not really. In 1964, as Achebe was delivering his paper in England, Lagos was in a state of unprecedented political turmoil. The population census, released in February, had revealed widespread corruption at the heart of the political machine. As Lindfors reports, in March of that year the Lagos *Daily Times* was warning explicitly that 'The Federal Republic of Nigeria faces the grave danger of disintegration.'[15] At the turn of 1965, however, the political situation was, for a while, comparatively calm. President Nnamdi Azikiwe and Prime Minister Abubakar Balewa managed, as we have seen, to paper over their differences, and it seemed that the immediate crisis might have been averted. In the army coup accurately predicted by *A Man of the People*, which took place in January 1966, Balewa would be assassinated along with the premier of Northern Nigeria, Ahmadu Bellow and the Nigerian Finance Minister, Festus Okotie-Eboh. Between the publication of Achebe's address 'The Novelist as Teacher' and the publication of *A Man of the People*, however, there is no reason to suspect an abrupt change of political sensibility on Achebe's part.

In the address, he had set out the terms of 'an adequate revolution for me to espouse – to help my society regain belief in itself and put away the complexes of the years of denigration and self-abasement'.[16] If *A Man of the People* is part of that revolution, the lessons it seems to offer Nigerians in rediscovering self-belief and self-value are very harsh ones indeed. What the novel depicts, as we have seen, is not the renaissance but the final degeneration of the Nigerian public sphere. The indigenous ruling class, represented by Nanga, are shown as weak, unproductive and steeped in a culture of nepotism and corruption that they inherited directly from the people. The educated young, represented by Odili, Max and their comrades, are depicted as naïve, deracinated and self-serving. When the military seize power, suspending democracy and jailing the entirety of the elected government, the fickle and selfish mood of the nation remains unchanged. Contrasting traditional culture with the corrupt modernity bequeathed by colonialism, Odili observes finally that 'the village had a mind; it could say no to sacrilege. But in the affairs of the nation there was no owner, the laws of the village became powerless' (*MP*, 148).

As we see here, just as clearly as in *No Longer at Ease* and the historical novels, the idea that Achebe's educative project with his fiction is to proselytise the virtues of Nigerian nation-

A Man of the People and the Biafran writings 151

hood is very difficult indeed to sustain. In the work of critics like Simon Gikandi, he is often aligned with the ideas of cultural nationalism associated with Frantz Fanon. There are indeed, as we will see, certain important commonalities between Achebe's fictional project and Fanon's thinking, especially in *The Wretched of the Earth*. As far as Nigeria is concerned, however, it is Fanon's critique of the failings of newly independent nations that Achebe draws on, rather than his thinking on the organic emergence of national consciousness. In *A Man of the People*, we see nothing whatever of authentic national culture in the way Fanon imagines it, as 'the whole body of efforts made by a people in the sphere of thought to describe, justify and praise the action through which that people has created itself and keeps itself in existence'.[17] What we do see, on the other hand, is a clear echo of Fanon's scathing commentary on the new African bourgeoisie. Indeed, in his portrait of Nanga's ignorance and self-serving complicity with neo-colonial interests, ultimately displaced by military force, it is possible to see a precise parallel between Achebe and Fanon, writing in the same era:

> As we see it, the national bourgeoisie of certain under developed countries has learned nothing from books. If they had looked closer at the Latin American countries they doubtless would have recognised the dangers which threaten them. We may thus conclude that this bourgeoisie in miniature that thrusts itself into the forefront is condemned to mark time, accomplishing nothing. In underdeveloped countries the bourgeois phase is impossibly arid. Certainly, there is a police dictatorship and a profiteering caste, but the construction of an elaborate bourgeois society seems to be condemned to failure. The ranks of decked-out profiteers whose grasping hands scrape up the bank-notes from a poverty-stricken country will sooner or later be men of straw in the hands of the army, cleverly handled by foreign experts. In this way the former mother country practices indirect government, both by the bourgeoisie that it upholds and also by the national army led by its experts, an army that pins the people down, immobilising and terrorising them.[18]

Out of the mouth of Achebe's callow, self-regarding narrator, the arrival of the army at the conclusion of *A Man of the People* is a welcome, rather than a terrifying development, of course. The actions of 'our young Army officers' (*MP*, 147) in imposing martial law in fact serve Odili very well, eliminating his rival and facilitating his conquest of the girl Edna. What is the reader to make of this disturbing development, however? The violent imposition of dictatorship in place of (even a flawed) democracy would seem, on the face of it, to go entirely against the liberal aspirations expressed in 'The Novelist as Teacher' and elsewhere. Should the ending of *A Man of the People* therefore be read as a *warning* of the consequences for Nigeria of neglecting core democratic values of probity, law and public accountability? Once again, it is difficult to square this easy interpretation with Achebe's public interventions at the time. In an interview for the Kenyan *Sunday Nation* in January 1967, he admitted that even by that stage, his thoughts on the overthrow of democracy by the Nigerian army were 'not fully clarified'.[19] Although the coup was 'unfortunate', Achebe's public position was that 'military takeovers are not always bad in themselves. You see, the Nigerian situation left no political solution. The political machine had been so abused that whatever measures were taken, it could only produce the same results. We had got to a point where some others force had to come in.'[20] It is clear here that in Achebe's eyes, the revolution of January 1966 that his novel accurately predicted was, indeed, founded in an idealism that he found admirable. The fact that, in only a few months, it was superseded by a counter-revolution 'that has no basis other than tribalism'[21] should not, he argues, obscure the necessity for that first, radical intervention.

In Fanon's analysis in *The Wretched of the Earth*, it is not merely the new bourgeoisie that are responsible for choking off the development of nations in the first stages of postcoloniality. The new university educated elite must also take their share of the blame for societal stagnation. 'Each generation must, out of relative obscurity, discover its mission, fulfil it, or betray it',[22] he suggests. Read in these terms, *A Man of the*

People is unambiguously an account of the historic failure of the class which includes Achebe himself, to found a prosperous, democratic Nigeria. For Fanon, it is worth noting, even the reclamation of pre-colonial culture that we see in texts like *Things Fall Apart* and *Arrow of God* by no means, in itself, necessarily indicates freedom from a colonial mind-set. 'Perhaps this passionate research and this anger are kept up', he speculates, 'by the secret hope of discovering beyond the misery of today, beyond self-contempt, resignation and abjuration, some very beautiful and splendid era whose existence rehabilitates us both in regard to ourselves and in regard to others.'[23] The aim of such writing is, at root, to contest the European equation of Africa with barbarism, and as such must be recognised as irremediably caught up in a dialectic with colonialism, rather than focused on national renaissance. Even if efforts (such as Achebe's) to challenge the hegemony of colonialism's demeaning representations are historically necessary in the journey towards liberation, Fanon suggests, they also carry an inherent ambivalence. Native intellectuals in nations at the time of independence – like Odili and like Achebe himself – who were reared to a mediating, and hence intermediate position between colonialism and their own culture, are never secure or grounded. Their efforts (in Achebe's case) to reclaim their people's history are, on one level, a clearly redemptive gesture. At the same time, however, it is also 'symptomatic of the intellectual's realization of the danger that he is running of cutting his last moorings and of breaking adrift from his people'.[24]

In Odili, Achebe paints a portrait of a young educated African who is very clearly 'becoming estranged', as Fanon put it, who is indeed already 'the living haunt of contradictions which run the risk of becoming insurmountable'.[25] From the first, Achebe is careful to draw Odili's sensibility as vacillating and conflicted. In the first confrontation with the minister, high-minded disapproval is easily tempered by the latter's appeal to his vanity and ambition. Immediately Odili confesses, 'I found myself wondering whether – perhaps – I had been applying to politics stringent standards that didn't belong to it' (*MP*, 9). He is, we learn in chapter 2, keenly committed to the principle of progressing on his own merits without using powerful connections to unfair advantage. When he is invited to stay at Nanga's house (while the latter touches the Minister for Overseas Training for an international scholarship) however, we soon find how flimsy that moral commitment is. In an ironic gesture to *Things Fall Apart*, as we have seen, he indicates that he is interested in writing a work of fiction about colonialism and traditional culture in his home district. When he observes the life of the people all around him, however, Achebe is careful to stress how Odili's elitism and self-absorption prevent any meaningful connection:

> I walked for hours, keeping to the well-lit streets. The dew settled on my head and helped to numb my feeling. Soon my nose began to run and as I hadn't brought a handkerchief I blew it into the roadside drain by closing each nostril in turn with my first finger. As dawn came my head began to clear a little and I saw Bori stirring. I met a night-soil man carrying his bucket of ordure on top of a battered felt hat drawn down to hood his upper face while his nose and mouth were masked with a piece of black cloth like a gangster. I saw beggars sleeping under the eaves of luxurious department stores and a lunatic sitting wide awake by the basket of garbage he called his possession. The first red buses running empty passed me and I watched the street lights go off finally around six. I drank in all these details with the early morning air. It was strange perhaps that a man who had so much on his mind should find time to pay attention to these small, inconsequential things; it was like the man in the proverb who was carrying the carcass of an elephant on his head and searching with his toes for a grasshopper. But that was how it happened. It seems that no thought – no matter how great – had the power to exclude all others. (*MP*, 71)

Here the 'inconsequential' existence of the poor and dispossessed is figured as nothing but a distraction from the 'great' concerns of Odili's social and sexual standing.

When the question of principled political resistance is introduced with the entrance of Max and the CPC, Odili's interests are again conflicted. In an effort to impress his radical friends, he questions the class basis of the young movement, which takes it as unproblematic that 'a party calling itself the Common People's Convention should be made up of only professional men and women' (*MP*, 78). The core motivation for his involvement, as we see again and again however, is the pursuit of his rivalry with Nanga. In this context, it comes as little surprise at the end of the novel when he corruptly pays Edna's bride price and the costs of her education to Nanga, out of funds that were donated to the party precisely to fight corruption and graft. At the narrative's climax, as the political turmoil escalates and real change seems to peep over the horizon, the terms in which Odili perceives that change are again chosen carefully by Achebe. The nation, far from lean and impoverished as Achebe has allowed us to see it, appears through his eyes as indolent, lethargic and ripe to shed its 'lazy folds of flabby skin and fat it had put on in the greedy years' (*MP*, 100). Even as, in Odili's mind, Nanga and the nation seem to morph together, change becomes inseparable from his desire to do personal battle with the minister. As he meditates on the revolution to come, Achebe shows his protagonist revelling in his possession of a brand new motor car, symbol *par excellence* of the privilege and inequality that the party purports to oppose. As the narrative draws to a close, he is just as much out of sympathy with the people of his nation as he was at the start.

On 14 January 1966, the recently formed Society of Nigerian Authors put on a special evening to celebrate the launch of the novel. In his memoir *There Was a Country: A Personal History of Biafra*, Achebe writes of the Society that it was founded with the aim of protecting the liberty and autonomy of writers, and to express that solidarity of purpose between them:

> We thought it would keep our members safe and protect other artists as well. We hoped that our existence would create an environment in Nigeria where freedom of creative expression was not only possible but protected. We sought ultimately through our art to create for Nigeria an environment of good order and civilization – a daunting task that needed to be tackled in a country engulfed in crisis.[26]

The stark warning of impending crisis that *A Man of the People* embodies can certainly be seen as being in tune with that project. Indeed *There Was a Country* encourages a reading of the novel in exactly the terms he sets out, as a work that aimed to expose unpleasant truths about the state of the nation in terms uncompromising enough to render them un-ignorable.

Achebe was president of the new society, one of the pre-eminent figures in African publishing and a well-known media figure. To see, from his pen, a military takeover depicted as the only 'happy ending' for a nation mired in corruption would, it is easy to assume, have been profoundly shocking to Achebe's contemporaries. In fact, however, as Bernth Lindfors argues in 'Achebe's African Parable', it is likely that the drift of Achebe's thoughts were not dissimilar to those of many others. As we have already seen, in the mid-1960s, the reputation of the Nigerian armed forces was very different from what it became in later decades. In December 1960, as Lindfors writes, 'Nigerian troops had been sent to the newly-independent Republic of the Congo (Leopoldville) to help United Nations forces keep order, and in April, 1964 they had been dispatched to Tanganyika to relieve British troops who had put down a Tanganyika Army mutiny. In Nigeria, Army troops had quelled a Tiv riot in 1960 and had maintained order in the Western Region during the 1962 state of emergency.'[27] As he argues, while the armed forces of other African nations had been seen to have acted in inflammatory and disruptive ways, the Nigerian military had, by 1966, acquired a reputation for effective law enforcement and peacekeeping. In the region more generally, moreover, the idea of military rather than democratic rule was becoming increasingly commonplace. Back in February 1964, the Lagos *Daily Times* had been fearful that the 'constant cataclysms which have recently disrupted peace and order in Africa have produced a dangerous trend towards replacing the growing pattern of parliamentary rule with military juntas'.[28] By the time Achebe completed his manuscript in early 1965, however, the expectation that Nigeria might follow the path of Togo, Dahomey, Tanganyika, Uganda, Kenya, Zanzibar and many others was widespread. Lindfors quotes an article from the popular Lagos *Sunday Express* from 3 January 1965, calling openly for dictatorship as the solution to Nigeria's ills:

> Democracy has bred corruption in our society on a scale hitherto unknown in human history.
>
> Nigeria needs a strong man with a strong hand. By this I mean, that Nigeria needs to be disciplined. Nigeria needs to be drilled.
>
> The leadership we want is the leadership of a benevolent dictator who gets things done; not that of 'democratic administrators' who drag their feet.[29]

On the very night of *A Man of the People*'s launch, the paper got its wish. Achebe and his colleagues woke up on the morning of 15 January 1966 to discover soldiers patrolling key areas of Lagos, and the news that the Prime Minister and key members of his regime had been assassinated. The spokesman for the coup, Major Chukwuma Kaduna Nzeogwu, who Achebe later described as a 'disciplined, no-nonsense, nonsmoking, nonphilandering teetotaler and ... anti-corruption campaigner',[30] announced its initial successes and set out its justifications on national radio:

> Our enemies are the political profiteers, swindlers, men in high and low places that seek bribes and demand ten per cent, those that seek to keep the country permanently divided so that they can remain in office as Ministers and VIPs of waste, the tribalists, the nepotists, those that make the country look big for nothing before international circles.[31]

As Ezenwa-Ohaeto writes, however, Nzeogwu's coup was not destined to accomplish what it set out to, even in the first instance. Most significantly, the plotters failed in their bid to eliminate the commander of the army, Major General Aguiyi Ironsi. In the following weeks and months, Ironsi was able to manoeuvre himself into the position of Head of State and to neutralise most of those, including Nzeogwu, who had carried out the January coup. With ethnic tension escalating, Ironsi himself did not survive for long. An Igbo with strong One-Nigeria sentiments, he embarked on a tour of the Northern and Western regions with the aim of underlining his commitment to national unity, but was assassinated by Northern officers in his own guard on 29 July 1966. His death was just one of thousands of Igbo army officers who were killed in that second coup. As Ezenwa-Ohaeto writes, in his position at the NBC in Lagos Achebe was acutely aware of the implications of this turn of events, as country-wide pogroms began, targeting all Igbo professionals and their families who were living outside their traditional homeland in the South East. As a well-known public figure whose own Igbo heritage was common knowledge, Achebe was not exempt from the threat. According to Ezenwa-Ohaeto's account:

> Somebody on Achebe's staff telephoned him on Sunday, at the height of the violence against Easterners, and gave him information that a group of soldiers had come to Broadcasting House looking for him. If those soldiers had gone to that office the previous day, or if they had waited till the next day which was a Monday, they would have caught and killed their quarry. The telephone message from that worried staff member was succinct: 'If I were you, I should leave your house.' When Achebe asked for the reason, the man answered: 'The troops are looking for you.' Achebe felt that he had done nothing and that he was not a criminal either, so he telephoned Victor Badejo, Director-General of the NBC, to ask why soldiers should be looking for him. 'Where are you calling from?' inquired Badejo anxiously. 'From my house of course', answered Achebe, 'from Turnbull Road.' 'You better leave immediately,' advised Badejo, 'You better take Christie and leave.'[32]

Achebe, his children and his wife who was pregnant at that time moved to a new residence built by the NBC for the Director of External Broadcasting. The fact that the soldiers went first to their old home provided vital extra time for them to find somewhere to hide. Achebe contacted Frank Cawson, the British Council representative in Lagos, and the family were able to take shelter in his house for a few days. In an account for *Transition* of the situation for Easterners in Lagos at that time, the journalist Peter Enahoro wrote:

> Two friends drove up to the house and gave me a first-hand account of the Northern revolt in progress. Ibos were being abducted from offices and taken away to 3rd Battalion Barracks. There was a road-block between us and Lagos. There were roadblocks on the two routes out of Lagos. They had seen Ibo policemen being marched off by Northern troops and they were scared ... A woman ran into my house. She was hysterical. She had been among a group of people walking past a road-block; suddenly one of the soldiers called to them to line up. They obeyed. They were asked what part of Nigeria they came from. Those who said, 'East', were separated from the others. Then right before their eyes, the 'Easterners' were gunned down ... Abductions were being carried out by marauding soldiers and executions were going on all the time ... A burst of machine gunfire exploded so loud it seemed to have come from the sitting room downstairs. The fighting was literally at my door step. My house was situated in an isolated area and my only neighbours – white employees of a Dutch Firm – had evacuated their complex of bungalows the previous day. Some fleeing Ibo soldiers had hidden in the garage of one of these bungalows. The Northerners, conducting a search-and-destroy operation, found the Ibos and calmly fed ammunition into their bodies.[33]

After a week – by which time soldiers had identified their hiding place – Achebe was able to find a sailing from Lagos to Port Harcourt that could take Christie and the children. As they boarded the ship, he recalled to Ezenwa-Ohaeto 'hearing the laughter of those he had lived with in Lagos for almost ten years',[34] as they revelled in the plight of the Igbo refugees fleeing for their lives. Achebe himself was able to exploit a 'lull in the killings'[35] to make his own way back to Igboland and Ogidi, his home village. As Ezenwa-Ohaeto says, 'such arrivals were occasions for celebration because some families had been wiped out entirely, while in other cases only the children managed to return to the East, their parents having been killed'.[36]

The succession of events that followed the publication of *A Man of The People* was to have a profound formative effect on Achebe's consciousness as a thinker and writer. As I will argue in the remainder of this book, indeed, the importance of his experiences in this period for the direction of his later work can hardly be overestimated. *A Man of the People*, in this sense, can be seen as marking a crucial turning point in his work. From then on, as his memoir records, the progression of events served to reinforce, rather than weaken, his conviction in the analysis offered by the novel:

> As we reached the brink of full-blown war it became clear to me that the chaos enveloping all of us in Nigeria was due to the incompetence of the Nigerian ruling class. They clearly had a poor grasp of history and found it difficult to appreciate and grapple with Nigeria's ethnic and political complexity. This clique, stunted by ineptitude, distracted by power games and the pursuit of material comforts, was unwilling, if not incapable, of saving our fledgling new nation.[37]

Until that time, Achebe suggests, as a writer and intellectual he had regarded the social and political problems experienced by Nigeria as necessary or understandable staging posts in its journey from independence. The wave of ethnic violence that followed the coups of 1966, however, seem to have forced an abrupt change of perspective. 'Suddenly', he writes, 'I realized that the only valid basis for existence is one that gives security to you and your people. It is as simple as that.'[38]

The Biafran writings

As Achebe shows in his memoir *There Was a Country: A Personal History of Biafra*, the backlash of violence against the Igbo across the North and West of Nigeria in late 1966 did not just target the plotters of the January coup or even their sympathisers within the army. Instead, a wave of mass killing was unleashed, apparently directed at any and all Igbo outside the East. What had been presented by Nzeogwu and his comrades as a patriotic revolution against corruption was now painted by politicians and the media as an Igbo bid for supremacy over

Nigeria's other ethnic groups. For Achebe, what the nation then witnessed was not simply a spontaneous expression of popular resentment, but the beginning of a planned campaign of ethnic cleansing:

> Thirty thousand civilian men, women, and children were slaughtered, hundreds of thousands were wounded, maimed, and violated, their homes and property looted and burned – and no one asked any questions. A Sierra Leonean living in Northern Nigeria at the time wrote home in horror: 'The killing of the Igbos has become a state industry in Nigeria.'
>
> What terrified me about the massacres in Nigeria was this: If it was only a question of rioting in the streets and so on, that would be bad enough, but it could be explained. It happens everywhere in the world. But in this particular case a detailed plan for mass killing was implemented by the government – the army, the police – the very people who were there to protect life and property. Not a single person has been punished for these crimes. It was not just human nature, a case of somebody hating his neighbor and chopping off his head. It was something far more devastating, because it was a premeditated plan that involved careful coordination, awaiting only the right spark.[39]

When the Eastern Region seceded from the Nigerian Federation on 30 May 1967, citing the concerted failure of the national government to guarantee the rights of its people or protect them against genocide, Achebe became a citizen of the new Biafra.

Nigeria itself, it immediately became clear, was unwilling to countenance Biafran independence. In Achebe's analysis in his memoir, one of the reasons for this was the fear that if Igbo-dominated Biafra found it possible to secede from the Federation, then a number of other 'ethnic nationalities' might seize the opportunity for self-determination.[40] Another reason – whose role became increasingly clear during the ensuing conflict – was the recent discovery of oil in the Niger Delta. After fifty years of failed exploration, British Petroleum (BP) and others had managed to tap commercially exploitable reserves in Olibiri near Port Harcourt from 1956. Outputs were initially small, but as the political historian Phia Steyn argues in an account of oil exploration in the region, the political as well as economic implications of the discovery were immense.[41]

After the Suez crisis of the same year, Steyn suggests, it had become clear to Britain and its neighbours that over-reliance on oil from the Persian Gulf was a major strategic weakness. If free passage for oil tankers through the Suez canal was not guaranteed, security of energy supply to the industrialised economies of Western Europe was similarly compromised. From the late 1950s, therefore, the development of South East Nigeria as an alternative source of oil began to assume increasing importance both for Britain and for the Nigerian federal government. From early in the Biafran conflict, it was clear to Achebe and others that the control of oil in the Niger Delta was a – if not the – major driving force of the military onslaught suffered by the new nation between 1967 and 1970 at the hands of its erstwhile countrymen. His poem '1966', first published in the collection *Beware Soul Brother*, ominously merges the imagery of oil exploration with images of mortal conflict, to the point at which the two become inseparable:

> slowly downward in remote
> subterranean shaft
> a diamond-tipped
> drillpoint crept closer
> to residual chaos to
> rare artesian hatred
> that once squirted warm
> blood ...[42]

In 'Agostinho Neto', he imagines the new rulers of independent Africa as 'idiot-kings',[43] lulled into luxurious complacency while an alien race butchers their own people. 'Biafra, 1969', meanwhile, likens the deadly violence of neo-colonialism to the ravages of 'voracious white ants' on a great hardwood statue:

> In our time it came again
> In pain and acrid smell
> Of powder. And furious wreckers
> Emboldened by half a millennium

Of conquest, battening
On new oil dividends, are now
At its black throat squeezing.[44]

Was Achebe correct in making the assumptions that so clearly underlie these writings, of Britain's violent determination to see the Biafran project fail? It is not difficult to see that secession from the Nigerian Federation would have been seen by Britain as a potential threat to its interests. While during the conflict itself, the UK maintained strong military, diplomatic and trading links with Nigeria, its relationship with Biafra was strained, with the implication that supply of oil from Biafran territory was capable of becoming as problematic as that from the Persian Gulf. In the early phase of the conflict, Achebe writes, Biafra's bid for independence provided a strong platform for anti-colonial sentiments. Further, there was every reason to believe that its example might inspire other areas of the Federation, perhaps including Lagos itself. In *There Was a Country*, Achebe's analysis is that Biafra's early success 'alarmed Britain, the former colonial power, anxious for its big oil holdings'.[45] As a roving ambassador for Biafra, frequently attending meetings in London, he was able to witness first-hand the rapid hardening of Prime Minister Harold Wilson's administration against Biafra, despite widespread public protest. At that time Achebe obviously did not have access to the debates going on within the British government itself. What was absolutely unmistakable, however, was the strength of its determination to support Nigeria whatever the political cost.

As internal records from the Ministry of Defence and the Foreign and Commonwealth Office reveal, in fact Britain made available arms and ammunition to the Nigerian Federation in quantities that were unprecedented in Britain's history as a nation. On 4 December 1967 Secretary of State for Defence Dennis Healey received confidential advice from George Thomson at the Foreign Office setting out the massive scale of Nigeria's request for arms. Thomson's clear and cold advice at that time – setting the tenor for British policy throughout the conflict – was that a vigorous campaign to arm the Nigerian military was clearly to Britain's advantage. As Thomson urged, 'I realize that a sudden demand of this kind is extremely difficult to meet, but as I see it ... it would be greatly to our advantage to do whatever we can to meet it.'[46] Firstly, it was unlikely that such a policy would attract major dissent from within the cabinet, where the issue of Britain's strategic interests in Nigeria had already been discussed. Secondly, Nigeria's request for arms avoided mention of politically sensitive assets such as warplanes (which the Federation was able to source from the Soviet Union). As Thomson then explains:

> (c) There is no doubt that the F. M. G. [Federal Government of Nigeria] have had their fingers burned in other countries, and a favourable response ... ought to give us every chance of establishing ourselves again as the main supplier of the Nigerian forces after the war ... the Nigerian economy ought to be able to recover and start to expand again, and there should be valuable business to be done.
> (d) Anything that we can do to assist the F. M. G. should help our oil companies to re-establish and expand their activities in Nigeria.

From Britain's point of view, as journalist Michael Leapman showed in a retrospective on the Biafran war for the London *Independent on Sunday* (which Achebe cites in his memoir), a crucial strategic priority was to back the 'likely winner' of the conflict. Offering heavy military support to a Nigeria that then went on to fail in its bid to crush Biafra would have been disastrous for the security of Britain's oil operations in the South East. Leapman quotes a Commonwealth Office briefing direct to Harold Wilson as Prime Minister setting out unambiguously that 'the sole immediate British interest is to bring the Nigerian economy back to a condition in which our substantial trade and investment can be further developed'.[47] In response to the suggestion that, since the oilfields were in Biafra, British Petroleum should consider paying oil royalties to the new republic, Wilson's response was clear. '"Dangerous argument – c. f. Rhodesia" he scrawled in the margin of the policy paper. Rhodesia unilaterally declared independence in 1965 but Britain was urging that nobody should recognize it, despite the regime's de facto control.'[48] When George Thomas was dispatched to Lagos to negotiate the terms of Britain's support with Nigeria's Premier, General Gowon, Wilson was briefed again by the Commonwealth Office: 'If Gowon is helpful on oil, Mr. Thomas will offer a sale of anti-aircraft guns.'[49] Biafra had no warplanes, at that time receiving mainly medical supplies and small amounts of food by air, so the aggressive intent of this offer would have been clear on all sides. With Britain guaranteeing overwhelming superiority of arms to Nigeria, determined Biafran resistance was unable to prevent the Federation from regaining control of the oil fields. Thereafter, Wilson's government negotiated a mutually convenient trading arrangement with Gowon: oil formerly belonging to Biafra would be extracted by British Petroleum, in exchange for extensive supplies of arms from Britain capable of facilitating a full siege of the rebel republic.

British governmental records which have now been opened for public access reveal that, within the inner circles of Wilson's administration, there was serious concern in some quarters about the ethical implications of arming a campaign that was rapidly turning into a massacre. In secret correspondence to John Morris at the Ministry of Defence in January 1969, for example, Foreign Office Minister Maurice Foley wrote that 'none of us [are] happy about having to go on providing arms and ammunition to Nigeria while the civil war continues with no immediate end in sight'. The only alternative, however, was 'to set ourselves on the slippery slope towards the loss of the very extensive British interests in Nigeria',[50] and this could not be countenanced. Two months previously, Morris had confirmed a shipment including fifteen million rounds for small arms and twenty thousand artillery shells to the Nigerian Federation. By that point, as Morris wrote to Lord Malcolm Shepherd on 13 November 1968, the Ministry of Defence had supplied arms to Nigeria 'equivalent to 60% of the British Army's total reserve stocks to meet its world-wide liabilities' despite the fact that, as he freely admitted, there had been no 'objective assessment ... whether these munitions are likely to be a conclusive factor in ending the fighting in Nigeria'.[51] Correspondence of the time between senior civil servants at the Foreign and Commonwealth Office and at the Ministry of Defence reveals significant disquiet at this within the cabinet. In a secret memo, one (unnamed) aide warns that his minister was 'becoming increasingly restive on the subject of the supply of arms and ammunition to Nigeria [and] is now muttering darkly about either writing or going to see the Prime Minister himself'. Setting his concerns in context, the memo candidly summarises the gains anticipated for Britain from aiding the campaign against Biafra:

> Present British policy seems to be to provide conventional weapons and ammunition to Nigeria (on a rather more lavish scale than we would probably be keen to admit in public), in the knowledge that while this is not doing very much towards bringing the war to an end, Nigeria could almost certainly buy the stuff somewhere else if we didn't provide it, and by letting her have it we retain a certain degree of influence in Lagos and the possibility of emerging with good relations when Nigeria ultimately wins, thereby ensuring access to the oil reserves in East Nigeria.[52]

Exchanges between Morris and Shepherd, copied to Harold Wilson as Prime Minister, confirm this view. The genocide being waged against the Biafrans might be regrettable, certainly from a public relations standpoint, but nothing could be allowed to over-ride Britain's economic interests in the region. As Secretary of State for Defence, Dennis Healey's position was that it was not his role to question the ethics of the arms deals over which his department presided. This view was made clear to the Foreign Office in a confidential memo of 14 November 1968, written by his parliamentary secretary J. F. Mayne. As far as Healey was concerned, he writes: '[o]ur role in any arms deal with Nigeria is that of supplying agents; the question of whether we ought or ought not to supply is one for the Foreign and Commonwealth Secretary to defend'.[53]

For the Biafrans, as Achebe's memoir graphically illustrates, the effects of Thomson and others' hawkish pursuit of

British interests was catastrophic. While France, in particular, was willing to take up a stance in clear opposition to Britain, supplying the rebels with aid and a limited amount of ordnance, the help it was able to provide was tiny in comparison. Once the strategically crucial oilfields were lost, there was nothing Biafra could do to prevent complete encirclement by the British-armed Nigeria army. For families like Achebe's, as *There Was a Country* recounts, the tightening siege meant repeated retreats as one town after another ceased to be defensible. From Ogutu, they fled to Owerri, where Christie who was expecting another baby was admitted to a Roman Catholic hospital. During her hospital stay the family heard that Nigerian soldiers had again broken Biafran defences and were pushing towards Owerri. 'It had clearly become quite serious when we noticed Biafran soldiers coming into the hospital to warn the clinical staff to leave and evacuate all the patients. Christie was summarily discharged.'[54] As federal forces began to appear, the family were able to flee to Okporo, but Nigerian soldiers were again hot on their heels. In the makeshift medical clinic there, Achebe recalls, 'the visitor was greeted by the strong smell of vomit, diarrhea, and bodily fluids that are kept private in sunnier times. In the distance one could hear the screams of pain from what appeared to be a makeshift operating room, where surgeons performed procedures with woefully limited anesthesia.'[55] Soon federal troops were in Okporo too, accompanied by 'horrendous stories of nurses and local women being raped and violated in unthinkable ways'.[56] Achebe and his wife believed enough of these stories to think it necessary to hide their eight-year-old daughter Chinelo when the soldiers arrived. Achebe describes speaking to them, 'overwhelmed by the strong smell of *kai kai*, a local gin, on their breath'.[57] He managed to negotiate that they would take a goat as plunder, in lieu of other spoils.

In the poem 'Vultures' he captures something of the everyday horror of the siege of Biafra, as two birds incline affectionately together in good fortune, having 'picked / the eyes of a swollen / corpse in a water-logged / trench'.[58] With arms from the Wilson government, Nigeria had succeeded in cutting the republic completely off from the sea, shutting off humanitarian supplies from its people almost completely. As *There Was a Country* records:

> By the beginning of the dry season of 1968, Biafran civilians and soldiers alike were starving. Bodies lay rotting under the hot sun by the roadside, and the flapping wings of scavengers could be seen circling, waiting, watching patiently nearby. Some estimates are that over a thousand Biafrans a day were perishing by this time, and at the height of Gowon's economic blockade and 'starve them into submission' policy, upward of fifty thousand Biafran civilians, most of them babies, children, and women, were dying every single month.[59]

One of the key weapons Biafra deployed in its struggle against Nigeria's overwhelming military strength was the media. Providing unprecedented access to the war zone for international correspondents enabled detailed coverage of the conflict on TV screens across the West, as well as in high-profile periodicals such as *Time* magazine. Over the course of the war, it seems likely that just under three million Biafrans lost their lives, and of these an estimated 90 per cent were children who died of starvation or associated illnesses such as *kwashiorkor*. Iconic images by photojournalists such as Don McCullin, depicting children in the terminal stages of malnutrition, gained rapid, global circulation. Although these helped to fuel mass condemnation of the conflict, especially in London, they did nothing in practice to moderate Britain's focus on its oil and other interests in the region, or to interrupt Nigeria's apparently genocidal campaign.

For Achebe and other intellectuals in Biafra, the extraordinary violence their fledgling state faced became, in itself, a political and ideological challenge. Their primary response, spearheaded jointly by the Biafran leader Emeka Ojukwu and by Achebe as its highest-profile writer and commentator, was a statement of the principles of the Biafran revolution, which was delivered as *The Ahiara Declaration* in June 1969. While, in Ezenwa-Ohaeto's biography and elsewhere, indications are given that Achebe had some involvement in the genesis of this key document, it was not until the publication of his memoir in 2012 that it became clear that, in fact, Achebe was the lead author of this historic document.

Towards the end of 1968, *There Was a Country* recounts, Ojukwu called on Achebe to draw together a group of intellectuals to articulate Biafra's revolutionary story. In scope and ambition, the project could hardly have been grander, as the group set out to grapple with the fundamental questions facing their new nation. As Achebe modestly describes in his account:

> It did not escape Biafra's founders that a great nation needed to be built on a strong intellectual foundation. Our modest attempt to put the beginnings of our thinking down on paper resulted in what would be known as the Ahiara Declaration.
>
> In the Harmattan Season of 1968, Ojukwu invited me to serve on a small political committee that the Ministry of Information was creating. The Ministry of Information was the only place that an author would be comfortable, he told me, because that was the venue of intellectual debate – where philosophy, cultural matters, literature, politics, and society with all its elements were discussed. The ministry had to play an important role in the new nation, he insisted, as Biafra tried to free itself from the faults it saw in Nigeria.
>
> So I joined this group and set to work. The questions that we raised within the committee and later presented for broader discussion included: How would we win this war and begin the creation of a new nation with the qualities we seek? What did we want Biafra to look like? What would be the core components of our new nation-state? What did we mean by citizenship and nationhood? What would be Biafra's relationship to other African countries? What kind of education would the general population need to aid Biafra's development?[60]

What began as a speculative and philosophical enterprise soon acquired harder political edges, as Ojukwu formalised the role of Achebe and his collaborators as the National Guidance

Committee for Biafra. The document they were writing would not merely be a statement of ideals, he decided, but would have the status of a constitution for the new republic. *The Ahiara Declaration* would be, in Achebe's words, 'a promulgation of the fundamental principles upon which the government and people of Biafra would operate'. The Biafran leader impressed on the group the historic importance of their work. 'The Biafran nation, Ojukwu explained, had to have special attributes – the very principles that we approved of and were fighting for: unity, self-determination, social justice, etc. The final version of this document, we hoped, would also tell our story to the world – how Biafra had been pushed out of Nigeria by Nigerians and threatened with genocide.'[61]

In *The Ahiara Declaration*, significantly, the Biafran conflict is never characterised simply as a civil war between formerly neighbouring regions in Nigeria. Indeed, Nigeria itself is not figured as the fundamental enemy. The real struggle, its authors argue, is instead the condition of abject neo-colonial subordination that Nigeria has come to embody. For Britain, the former imperial power, only one kind of independent African nation is welcome. That is, 'a corrupt and rickety structure … in a perpetual state of powerlessness to check foreign exploitation'.[62] For daring to challenge the integrity of Nigeria, 'that ramshackle creation that has no justification either in history or in the freely expressed wishes of the people',[63] the Biafrans now face the prospect of extermination. Their goal – their crime – is that of wishing to build a healthy, democratic African state on a foundation of true independence:

> Since in the thinking of many white powers, good, progressive and efficient government is good only for whites, our view was considered dangerous and pernicious: a point of view which explains but does not justify the blind support which these powers have given to uphold the Nigerian ideal of a corrupt, decadent and putrefying society. To them genocide is an appropriate answer to any group of black people who have the temerity to attempt to evolve their own social system.[64]

Nigeria's 'independence', the *Declaration* contends, was never anything but a mask for neo-colonialism, and nor was it meant to be for Britain, the imperial power. The motivation of Harold Wilson's government, it argues, is simple: pure economic self-interest. If an Igbo genocide was required to protect its oil holdings in the Niger Delta, then aiding and facilitating the necessary campaign of violence presented no special obstacle.

In this, Britain had form. In the eighteenth century, it had overseen a genocide against the native Americans, and in the nineteenth century had done the same in Tasmania and New Zealand. For centuries, Britain had been a pivotal slave-trading power. For Britain, the sacrifice of native peoples to its on-going entrepreneurial ambitions had, in fact, become deeply historically ingrained. In this sense, its quest for control of Biafran oil was nothing new at all. 'We see why the Shell-BP led the Nigerian hoards into Bonny, pays Biafran oil royalties to Nigeria, and provided the Nigerian army with all the help it needed ... We see why the oil and trading companies in Nigeria still finance this war and why they risk the life and limb of their staff in the war zones.'[65]

The authors of *The Ahiara Declaration* were not established politicians or ideologues, but scholars and creative intellectuals like Achebe himself. Eyo Ndem, a political sociologist, was a refugee from the University of Nigeria. Ifegwu Eke was an agricultural economist. Emeka Aniagolu was a practicing judge who would go on to become a major African law-maker. The committee secretary, Emanuel Obiechina, was a literary historian. Novelists such as Chukwuemeke Ike were among the figures summoned to give evidence. Ikenna Nzimiro brought expertise on Igbo traditional culture, while Chieka Ifemesia was a historian with specialist understanding of British colonialism. The latter's account of the committee's work, recorded by Ezenwa-Ohaeto, sheds interesting light on the open, democratic dynamics that Achebe tried to foster as chairman:

> [E]verything about the community was discussed, with people making suggestions. Recommendations were also made which people took home to their units. The meeting

of the committee was a two-way thing for the members also brought recommendations from their units. Ojukwu as the Patron always attended the meetings. There is scarcely any meeting he did not attend.[66]

While the group worked together on the *Declaration* in Umuahia, the town began to become a mecca for other artists and writers. In his 'Reminiscences', Chukwuma Azuonye recalls how they braved the air raids which 'had become menacingly more frequent and intense with gruesome bombing and strafing' to gather at the New Town Tavern. Poetry readings were held 'over palm wine, chicken and *odudu*. Umuahia gave birth to some of the finest poetry of the civil war.'[67] Achebe's memoir recounts that, as the Biafran situation became increasingly desperate, so its artistry seemed to flourish, producing 'an explosion of musical, lyrical, and poetic creativity'.[68] When the group finished *The Ahiara Declaration* and Ojukwu delivered it as a public address on 1 June 1969, he recalls his brother Frank's account, 'odika si gbabia agbaba [it was as if we were dancing to his words] ... People listened from wherever they were. It sounded right to them: freedom, equality, self-determination, excellence. Ojukwu read it beautifully that day.'[69]

As we have seen, *The Ahiara Declaration* set out a strident critique of the faults and flaws of 'Nigerianism'[70] together with a high-minded proclamation of the values Biafra would embody. Recalling some of Achebe's public statements of the mid-1960s, such as 'The Novelist as Teacher' and the affirmative rhetoric of the Voice of Nigeria, its tone is campaigning and committed. All the more interesting, then, to consider Achebe's few fictional writings of the period, which strike a much more troubled and ambivalent note. As with his earlier novels from *Things Fall Apart* to *A Man of the People*, it seems that for Achebe in Biafra, fiction once again became the space in which a counter-discourse to 'commitment' was allowed to express itself.

In the story 'Girls at War', published after the end of the conflict in 1972, Achebe paints a picture of Biafra very different from the egalitarian utopia conjured by *The Ahiara Declaration*. His narrative centres on the figure of Reginald Nwankwo, an official of the Ministry of Justice, and his encounters through the war with Gladys, a worker for the revolution. At the beginning of the war, we discover, Nwankwo has used his government car to give the girl a lift to Enugu where she wants to enlist in the militia. He is sexist and discouraging, advising her that the services of girls are not required for the nation's defence. Some months later, his car is stopped at a checkpoint: the official checking his car is the same girl. With unflinching efficiency, she subjects his official's car to the same rigorous examination as all vehicles, disregarding his attempts to over-awe her with his rank. In Nwankwo's objectifying gaze, the image of Gladys has already begun to metamorphose from that of volunteer for the civil defence to that of possible sexual conquest:

> Then she opened the rear door and bent down to inspect under the seats. It was then he took the first real look at her, starting from behind. She was a beautiful girl in a breasty blue jersey, khaki jeans and canvas shoes with the new-style hair-plait which gave a girl a defiant look and which they called – for reasons of their own – 'air force base.'[71]

In deft strokes, Achebe portrays Nwankwo's increasing ambivalence, caught as he is between an instinct to diminish all adult qualities in young women other than the sexual, and his growing recognition of the idealism, commitment and seriousness of purpose exhibited by Gladys and others of her generation.

Eighteen months later, in the days of the tightening siege, his ambivalence remains, but when Achebe's two characters meet once more, he is careful to show us just how much the power relation between them has changed. While the masses starve and refugee camps multiply, Nwankwo's place in the regime guarantees him privileged access to the scarce food and supplies brought in by air. As well as fuel for his car, a government driver and access to fish and meat, a connection with the manager of Nkwerri depot allows him rich pickings from the limited stocks of foreign aid. In a brave new republic purportedly founded in egalitarian values, Achebe's narrative points up the grossness of the inequality Nwankwo's position has come to symbolise:

As his driver loaded tins and bags and cartons into his car the starved crowds that perpetually hung around relief centres made crude, ungracious remarks like 'War Can Continue!' meaning the WCC! Somebody else shouted 'Irevolu!' and his friends replied 'shum!' 'Irevolu!' 'shum!' Isofeli?' 'shum!' 'Isofeli?' 'Mba!'

Nwankwo was deeply embarrassed not by the jeers of this scarecrow crowd of rags and floating ribs but by the independent accusation of their wasted bodies and sunken eyes. Indeed he would probably have felt much worse had they said nothing, simply looked on in silence, as his boot was loaded with milk, and powdered egg and oats and tinned meat and stock-fish. By nature such singular good fortune in the midst of a general desolation was certain to embarrass him. But what could a man do? (*GW*, 107)

If *The Ahiara Declaration* seeks to portray a 'healthy, dynamic and progressive'[72] Biafra, united in equality and common purpose, 'Girls at War' offers a very different image indeed. On his way back to Owerri, Nwankwo orders his driver to stop for a 'very attractive girl by the roadside' (*GW*, 108) thereby initiating the third and final encounter with Gladys. His inference from her health and expensive clothing is that 'she had to be in the keep of some well-placed gentleman, one of those piling money out of the war' (*GW*, 109). Achebe's text, however, opens up a second possibility, with the revelation that she is now working for the Fuel Directorate, and therefore might have established her own illicit sources of income. Invited into his home, she quickly installs herself, changing into a 'house dress' (*GW*, 111) and busying herself in the kitchen. After the fright of an enemy airplane flying overhead, she allows him to kiss her and squeeze her breasts. Later, she shocks Nwankwo 'by the readiness with which she followed him to bed and by her language. "You want to shell?" she asked. And without waiting for an answer said, "Go ahead but don't pour in troops!"' (*GW*, 118). Likening her to a prostitute, Nwankwo responds by meditating on the negative transformation wrought by war. 'Gladys, he thought, was just a mirror reflecting a society that had gone completely rotten and maggotty at the centre' (*GW*, 119). He reflects on the war profiteers in Biafra 'sending young men to hazard their lives bartering looted goods for cigarettes behind enemy lines' and the contractors receiving 'piles of money daily for food they never deliver to the army' (*GW*, 119).

In an unusual display of civic responsibility the following day, he picks up a child soldier on the road. The boy has lost a leg to the war and, when an enemy warplane screams overhead, he cannot manoeuvre himself from the car to the safety of the bush. While Nwankwo runs to save himself, it is Gladys who goes back to help the boy. The complex image with which Achebe then concludes the story works to throw his protagonist's judgement radically into doubt. 'From afar he saw his driver running towards him in tears and blood. He saw the remains of his car smoking and the entangled remains of the girl and the soldier. And he let out a piercing cry and fell down again' (*GW*, 123). Balancing ideas of corruption and exploitation, heroism and loss, Biafra's portrayal in 'Girls at War' is like nothing the chair of its National Guidance Committee could possibly have countenanced for inclusion in *The Ahiara Declaration*. Instead, in a way that recalls *No Longer at Ease* and *A Man of the People*, the story goes about exposing the dirtiness and difficulty of nation-building, to the point where hope for the future seems to be all but extinguished.

In Achebe's only other fictional work dealing directly with the Biafran war, the children's story *How the Leopard Got His Claws*, similarly troubled thematics are again discernable. In 1967, he collaborated with the poet Christopher Okigbo in setting up a publishing house, the Citadel Press, in an attempt to address the lack of suitable educational materials for Biafra's children. Early in its life, the press received the manuscript of a work for children by the writer John Iroaganachi, comprising a re-telling of the well-known West African folk tale 'How the Dog Became a Domesticated Animal'. In the traditional tale, whose multiple iterations arise from its popularity in numerous oral traditions, the main character is a dog whose trusting nature leads him to be tricked and cheated by other animals. In a move that seals his fate forever, the dog makes a deal with man. In exchange for the protection and the privileges of the latter's house, he abandons the freedom of the wild and accepts domestic slavery.

In the circumstances of Biafra's revolution, for reasons that are understandable, the metaphorics of this tale seemed jarring and unsuitable to Achebe and Okigbo. While the latter pursued the armed struggle against Nigeria (he died defending Nssuka later that year), Achebe decided to embark on a radical rewriting of Iroaganachi's text. In this context, it would be easy to assume that his finished narrative *How the Leopard Got His Claws* would be affirmative and patriotic in tone, but once again that is far from the case. Achebe makes major changes in the area of characterisation. With the dog, he paints a picture of a selfish and violent animal, marked out from other beasts by his sharp teeth. The forest they all inhabit is an Edenic space with room for everyone, but the dog's laziness and selfishness soon brings trouble to paradise. When rain begins to fall in the forest, the other animals, guided by their wise and gentle ruler the leopard, resolve to work together to build themselves a shared house:

> The tortoise copied the pattern on his back and made the plan of the roof. The giant rat and the mouse dug the foundation. Some animals brought sticks, some ropes; others made roof mats. As they built the house, they sang many happy songs. They also told many jokes. Although they worked very hard, everyone was merry. After many weeks, they finished the building. It was a fine building. The animals were pleased with it. They agreed to open it with a very special meeting. On the opening day, the animals, their wives, and their children gathered in the hall. King leopard then made a short speech. He said: 'This hall is yours to enjoy. You worked very hard together to build it. I am proud of you.'[73]

While all others are labouring to build the common shelter, the dog keeps his distance, but once it is finished he is quick to seize it for himself. When the deer objects, he bites and wounds him. When the leopard challenges him to come out, the dog tears and bites him too. As the leopard slinks away into the forest, the other animals unite in cowardice, adopting the dog as their new king.

In a clear parallel to Biafra's secession, the leopard resolves to make his own way. For the dog, however, this choice is unacceptable. Fearing that on his example, others might leave the village, he orders six strong animals to bring the leopard back, with violence if necessary. Caught and stoned by his former compatriots, the leopard's mind turns to self-defence. From the blacksmith he takes teeth of iron and claws of bronze. From the house of Thunder he takes a fearsome roar. Returning to reclaim his birthright, he strikes fear into the other animals:

> The leopard seized the dog and bit and clawed him without mercy. Then he threw him out of the circle.
> All the animals trembled. But they were too afraid to run. The leopard turned to them and said, 'You miserable worms. You shameless cowards. I was a kind and gentle king, but you turned against me. From today I shall rule the forest with terror. The life of our village is ended.'[74]

Each animal is forced to take from the shelter whatever he put into it, until the hall is pulled apart. The dog, bleeding and fearful, seeks protection in the house of the hunter. In exchange for the privilege of hunting and killing with man, he relinquishes his freedom for slavery. Achebe ends his tale with the animals locked in self-destructive conflict:

> Today the animals are no longer friends, but enemies. The strong among them attack and kill the weak. The leopard, full of anger, eats up anyone he can lay his claws on.
> And the hunter, led by the dog, goes to the forest from time to time and kills any animals he can find. Perhaps someday the animals will make peace among themselves and live together again. Then, at last, they will be able to keep away the hunter, who is their common enemy.[75]

Here, themes from *The Ahiara Declaration*, especially the damaging influence of neo-colonialism (here presented in the guise of the blacksmith and the hunter), are clearly present. As in the story 'Girls at War', however, what shines through Achebe's narrative most clearly is not clarity of commitment but ambivalence and disquiet. The leopard (Biafra) is shown initially as wise and slow to seek conflict. The end point that is envisioned for him, however, is not victory and the restoration of peace, but an implacable cycle of resentment and revenge. The dog, who is lazy and selfish, attains a measure of power as the one animal who all others must fear. He buys this, however, not only by betraying his own kind but by accepting a despicable contract of never-ending servitude. In this sense, what the story seems to impart to the children of Biafra is not some lesson in standing up for your principles and defending your right to freedom, but rather a strong sense of unease about the future trajectory of their nation. If *The Ahiara Declaration* projects the possibility of a society founded on liberty and justice, the image offered by *How the Leopard Got His Claws* seems almost diametrically opposed to that. What it shows is a tropical African kingdom destroyed by selfishness and corruption of spirit.

After the end of the conflict, Achebe returned to Enugu and to the offices of the Citadel Press on Okpara Avenue. Among the other buildings that stood, unscathed, where they had always been, he vividly recalls in his memoir how the Citadel had been 'pummeled into the ground', its parts scattered, 'pulverized as if with a jackhammer'.[76] It was, he says, 'the work of someone or some people with an ax to grind. It appeared as if there was an angry mission sent to silence the Citadel – for having the audacity to publish *How the Leopard Got His Claws*.' His own response was telling. 'Having had a few too many houses and offices bombed, I walked away from the site and from publishing forever.'[77]

As we have seen throughout this book, Achebe's attitude towards Nigeria was an ambivalent one almost from the start. The fissures in his thinking and feeling that appeared in the gap between his broadcasting and public commentary, on the one hand, and his fiction on the other, did not disappear with the birth of Biafra. Looking back to the 1960s in his memoir, he reflected that Nigeria's writers at that time had 'found themselves with a new, terrifying problem on their hands: They found that the independence their country was supposed to have won was totally without content. In the words of Dr. Nnamdi Azikiwe, Nigeria was given her freedom "on a platter of gold." We should have known that freedom should be won, not given on a plate.'[78] In Biafra, as we can see from the idealism of *The Ahiara Declaration*, Achebe and others clearly were, on one level, keen to make a fresh start. The *Declaration* called, in unambiguous terms, for a departure on fresh principles that would circumvent the weakness, corruption and enslavement to neo-colonialism that Nigeria had come to embody in their eyes. His fiction of the period, as ever telling the other side of the story, sheds cold light on that dream. In the story 'Civil Peace', set in the immediate aftermath of the conflict, indeed, we are confronted with the hard realisation of how little has changed after all the bitter struggling. Jonathan Iwegbu, an erstwhile Biafran, begins by celebrating that he, his wife, each of their three children and even their little house in Enugu have come out of the war unscathed. Using his bicycle as a taxi service, he begins to rebuild a life. His children pick mangoes, his wife begins a trade in cooked breakfasts, he gathers palm wine from surrounding villages and sets up a makeshift bar. Turning in the (soon to be defunct) Biafran money he has made over to the local treasury in exchange for twenty Nigerian pounds, he cannot believe his good fortune. That night, however, ex-Biafran soldiers brandishing automatic weapons come to the house demanding money. They mock his cries for help and sarcastically offer to call the army. In the morning, poor once again, the family continue with their meagre work. As Jonathan muses to his commiserating neighbours, toil and poverty are nothing but what he expects.

In *The Wretched of the Earth*, first published in English at around the time Achebe was working on *A Man of the People*, Fanon had castigated the new middle class in African nations for their failures to the people. 'The national bourgeoisie of underdeveloped countries', he argued 'is not engaged in production, nor in invention, nor building, nor labour; it is completely canalized into activities of the intermediary type. Its innermost vocation seems to be to keep in the running and to be part of the racket.'[79] If *A Man of the People* works to confirm that diagnosis through the weak and self-serving figure of Odili, the spirit of *The Ahiara Declaration* address it too, calling for national renewal in Africa to be carried out along very different lines. 'In an underdeveloped country', demands Fanon, 'an authentic middle class ought to consider as its bounden duty ... to put itself to school with the people: in other words to put at the people's disposal the intellectual and technical capital that it has snatched when going through the colonial universities.'[80] With the birth of Biafra, leading the group that would write the new nation's constitution, Achebe had the opportunity to rise to Fanon's challenge, in a way few African writers and intellectuals had. As a central member of the new republic's regime, his values and principles treated with importance and seriousness, he was privileged to share in the making of an idealistic new nation. *The Ahiara Declaration* was, certainly, as close as his writing would ever get to untempered nationalism. In his fiction, characteristically however, we find the other side to the story.

As *There Was a Country* reveals, deep involvement with the Biafran regime was challenging for Achebe on both intellectual and ethical levels. As well as chairing the National Guidance Committee, Ojukwu also had him working for the Biafran Organization of Freedom Fighters (BOFF), a propagandist arm of government whose brief was to project a positive image of the military to the people. In the context that Biafra was, from its inception, a nation focused on violent resistance to incursion, many of the actions taken by its armed forces must have been very hard to mediate, even for a broadcaster with Achebe's experience. Ntieyong Udo Akpan, Chief Secretary to the government of Biafra, sheds illustrative light on the challenges Achebe must have faced, in his book *The Struggle for Secession: 1966–1970*. During the Nigerian advance into the oil-rich Niger Delta, non-Igbo minorities were suspected of collaborating against Biafra, and despite a lack of substantial evidence, the response of the regime was shocking:

> Whole villages were burnt and individuals murdered ... and it was quite shocking to know those who were the actual leaders of the bloody and destructive rampage –

professional men, university lecturers, and others. The Governor [Ojukwu] himself gave at least tacit approval to these acts of brigandage.[81]

After Port Harcourt had fallen, Akpan reports being 'terribly shocked by the number of bodies being carted into mass graves – bodies of persons not killed by bullets but by cruel handling'.[82] Achebe's brief, to shape a public 'education strategy'[83] fostering patriotism and support for the army, necessarily forced him into direct confrontation with the ethics of pursuing war with such careless use of power. In an interview with Kalu Ogbaa some time after the end of the conflict, further light was shed on the nature of the ambivalence that shines through all of his creative writings from Biafra. The project of the new republic was, in ideological and political terms, a noble one, an attempt to erase colonialism's negative legacies in a way Nigeria had been patently unable to. In practice though, formed as it was in the shadow of a genocidal campaign for its extinction, the reality of building and defending Biafra had been very different:

> In a revolutionary situation, in a situation of great danger, in an institution and regime of violence, for instance, what does a creative artist do? ... I decided that I could not stand aside from the problems and struggles of my people at that point in history. And if it happened again, I would not behave differently.
>
> But there are limitations, you know. For instance, in that kind of situation there is bound to be pressure to think alike. There is bound to be pressure, maybe, to surrender some of your cherished ideals. There may even be the danger ... of forgetting that art is not 'brother' to violence.... It's tricky to get into that situation. I cannot say more than I have said, but I'll simply say again that an artist has to have his wits about him because he is stepping into a very dangerous domain.[84]

After Biafra, Achebe found it impossible to live in Nigeria, continually confronted by the violence and betrayals wrought by the civil war. Having gone into exile with his family in the United States, he gave up editorship of the African Writers Series in 1972. In 1976, he returned to the country of his birth once again, but with a consciousness still clearly scarred and troubled by the conflict. Interviewed for *Okike* in 1976, he spoke in very personal terms about the ways in which the Biafran experience had disrupted his sensibility as an artist. Ten years had elapsed since the publication of *A Man of the People*, and yet despite his efforts, no fifth novel was forthcoming. After the civil war, he said, the fundamental problem was that of 'finding the kind of emotional and artistic stability – peace of mind, if you like – that is needed'.[85] One attempt had already been abandoned, and the questions of critics and fans keenly expecting another work were becoming oppressive. 'You may think this is just an excuse', he says, but 'I think the job of my readers is to get the maximum out of what I have done.'[86] For him, reassessment and 'a new departure' were needed. 'I have to ask myself: "What happened to Nigeria? What happened to my relationship to Nigeria? What happened to the Igbo people in relation to Nigeria? And how are we going to deal with this in future?"'[87] As must have been clear to his interviewer Onuora Enekwe, his questions were fundamentally political ones. Achebe's next major work, *The Trouble with Nigeria*, would indeed be thoroughly political in form. It was not until the mid-1980s with *Anthills of the Savannah*, though, that he was able to return at full strength to the challenge of the novel.

5

Anthills of the Savannah

Anthills of the Savannah is structured around a quartet of characters, members of the elite in the postcolonial West African state of Kangan. Sam, Kangan's Head of State, has come to power in an army coup that overthrew a corrupt and ineffectual civilian regime some time before the opening of the novel. He is a product of a colonial school, Lord Lugard College, and Sandhurst, the most prestigious military training academy in England. Chris Oriko, a friend of Sam's since their boyhood at college, is a senior journalist whose fortunes have risen significantly since the latter became His Excellency. Chris is now Commissioner for Information with control of Kangan's media. Ikem Osodi, another alumnus of Lord Lugard College, is their idealistic long-time friend. He is a poet of repute and editor of a leading newspaper. Ikem is one of the few members of the elite who is still willing to take the risk of 'speaking the truth to power', priding himself on his crusading editorials. Achebe's fourth protagonist is Beatrice, a little younger than the others but, like them, carrying all the signs of a top-notch international education, including a first class honours degree from St Mary's College, University of London, with its reputation for feminist intellectualism. Beatrice is Chris's girlfriend and friend to both Ikem and the president. At the end, it will be up to her to pick up the pieces when her male counterparts have played out their dramas.

With *Anthills*, Achebe broke a two decades long block with the novel. Immediately after the Biafran war, he had published a collection, *Girls at War*, including some new and some older short stories, and in the years following occasional poems appeared in *Okike* and elsewhere. As a critic and commentator, his writing and reputation had continued to develop, with a volume of essays, *Morning Yet on Creation Day* appearing in 1975. Multiple attempts at producing a fifth novel, however, had failed to bear fruit. As we saw in chapter 4, the experience of Biafra – of being turned on by former countrymen and oil-hungry Britain, and bombed and starved into submission – was one that left Achebe struggling to find 'the kind of emotional and artistic stability'[1] he needed for novel writing.

Perhaps unsurprisingly therefore, as Lyn Innes observes,[2] one of the most striking features of *Anthills* is how strongly it seems to be preoccupied with the problem of finding the words, finding the voice with which to speak of Nigeria and its situation. In terms of form, the narrative is fragmentary. Instead of being directed by a single eye view, it is framed around 'witness statements' that offer very different perspectives on the military dictatorship they describe, as well as the question of the ethical responsibilities its excesses might impose on those with the capacity to resist. In intervening sequences, these first person testimonies alternate with third person narration in which the perspectives and interests of other characters are represented, including the President Sam (who interestingly is not given his own witness statement). Other figures, including Kangan's duplicitous Attorney General, and 'Mad Medico', an eccentric Englishman busy creating his own legend around the capital, appear and disappear during the course of the narrative. Not until chapter 7 – a full third of the way into the novel – does Achebe reveal the metafictional device by means of which these disparate perspectives will be unified. Beatrice, it seems, has taken on the challenge of 'bringing together as many pieces of this tragic history as I could lay my hands on' (*AS*, 78). The text – or collection of texts – we are reading, then, is the fruit of her labour.

More than any of Achebe's previous four novels, as this makes clear, the texture of *Anthills* is self-consciously editorial in orientation. In place of the bold, formal simplicity of a text like

Things Fall Apart, its narrative is discontinuous, with revelations tortuously circled and worked towards. As a number of critics have noted, moreover, this change in narrative approach also has a gendered dimension, as Achebe makes his first fully developed attempt at voicing a female main character. While in previous works, the wives and girlfriends of his various protagonists such as Ekwefi (*Things Fall Apart*), Clara (*No Longer at Ease*) and Elsie *(A Man of the People)* are primarily used to focalise more central concerns such as male rivalry, ambition and egocentrism, it is only with the appearance of Gladys in the short story 'Girls at War' that we see Achebe begin to develop a balancing female presence with equal concentration and complexity. In *Anthills*, that changing consciousness of gender is extended at novel length.

Finally, as much as his previous novels, this is a text that is seriously concerned with questions of community. As I have argued throughout this book, Achebe's writing as a whole has too often been yoked by critics to doctrinaire conceptions of nationalism that do little to illuminate the questioning, dissident nature of his sensibility. When it comes to 'nation', as we will see in this chapter, his fifth novel is as problematic as ever. Contemporary as it is with the upsurge of political and historical thinking about national identity associated with such figures as Ernest Gellner and Benedict Anderson, *Anthills* can certainly be said to be concerned with 'imagined communities'.[3] Those imaginings, however, are no less tortuous than they were in *No Longer at Ease* and *A Man of the People*. In Nigeria like many other former European colonies in the mid-1980s, the meaning of 'nationhood' and of what it was to be 'Nigerian' remained difficult and thorny questions which were not merely the subject of liberal debate, but which regularly asserted themselves in political unrest, violence and in the succession of military coups (each styled in terms of national redemption) that defined the period. On the level of ethnic community, as we saw in earlier chapters, the whole of Achebe's *oeuvre* is strongly Igbo in focus, and in *Anthills* that flavour remains. Igbo proverbs and traditional sayings are, so to speak, the palm-oil with which his fiction is eaten. Considering the context within which *Anthills* was written, however, the question of whether he is able to bridge the gap between ethnic and national community – between Igbo and Nigerian nation – is a crucial one. Drawing on the region's troubled history of civil war, coups and counter-coups, the novel presents itself, on one level, as an explicit Fanonian call for the nation's elite to 'to put itself to school with the people',[4] to re-mould the state as the expression of the whole people's self-actualisation. Who is that people, though, and where (other than in imagination) might we place that state?

Anthills was published in 1987, under the dictatorship of the colourful General Ibrahim Babangida, 'more generally known', as Nahem Yousaf says, as 'the evil genius'.[5] Nigeria was experiencing a disastrous economic meltdown at that time, accompanied by a seemingly continual round of state- and opposition-sponsored violence. What Achebe offers us is not, however, merely a documentary account of that moment. *Anthills* was a novel with a long gestation, and as I will be arguing in this chapter, the thought processes it embodies reflect more than just an engagement with the immediate political circumstances of the mid-1980s. The experience of the Biafran struggle at the end of the 1960s and – just as importantly – that of Biafra's defeat at the beginning of the 1970s had radicalised Achebe's consciousness in a wholly new way. Although it was a long time coming, *Anthills* was the product of that development. In this sense, ideologically as well as stylistically, the novel represents a major new departure in his writing.

Dictatorship

Immediately after the 1967–70 civil war, as he recalled in his memoir *There Was a Country*, one of the first things Achebe did was to return to the Citadel Press, the publishing house he had established with Christopher Okigbo. His friend had been killed during the conflict, and arriving alone at the modest premises they had set up together, Achebe was shaken to find that they had been 'pummelled into the ground' by supporters of the Nigerian military government, for daring to raise a dissenting voice in the children's story *How the Leopard Got His Claws*.[6] In the wake of the Federation's victory, the first peacetime move of Nigeria's Yoruba Finance Minister Obafemi Awolowo had been to bankrupt the Igbo middle class by nullifying the bank accounts of all former Biafrans, while the towns and villages of Biafra itself lay across the South East as 'a vast smouldering rubble'.[7] Feeling that he had no place in Nigeria, Achebe took his family into exile in the US.

In important ways, as we saw in chapter 4, the Biafran war had revolved around control of newly discovered oil reserves in the Niger Delta, and while Achebe was away from Nigeria in the early 1970s, oil was to change the Nigerian scene dramatically. As soon as Shell-BP and the other international oil firms with interests in the recaptured Biafran territory were ready, Nigeria's military government stepped up production exponentially. As Falola and Heaton report in their *History of Nigeria*, in 1966, before the civil war, production had stood at 417,000 barrels per day. During the 1970s it mushroomed to an average of 2.3 million. Huge amounts of oil money began to flow into Nigeria, such that in a single decade, government revenues from oil rose thirty-fold from 166 million to 5.3 billion Naira. The crucial effect of this, as Falola and Heaton show, was that by 1974, more than four-fifths of all government revenues in Nigeria came from petroleum.[8] In a few years, in other words, the nation's economy had been transformed into one that overwhelmingly depended on the international demand for oil. As Nigerians would soon discover, this also implied great vulnerability in the face of changing market conditions. At the same time, however, under the rule of General Yakubu Gowon, 'there was minimal oversight of how petroleum revenues were spent. Millions of Naira went missing as government officials at the federal and state levels lined their own pockets with revenues earmarked for other purposes.'[9]

Competition for power in Nigeria, coming as it did with control over vast state contracts, was intense. By the time

Achebe returned in 1976, two further coups (one successful, one abortive) had shaken the country. As Falola and Heaton observe, however, extreme economic and social inequality remained entrenched. The new wealth – at least part of which might have been expected to trickle down to the general population in the form of improved opportunities and infrastructure – was instead monopolised by an elite who were able to secure themselves control over petrochemical licenses and contracts. The result of this, Falola and Heaton argue, was 'a government that became increasingly divorced from its subjects, creating a stark disconnection between the will of the people and the actions of government officials'.[10] *Anthills*, as well as Achebe's more explicitly political pamphlet *The Trouble with Nigeria*, can be seen as direct responses to this new era of Nigerian 'kleptocracy'.[11]

Throughout the 1970s and most of the 1980s, Nigeria was ruled by a series of military dictatorships, each of which in one way or another find their way into Achebe's portrait of Sam's regime in *Anthills*. In 1979, for a brief while, things seemed set to change, when General Olusegun Obasanjo became the first military Head of State in modern African history to voluntarily introduce democratic elections. Civilian rule, it appeared, was returning, and as A. E. Afigbo argues in his *Nigerian History, Politics and Affairs*, the terms of the 1979 constitution for Nigeria were framed in lofty terms. Its two stated purposes were to promote 'the good government and welfare of all persons in our country on the principles of Freedom, Equality and Justice' and to consolidate 'the unity of our people'.[12] In practice, however, the Nigerian economy's overwhelming domination by the petroleum sector posed a strong counter-force to such egalitarian and democratic ambitions. In purely economic terms, the relative importance of ordinary Nigerian taxpayers was dwarfed by that of the oil companies which, directly or indirectly, bankrolled the vast bulk of state expenditure as well as the lifestyles of the elite. On the political level, as Tom Forrest argues in an essay on the Nigerian crisis of 1979–1984, the predictable effect of this was that meaningful democratic debate was comprehensively side-lined in favour of 'intense political competition for access to the state and over the distribution of state resources'.[13] Writing in the mid-1980s, Forrest describes the situation that Achebe and others had to contemplate every day, where every official working for or with the government was 'subject to great pressure over the distribution of state patronage'.[14] Even under Shehu Shagari's new civilian government, policy was never defined according to a consistent ideology or programme. Rather, the government held its support (and thereby itself) together through a careful distribution of office and rewards to regions, groups and individuals, with ministerial appointments and other strategically important roles allocated according to a system of 'zoning ... in return for the mobilisation of support for the party'.[15] Instead of the National Party of Nigeria (NPN), Forrest comments sardonically, Shagari's organisation might as well have been named the 'Party of National Patronage'.[16]

In 1983, the army abruptly seized back control of Nigeria, citing corruption in the civilian government and declaring a 'War on Indiscipline'. In *Anthills*, this is the situation Achebe dramatises, in which a military dictatorship lacking legitimacy seems at first to be a less bad option than the democratically elected administration it replaces. In Achebe's Kangan, we see few tears being shed for the outgoing civilian administration, and looking at the record of Nigeria's brief interlude of democratic rule between 1979 and 1983, it is possible to see where Achebe might have drawn the inspiration for representing things that way. Inter-ethnic conflict had bedevilled Nigeria from its foundation, and Shagari's government had done little to assuage that, promoting a culture that was corrupt and fundamentally anti-meritocratic. As Achebe tried to illustrate in *The Trouble with Nigeria*:

> Let us take a hypothetical case where two candidates A and B apply to fill a very important and strategic position. A has the right qualification of competence and character but is of the 'wrong' tribe, while B, less qualified, belongs to the 'right' tribe, and so gets the job. A goes away embittered. B throws a party and then messes up the job. The greatest sufferer is the nation itself which has to contain the legitimate grievance of a wronged citizen; accommodate the incompetence of a favoured citizen and, more

important and of greater scope, endure a general decline of morale and subversion of efficiency caused by an erratic system of performance and reward.[17]

For Achebe, the suffocating dominance of patronage in Nigerian politics placed a great long-term cost on Nigeria, because it ensured the systematic triumph of mediocrity over talent. In terms of public policy, it meant that issues of wealth distribution among the various states and interest groups dominated over all other priorities, so that serious real-world problems – such as the persistence of terrible poverty in the rural areas – were never addressed. In government, if ministers failed in their undertakings, the president was powerless to reshuffle his team like any other Head of State, bringing in new faces and ideas. Instead, as Forrest argues, the system spawned a new class of power-mongers in government who, untouchable themselves, set about monopolising huge swathes of state activity.

During this period, as *The Trouble with Nigeria* shows, Achebe's own ideas about leadership developed in response to the scene around him. Importantly – in the context within which he was writing – it is clear that he was not absolutely opposed to the idea of dictatorship, at least of a certain sort. On the pamphlet's opening page, indeed, he observed the effects of powerful leadership with apparent approval:

> On the morning after Murtala Muhammed seized power in July 1975 public servants in Lagos were found 'on seat' at seven-thirty in the morning. Even the 'go-slow' traffic that had defeated every solution and defied every regime vanished overnight from the streets! Why? The new ruler's reputation for ruthlessness was sufficient to transform in the course of only one night the style and habit of Nigeria's unruly capital. That the character of one man could establish that quantum change in a people's social behaviour was nothing less than miraculous. But it shows that social miracles *can* happen.[18]

In a decade in which billions of Naira had unexpectedly poured into Nigeria as if granted by providence, the dominant response of the powerful had been to embezzle, monopolise and squander the new wealth, creating 'an increasing army of party loyalists who have neither the desire nor the competence to execute their contracts' and 'a grossly overstaffed and unproductive public service'.[19] What was needed in such circumstances, he argues, was a display of 'true patriotism' from the very top. Like President Nyerere of Tanzania, who showed that he would rather debase himself by begging his bank manager for time to pay his mortgage than co-opt a cent of state money, it is those with absolute power who should display the finest ethical examples and the most scrupulous integrity. 'One shining act of bold, selfless leadership at the top, such as unambiguous refusal to be corrupt or tolerate corruption', he optimistically claimed, 'will radiate powerful sensations of well-being and pride through every nerve and artery of national life.'[20]

Ever since his return to Nigeria in 1976, Achebe had argued that in matters of public integrity, intellectuals as well as politicians should take the lead. The typical Nigerian thinker or writer, he told John Agetua in that year, was less 'committed to the intellect [than to] status and stomach. And if there's any danger that he might suffer official displeasure or lose his job, he would prefer to turn a blind eye to what is happening around him.'[21] According to biographer Ezenwa-Ohaeto, Achebe watched the progress of civilian rule under President Shagari with increasing disillusion. This is not to say that, in principle, Achebe was opposed to the idea of democracy itself, but it certainly does seem to have been clear to him that democracy, on its own, was not going to solve Nigeria's ills at that time. In 1982, he decided to make a more direct contribution to Nigeria's political future by joining the People's Redemption Party, led by Mallam Aminu Kano, a Muslim from a prominent Northern family. Among Achebe's key contributions to the PRP's attempt to unseat Shagari at the 1983 general elections was the publication of *The Trouble with Nigeria* itself. In that work, he presents Kano himself as the shining exemplar of the selfless leadership the nation required. He was literary and intellectual in orientation, and placed great political stress on the importance of improving conditions and opportunities for Nigeria's impoverished masses.

According to Achebe's pamphlet, Kano might be thought of as Nigeria's Gandhi:

> The importance to society of people like Aminu Kano or Mahatma Gandhi is not that every politician can become like them, for that would be an impossible and totally unrealistic expectation. But the monumental fact which they underscore and which no one can ignore again after they have walked among us is this: Gandhi was real; Aminu Kano was real. They were not angels in heaven, they were human like the rest of us, in India and Nigeria. Therefore, after their example, no one who reduces the high purpose of politics which they exemplified down to a swinish scramble can hope to do so without bringing a terrible judgement upon himself.
>
> Nigeria cannot be the same again because Aminu Kano lived here.[22]

As Achebe's past tense already signals, the high hopes expressed here for a democratic renaissance under Kano in 1983 were dashed by the succession of events in that year. On 17 April Kano himself had died unexpectedly at his home in Kano city. In the wake of that huge blow, splits in the People's Redemption Party left it crippled as an electoral force. Nigeria had already entered an economic crisis, as the price of crude oil fell sharply while the nation's corrupt internal markets saw rapid inflation. Amid dubious scramblings for position among rival parties in the August elections, the NPN won a second term under President Shehu Shagari. Within months, however, his administration was abruptly terminated when another army coup under General Muhammadu Buhari suspended democracy and re-imposed martial law.

In *Anthills*, although the fictional West African country of Kangan (whose major river is the Niger) closely resembles Nigeria, and while the situation of military dictatorship it describes in many ways resembles the regime under which he lived while he was writing it, Achebe by no means slavishly reproduces the history I have outlined blow-by-blow. Instead, he builds his narrative by patchworking together aspects of

Nigeria's contemporary situation with other elements drawn from its recent history. In his portrait of the soldier-President Sam, for example, we see echoes of Buhari's regime in the 1980s, Olusegun Obasanjo's in the 1970s, and Emeka Ojukwu's regime in Biafra in the late 1960s. In 1983, Buhari was swept to power by fellow army officers who enjoined him to instil discipline and order to their nation's corrupt and troubled polity, and this is exactly how Achebe chooses to represent Sam's coming to power. Like Buhari's, Sam's regime is shown as paranoid, intolerant of criticism and quick to muzzle dissenting opinion. Like Obasanjo's administration, however, he also portrays Sam as a leader who is vexed by his lack of democratic legitimacy. The reason Sam has failed in his bid to be ruler-for-life over Kangan is, precisely, because he decided to put the proposal to a referendum, rather than simply to affirm it by presidential decree. In the novel, this paradoxical attempt to gain a democratic mandate for absolute power that has been seized by force is frustrated by the non-cooperation of the people of Abazon. Sam's method of subduing the rebel province by starving it of water, moreover, introduces another powerful historical referent – the blockade imposed by General Gowon on the breakaway people of Biafra during the Nigerian civil war. While, after their humiliating defeat, the Biafrans may have accepted the necessity of coming back within Nigeria's fold, the wounds and resentments engendered by the conflict could not easily be assuaged by facile calls for solidarity and unity in the years to come.

Under Sam's regime in the novel (as in Buhari's) state-sponsored political violence is commonplace, while the neo-colonial influence of Britain, the former imperial power, is everywhere in evidence. When Ikem, as editor of the *Gazette*, takes an interest in a delegation from Abazon that has come to lobby the President, Sam's immediate instinct is to gag him, demanding his suspension from the newspaper and initiating a security investigation into Chris's activities as Commissioner for Information. Before long, Ikem is in custody, with little time left to live, and Chris is on the run. In these plot developments, *Anthills* reflects the oppressive atmosphere experienced by journalists in the mid-1980s when Achebe was working on the novel. Under the incredibly draconian 'Decree Four' during Buhari's presidency, reporters and others were deemed guilty of an imprisonable offence if they expressed 'in any form, whether written or otherwise, any message, rumour, report or statement ... which brings, or is calculated to bring, the Federal Military Government ... to ridicule or disrepute'.[23] Any writer who did not reflect regime policies and priorities to the letter, in effect, ran the gauntlet of the regime's courts or summary incarceration. In 1984, as Adegboyega Ajayi reports in a study of the military and the state in Nigeria, two journalists from the *Guardian* newspaper, Nduka Trabor and Tunde Thompson, were convicted and imprisoned under the decree. The government's ready willingness to put these two behind bars must have concentrated the minds of journalists and other writers in that year: Trabor and Thompson's offence was not calling for the overthrow of the regime, but merely that they had published a list of ambassadorial postings before it had received official authorisation.

In this sense, it is possible to appreciate the risks, even for a writer as well established as Achebe, in publishing a novel about a paranoid dictatorship in a nation closely resembling Nigeria. While Achebe was in the last stages of composing *Anthills*, Buhari was himself ousted in a further coup, and the revelation of Sam's own vulnerability to overthrow at the end of the novel reflects the sense of popular disorientation and fear in Nigeria that such sudden and repeated switches of power engendered. *Anthills* was nearing completion when Ibrahim Babangida became Nigeria's fifth military dictator in just over ten years, but distinctive aspects of his style of rulership also find their way into Achebe's portrayal, especially in the atmosphere of veiled corruption that surrounds His Excellency. As Daniel Jordan Smith writes in a study of corruption in Nigerian regimes, one of Babangida's most popular nicknames in the period was 'Maradona', after the famous Argentinean footballer, because of the amazing skill and subtlety he showed in evading all opposition. A man of many faces, as Smith says, Babangida 'managed simultaneously to placate Western governments and financial institutions, establish new mechanisms for the enrichment of the military elite and their civilian cronies, and sell the idea that he was acting in the national interest'.[24] As Nahem Yousaf reports, Babangida was known internationally as a smooth operator who 'gave Mercedes cars to visiting national leaders and reputedly siphoned off around 12 billion US dollars from the nation's oil reserves'.[25] In *Anthills* Achebe alludes directly to this presidential wheeling and dealing by suggesting a shady relationship between Sam and a business proxy, Alhaji Abdul Mahmoud, who mysteriously steers great wealth past the eyes of international authorities. As Chris says, '[n]o customs officials go near his jetty and so, say rumour-mongers, he is the prince of smugglers. What else? Fifty odd companies, including a bank' (*AS*, 111).

If in *Anthills*, Sam's administration is shown as increasingly turbulent and paranoid, this is also a characteristic Achebe might well have observed in Babangida's. As the travel writer Mark Weston observes, during the first four decades after independence, three in every five African leaders were either assassinated or forced into exile. Weston quotes Babangida himself on the experience of ruling Nigeria: '"I expected a coup every day.... From day one I was there, I knew that somehow, some day there would be a coup. Because we took it by force, somebody is going to try and take by force." You will need eyes everywhere – in the villages, in the cities, among your friends and close colleagues, even within your own family – to protect you against usurpers.'[26]

In the novel, Sam is tensely alert to the threat of dissent and sedition, moving quickly to muzzle the press, even to the extent of having his long-time friend Ikem executed without trial. Right from the beginning of the novel, nevertheless, dictatorship is portrayed as a childish game of domination for him. When Chris (as Commissioner for Information) disagrees with him on the problem of Abazon, Chris must lower his gaze 'in ceremonial capitulation' (*AS*, 1) to appease His Excellency's ego. When speaking to his Attorney-General, Sam chooses to speak unusually softly 'to put his hearer at a disadvantage' (*AS*, 20). When he chooses to be conciliatory rather than combative towards the members of his cabinet, Achebe takes his portrayal even closer to parody. As Chris says, 'In that instant the day changes. The fiery sun retires temporarily behind a cloud; we are reprieved and immediately celebrating. I can hear in advance the many compliments we will pay him as soon as his back is turned: that the trouble with His Excellency is that he can never hurt a man and go to sleep over it' (*AS*, 3).

Through Sam, then, we are shown a model of dictatorship that is interestingly multi-faceted. Simultaneously brutal yet refined, Sam is childlike in his demand for subservience yet subtle in his strategies of control. Through Chris, as one of the commissioners whose occupation is to stroke Sam's ego, we see the childish side. 'Days are good or bad ... according to how His Excellency gets out of bed in the morning' (*AS*, 2). Through Ikem, though, we see pragmatism, cynicism and even self-reflexivity. As Ikem says, '[h]e is basically an actor and half of the things we are inclined to hold against him are no more than scenes from his repertory to which he may have no sense of moral commitment whatsoever' (*AS*, 46).

Like Emeka Ojukwu – the soldier Head of State with whom, in Biafra, Achebe had most detailed, personal experience – Sam's personal style is built, outrageously, on apeing the English. He prides himself to the point of ridiculousness on his command of the Queen's English, which, like Ojukwu, he delivers by means of a cut-glass Received Pronunciation. As Ikem reflects in chapter 4:

> To say that Sam was never very bright is not to say that he was a dunce at any time in the past or that he is one now. His major flaw was that all he ever wanted was to do what was expected of him especially by the English whom he admired sometimes to the point of foolishness. When our headmaster, John Williams, told him that the army was the career for gentlemen he immediately abandoned thoughts of becoming a doctor and became a soldier ... after Sandhurst he was a catalogue model of an officer. *His* favourite expression after he came home was: *it's not done*, spoken in his perfect accent. (*AS*, 45)

Although the parallels with Ojukwu are clear enough for any contemporary Nigerian to pick up, they are not precise. Ojukwu went to an English public school followed by Oxford University to study Law (Sam does too, but goes to study Medicine). A ladies man and socialite (like Sam), early in his career Ojukwu made a radical change of direction by joining the armed forces (Sam does the same). After entering the army he attended a prestigious officer cadet school in England (Ojukwu went to Eaton Hall, Sam goes to Sandhurst). In colonial Nigeria, he rose rapidly through the ranks before finding himself the Head of State of a new African nation while still in his early thirties (Sam has come to power in a coup, rather than through secession, but the parallel is there). In his drawing of Sam's character it seems clear too that, at least in part, Achebe uses Ojukwu as a model, including distinctive aspects of the General's personal style. In an account of an interview with Ojukwu some years after the Biafran war, Michael Peel captures telling details which it is easy to see reflected in Sam, including the high-handed and imperious way he carries his own power:

> When General Ojukwu appeared in the living room, I could see immediately how he had become a leader of men ... He looked imposing physically, but even more striking was his facility with words, expressed in a clipped Southern English accent. This quirk, he said, laughing, meant he was referred to as the 'most Anglophile of all Nigerians,' talking of African nationalism in the timbre of the landed Home Counties gent ... He barely hesitated or wasted a word as he talked with the measured deliberation of someone who was used to being listened to intently and without interruption.[27]

In the novel as a whole, then, what Achebe offers us in *Anthills* is a nuanced view of dictatorship that resists any kind of doctrinaire critique. Indeed, towards the beginning of the novel, he even proposes something of a defence, through Chris, of the place of dictatorship in the formation of a robust, healthy nation. Here, like Achebe himself in *The Trouble with Nigeria*, Chris is willing to see a form of legitimacy in the powerful will of an autocrat:

Nations, he said, were fostered as much by structures as by laws and revolutions. These structures where they exist now are the pride of their nations. But everyone forgets that they were not erected by democratically-elected Prime Ministers but very frequently by unattractive, bloodthirsty medieval tyrants. The cathedrals of Europe, the Taj Mahal of India, the pyramids of Egypt and the stone towers of Zimbabwe were all raised on the backs of serfs, starving peasants and slaves. Our present day rulers in Africa are in every sense late-flowering medieval monarchs, even the Marxists among them. Do you remember Mazrui calling Nkrumah a Stalinist Czar? Perhaps our leaders have to be that way. Perhaps they may even need to be that way. (*AS*, 69–70)

As the plot of *Anthills* unfolds, however, we see how misplaced this sanguine outlook really is, as the effects of Sam's vanity, fallibility and vulnerability to manipulation by outside and inside forces emerge more and more clearly.

For Chris – as well as for the reader – the key tipping point that forces a re-examination of assumptions is the assassination of Ikem by Sam's security forces, and here once again, Achebe draws on controversial aspects of recent Nigerian history. As Larry Diamond points out in an early essay on the novel, in Ikem's death contemporary Nigerian readers would undoubtedly have recognised the assassination of Lagos-based journalist Dele Giwa, outspoken editor of Nigeria's *Newswatch* magazine, in October 1986. Giwa (much like Ikem) was the subject of intense interest by Nigeria's State Security Service, who accused him of inciting leftist elements towards revolution. Just hours after being interrogated by a senior security office, Giwa was killed in an explosion at his home.[28] As the author's historian daughter Nwando Achebe corroborates in a recent study, strong popular belief about the incident both at the time and since was that Babangida was personally behind the killing, which was carried out using 'a letter bomb bearing the Nigerian government's official insignia'.[29] Certainly, in the novel, Achebe leaves little doubt who is responsible for Ikem's death. Dictatorship might in theory sometimes be benign, or sometimes even necessary to a nation's progress, but as *Anthills* warns us, absolute power is a dangerous thing to concede to the unworthy.

The elite

In Sam's paranoid mind, the final offence that seals Ikem's fate is that he has pedalled sedition among the already excitable students of Kangan, and here again, Achebe draws on his own experience of the febrile atmosphere in Nigeria in the mid-1980s. At that time he was a serving university professor, as well as Pro-Chancellor of the Anambra State University of Technology. As such in the spring and summer of 1986 he would have had seen first hand the violence of clashes between students and police, and witnessed how rapidly they spread across the nation. A measure of Nigeria's brutality in response to protest is provided by the fact that, on one single day of unrest at Ahmadu Bello University – one of Nigeria's most prestigious – fifteen students were killed by police.[30] Achebe's own perspective on these events, as a senior member of university staff witnessing completely unjustified acts of violence on both sides, must have contained a measure of ambivalence. In the novel, correspondingly, when Ikem addresses the students of Kangan's University of Bassa, he does not simply endorse their struggle in the face of government oppression. While positively inciting them to seek political change, he is also insistent on confronting the students with their own shallowness and parasitism:

> 'Now what about students? I should really be very careful here as I am quite anxious to get home safely tonight.' Explosion of laughter. 'However, truth will out! I regret to say that students are in my humble opinion the cream of parasites.' Redoubled laughter. 'The other day, did not students on National Service raze to the ground a new maternity block built by peasants? Why? They were protesting against their posting to a remote rural station without electricity and running water. Did you not read about it?' The laughter had died all of a sudden. 'Perhaps someone can show me one single issue in this country in

which students as a class have risen above the low, very low, national level. Tribalism? Religious extremism? Even electoral merchandising. Do you not buy and sell votes, intimidate and kidnap your opponents just as the politicians used to do? [...] Do you not form tribal pressure groups to secure lower admission requirements instead of striving to equal or excel any student from anywhere? Yes, you prefer academic tariff walls behind which you can potter around in mediocrity. And you are asking me to agree to hand over my life to a democratic dictatorship of mediocrity? No way!' (*AS*, 152–3)

As this passage illustrates, in its address to the complex, deep-seated problems that confronted Nigeria in the 1980s, one of the most striking features of *Anthills* from a political point of view is the scale of its focus and ambitions. Notwithstanding all of the historical correspondences with Nigeria during the two decades in which the novel had its gestation, this is a novel of ideas that wants to reach far beyond that nation's immediate circumstances, into the deep causes of its malaise, and towards a vision of redemption that transcends the politics of the here and now. In this sense, although the novel is partly an examination of dictatorship in Africa, it is also necessarily concerned with the historic responsibilities of the educated elite.

Anthills' four protagonists Sam, Chris, Beatrice and Ikem represent the cream of Kangan society. Graduates of renowned universities and highly socially connected, they treat many of their privileges as if they were rights. Like Achebe and his educated contemporaries who secured plum positions in the media and public services as the British departed at the beginning of the 1960s, they are prime beneficiaries of decolonisation. Throughout the novel, one of the ways this reflects itself is in the way that each of them tends to see Kangan's story as inseparable from his or her own. In Sam's case, this equation could hardly be clearer, not least in his attempt to install himself as President for Life. The referendum he calls to ratify this ambition appears, on a surface level, like a deferral to the democratic wishes of the people. What it actually reveals, as Neil ten Kortenaar points out, however, is 'the paradox of Sam's power: it is his, and it belongs only to him, but it must be confirmed after the fact to demonstrate that it actually emanated from the people'.[31] Never are the people asked to vote on the legitimacy of the absolute power he has already arrogated to himself. With Ikem, although the rhetoric is more egalitarian, the case is not entirely dissimilar. Indeed, as we learn through Beatrice, the only reason Ikem is in Kangan at all, rather than living a bohemian writer's life in London, is that some 'friends at home finally persuaded him to join them in nation-building' (*AS*, 86). If Sam sees himself as embodying the nation, then as we see in Ikem's various speeches and pronouncements, Ikem is hardly less presumptuous in imagining himself as the muse of its revolution. Beatrice too, of course, also casts her narrative in a way that places her central to the nation's story. In the world of *Anthills* the manuscript we are reading is, at one and the same time, the story of four friends and the story of a nation, and she is its editor-compiler. Not only the various testimonies but also the climax of the story comes, therefore, exactly where she wants it to, in a symbolic celebration of rebirth and unity over which she presides, and which takes place in none other than her own home. Sam, Ikem and Beatrice, each in their own way, recognise the need for the educated elite to connect to the mass of the people, to see the nation's story as a thing much larger than themselves. Try as they might, however, they each struggle to narrate the nation in any way that does not in the end, once again, cast themselves as the indispensable protagonists.

With Chris, the situation is rather different. Once a senior journalist, Chris is now an apparatchik at the top of a regime whose stock-in-trade is suppressing dissent. Here again, Achebe draws on direct personal experience. During the civil war he was – from the point of view of a writer – privileged to gain a very rare kind of insight into the workings of a military regime from within its inner circle. For three years, he was a favoured adviser to the Biafran Head of State Emeka Ojukwu, through times in which the latter was frequently confronted with life-or-death tactical decisions, many of which also encompassed serious ethical challenges. As chairman of the National Guidance

Committee, Achebe was tasked by Ojukwu with articulating the values and principles that would set Biafra out as a nation. As a roving ambassador, he was enjoined to use his international reputation and contacts to proselytise for the new republic. As a member of BOFF, however, he also worked for a propagandist organisation whose brief was to ensure that a positive image of the Biafran military (including the government) was mediated to the Biafran people. This work was by no means always easy, as Achebe's memoir *There Was a Country* infers. When the Biafran army was implicated in violence against its own citizens in the border areas of the Niger Delta, for example, BOFF's role, like any state propagandist organisation during wartime, would have been to suppress negative coverage. Although Achebe himself is noticeably reticent about detailing such activities in his own account, other records from the war, such as Jerome Nwadike's memoir *A Biafran Soldier's Survival from the Jaws of Death*, are more graphic and forthcoming in the detail they provide. Nwadike recalls the motivational tactics used by Colonel Joe 'Hannibal' Achuzie, who freely confessed to recruits, 'yes, I have shot several [Biafran soldiers] on the spot. No one can stand up to bullets flying at him on the basis of good intention alone. There must be military discipline. If a man can be killed so that others will fight, we have to do it; look at what is at stake.'[32] Chinedu Agbodike, another survivor of the conflict, recalls being conscripted into BOFF at the age of ten, subjected to 'gruesome and intensive training' and drafted to the front line to spy on enemy troops.[33] Children like himself were armed only with a catapult and a long sharpened stick 'which we used with expert accuracy, for disarming, maiming or killing any enemy even wild animals especially during the time of danger'.[34] If caught by soldiers from Nigeria, he reports that he and his companions 'acted innocent, and harmless, always behaving like lost children left behind by their parents ... always crying, yet as dangerous as rattlesnakes on a bed'. He thanks the rebel leader Ojukwu 'who initiated these tactics'.[35]

There is no evidence whatsoever to show that as a senior member of BOFF, Achebe was aware of 'Hannibal' Achuzie's tactics and/or of Ojukwu's use of child soldiers at the time; his memoir suggests that he did not become aware of these things until after the conflict. In *Anthills*, which is set in peacetime, the worst Chris is asked to do is to suppress the work of a friend and fellow journalist by removing him from his post. By making Chris Commissioner for Information in Sam's regime, however, Achebe clearly draws on his own experiences under Ojukwu. Like his own in Biafra, Chris's position is bound to involve him to some extent in complicity with ethically questionable aspects of the regime's action. Two years before the novel opens Chris had, we infer, been less than entirely supportive of Sam's bid to become President for Life, allowing the later to be 'disgraced' in his own eyes. As time has gone on, however, the opportunity to assert his self-determination and stand on points of principle has dwindled to nothing. Like Achebe would have had at the time of Biafra, he has the option to live in exile, where he might 'drink a lot of booze in European capitals and sleep with a lot of white girls after delivering revolutionary lectures to admiring audiences seven worlds away' (*AS*, 113). Staying at home, however, the only choice he sees for himself and all those like him is that of hunkering down to weather the storm. 'Lie low for a while and this gathering tornado may rage and pass overhead carrying away roof-tops and perhaps ... only perhaps ... leave us battered but alive' (*AS*, 113).

Although, as I have suggested, Chris's situation in Kangan in some ways resembles aspects of Achebe's experience in Biafra, it is also clear that Chris is used in the novel as the mouthpiece for attitudes which *Anthills* does not want to endorse. Both as the former editor of a national newspaper and as Commissioner for Information, his attitude to the common people is scathing and dismissive. Not until he is forced to confront the reality of their lives on the journey to Abazon does he begin to re-examine his assumptions. Shaken from his complacency and complicity, it is only when Chris is close to losing everything that he begins to see his nation at all. Since returning from his university education in Britain, he has never had to stray outside the enclave of the elite. Travelling across the country, he is a stranger on the bus because, since the end of his childhood, he has never had to take a bus. Unlike the activists Braimoh and Emmanuel who travel at ease in their environment, having nothing to lose, Chris is 'a wide-eyed newcomer to the ways of Kangan' (*AS*, 193). It takes exile from his world of privilege and the 'hollow rituals' (*AS*, 196) of class and power, coupled with the emotional shocks of bereavement and fear, and the physical privations of the Great North Road, to engender his Damascene moment. In the vapid cocktail parties of the capital, the idea that the world of Bassa was not the world of Kangan has been expressed to him as an endlessly repeating cliché. Only when he has been forced to leave Bassa, however, does the novel allow him to realise the extent of his own deracination and that of the entire Kangan bourgeoisie:

> Now, as the overwhelming force of this simple, always-taken-in-vain reality impinged on each of Chris's five, or was it six, senses even as hordes of flying insects after the first rain bombard street lamps, the ensuing knowledge seeped through every pore in his skin into the core of his being continuing the transformation, already in process, of the man he was. (*AS*, 196)

From the point of view of influencing Kangan's politics, of course, Achebe provides Chris with his revelation too late to effect any political change. In the scene where he saves a young woman from rape by a police sergeant, however, the novel suggests something of its nature. Ensconced as Commissioner for Information in Sam's regime, Chris has been painted as a figure disabled by cynicism and mired in self-protective ambivalence. On the Great North Road, confronted with a real ethical choice – whether to defend the girl by risking his own personal safety – he does not hesitate to use his own physical power and the power of his position in a cause whose rights and wrongs his selfless actions make transparent. While other men stand back and laugh, Chris unflinchingly martyrs himself:

> Chris bounded forward and held the man's hand and ordered him to release the girl at once. As if that was not enough he said, 'I will make a report about this to the Inspector-General of Police.'

'You go report me for where? You de Craze! No be you de ask about President just now? If you no commot for my front now I go blow your head to Jericho, craze-man.'

'Na you de craze,' said Chris. 'A police officer stealing a lorry-load of beer and then abducting a school girl! You are a disgrace to the force.'

The other said nothing more. He unslung his gun, cocked it, narrowed his eyes while confused voices went up all around some asking Chris to run, others the policeman to put the gun away. Chris stood his ground looking straight into the man's face, daring him to shoot. And he did, point blank into the chest presented to him. (206–7)

In Kangan's political geography, Sam and Chris present two different faces of the ruling elite – the corrupt, self-aggrandising military ruler and the cynical, privileged civil servant. Both of them are destined for a fall, Sam into a shallow grave in the bush and Chris at a dusty roadside. Before his death, however, the latter is given a revelation. There is a yawning gulf of understanding that separates the elite from the masses and any hope of redemption must be based on filling it. The role of the elite is not to insulate itself in self-protective circles of privilege, but to re-connect with the people and lead them by example.

With the character of Ikem, *Anthills* presents a different face of the elite, in the figure of an arty, nationalist intellectual. As editor of the national *Gazette* and mascot of revolutionary workers and students, he gets plenty of chances to speak his mind. For him, it takes no Damascene epiphany to realise that the proper place to look for true national community is in the fabric of ordinary people's lives. Fanon's dictum that nation is the organic expression of the people is orthodoxy for him. On an emotional level, he is aware (in a way Achebe clearly intends to seem naïve) of 'a yearning without any clear definition, to connect his essence with earth and earth's people' (*AS*, 134). At the same time, however, he is also given sufficient self-knowledge to recognise the shallowness and hypocrisy of his own posturing. 'Of course', he admits to himself, 'we always take the precaution of invoking the people's name in whatever we do. But do we not at the same time make sure of the people's absence, knowing that if they were to appear in person their scarecrow presence confronting our pious invocations would render our words too obscene even for sensibilities as robust as ours?' (*AS*, 135). As Kortenaar acutely points out in his essay on *Anthills*, the contradiction that Ikem recognises here is one that runs to the heart of nationalism itself. In the thought of theorists on nationalism like Benedict Anderson whose work was so influential at the time *Anthills* was published in the late 1980s, nations are always, in a way, 'imagined communities'.[36] As much as they are projected as the expression of the people's being, they are also ideological constructs erected by vanguard nationalist movements, banners around which struggle can focus and organise itself. In order to lend themselves the aura of necessity and 'naturalness' that they need to fulfil their political goals, of course, nationalist movements of all kinds find it essential to mythologise their own programmes, in Fanon's words, as 'the all-embracing crystallization of the innermost hopes of the whole people'.[37] In practice, however, the societies they strive to create are typically more industrial and technocratic than traditional in orientation. In Kortenaar's essay on the novel, the effects of this paradox in Achebe's novel are teased out in an interesting way:

> As Ernest Gellner points out, nationalism 'claims to defend folk culture while in fact it is forging a high culture; it claims to protect an old folk society while in fact helping to build up an anonymous mass society.' [...] Ikem and his friends create the nation, but for the nation to have legitimacy, it must be supposed already to exist. So it is that Ikem discovers a nation among the taxi drivers and market women. The 'stubborn sense of identity' that Elewa and the taxi drivers share might also be interpreted as class consciousness, but Ikem sees it as an embryonic national identity because that is what he wants to find.[38]

In this sense, the nature of Ikem's double-consciousness is rather different from that of Chris. Balancing the latter's defeatism, Ikem brings unfocused idealism. In place of Chris's self-protectiveness, he brings a reckless willingness to do battle. What

Ikem lacks in *Anthills*, however, is clear-headed and consistent analysis.

Before we have even been introduced to him through his 'witness statement', indeed, the novel gives us a generous sample of Ikem's thinking in the form of his 'Hymn to the Sun', a self-consciously literary and metaphorical commentary on Kangan's situation. As editor of the African Writers Series for ten years, and editor of the important literary journal *Okike* for twelve more, it is well known that Achebe had first sight of some of the most significant and powerful works of African literature during the decades after independence. He would also, however, have been all too familiar with the attempts of keen but unfocused young writers who had yet to find a clear voice. Chris, reading Ikem's prose poem on the long bus ride to Abazon, seems to find great resonance in it, reading 'slowly with fresh eyes, lipping the words like an amazed learner in a literacy campaign class' (*AS*, 201). As Achebe hints here, however, what we are really offered through Ikem's hymn is a picture of a writer wrestling with half-considered political ideas, in a literary style ill-suited to carrying them. Where David Diop – whose powerful 'Africa' Achebe quotes at the beginning of chapter 10 – captures the idea of an interminable cycle of oppression and stubborn resistance in a few pared-down words, Ikem's verbose lyricism works to underscore the incoherence and lightness of his insights.

At the beginning of chapter 3, Ikem introduces the motif of the 'Wild Sun of April' in a satirical commentary on Sam's regime. While 'the weatherman on television reciting mechanically the words of his foreign mentors' (*AS*, 25) tries to assure the people that everything is fine with their lives, 'Brigadier Misfortune of the Wilting 202 Brigade' (*AS*, 25) arrives to inform them that nothing will be fine until the 'Sun' has been overthrown. His drift is easy enough to understand here. Two pages later, however, the basis of his political allegory seems to have unaccountably shifted. Now the people of Abazon are the harbingers of death, abandoning their mothers, wives and children to starvation in a desert wasteland, before seizing the land of others. Clearly, the piece is still an attempt at political satire, but its target – and indeed its politics – have completely changed:

> And now the times had come round again out of storyland. Perhaps not as bad as the first times, yet. But they could easily end worse. Why? Because today no one can rise and march south by starlight abandoning crippled kindred in the wild savannah and arrive stealthily at a tiny village and fall upon its inhabitants and slay them and take their land and say: I did it because death stared through my eye.
>
> So they send instead a deputation of elders to the government who hold the yam today, and hold the knife, to seek help of them. (*AS*, 30)

Stylistically, Ikem's hymn is hyperbolic and incoherent. Clouds which the sun has burnt away, 'cremating their remains … and scattering the ashes' (*AS*, 29) nevertheless lie 'suspended in a mist across the whole face of the sky' (*AS*, 29). Pigs fry in their own fat. Dogs and vultures battle over the corpse of a madman. What Ikem's piece needs – the reader is encouraged to speculate – is the directing hand of an editor. In his political arguments, as we hear from Beatrice later in the novel, Ikem is again as changeable as he is insistent. 'Whatever his audience is,' she explains, 'he must try not to be' (*AS*, 147). Faced with radicals, he will urge conservatism. Confronted by conservatives, he 'unleashes revolution' (*AS*, 147). Her own commentary is telling. 'It is not that he has ever sat down to reason it out … it just seems to happen that way' (*AS*, 147).

In ensuing scenes, one of the ways in which Achebe builds narrative tension in the novel is by foregrounding Ikem's precipitous, hot-headed approach to expressing himself. When at the novel's climax, he makes a speech to the assembled students of the University of Bassa, we hear straight away that his intention is to stage an intellectual *'coup d'etat'* (*AS*, 146) against them. He tackles them directly on the political status of their gathering, which purports to represent the views of workers and peasants when not a single peasant is in attendance. He berates the students about their own leadership, demanding how they expect to question the government when they cannot even hold their own leaders to account. In fact, however, as the reader is invited to see, the weakness of conviction and lack of self-examination with which Ikem is so keen to confront his student listeners, are precisely the qualities that he himself exemplifies. In his main address, he relates a story told to him by one of the elders of Abazon, now held in detention by the government. The story is one we have already heard in chapter 9, 'Views of Struggle':

> ... Once upon a time the leopard who had been trying for a long time to catch the tortoise finally chanced upon him on a solitary road. *Aha*, he said; *at long last! Prepare to die*. And the tortoise said: *Can I ask one favour before you kill me?* The leopard saw no harm in that and agreed. *Give me a few moments to prepare my mind*, the tortoise said. Again the leopard saw no harm in that and granted it. But instead of standing still as the leopard had expected the tortoise went into strange action on the road, scratching with hands and feet and throwing sand furiously in all directions. *Why are you doing that?* asked the puzzled leopard. The tortoise replied: *Because even after I am dead I would want anyone passing by this spot to say, yes, a fellow and his match struggled here.* (AS, 122–3)

The students of Bassa, according to Ikem's inference, are making a great deal of noise and fuss in protesting, but lack any coherent plan of resistance against those who are holding their nation hostage. Yet, as the reader observes, in almost the next breath we see Ikem defending his prerogative to offer no coherent plan of resistance. 'Now tell me', he demands with bizarre vehemence, 'can anything be more élitist, more *offensively* élitist, than someone presuming to answer questions that have not even been raised, for Christ's sake?' (AS, 15). Later, he castigates the students for doing 'too much parroting, too much regurgitating of half-digested radical rhetoric' (AS, 153) in concluding an oration that, itself, repeats plenty of half-considered slogans – 'the new radicalism' (AS, 151), 'the road to self-redemption' (AS, 153), 'purge yourselves' (AS, 153).

Having refused, on principle, to offer prescriptions, Ikem then cannot help himself from setting out what is, precisely, a prescription for national redemption. The negative influences of imperialism and capitalism should be forgotten, he argues. What matters is that ordinary workers try to do an honest and efficient day's work. Students and workers, more than government or business leaders are, he suggests, the ones who need to put their houses in order. Until they do so, lecturing the national leadership is out of the question. If the chairman of the student union is disturbed by this – confessing 'that he found Mr Osodi's concept of struggle too individualistic and adventuristic' (*AS*, 154) – so too is the reader. Ikem may be justified in castigating his audience for self-interestedness and 'mediocrity' (*AS*, 153), but in the context of a dictatorship growing more corrupt, paranoid and repressive by the day, his inability to do more than deliver a stern telling-off to the students of Bassa leaves an uncomfortable void at the heart of Achebe's narrative, that significantly intensifies its narrative tension.

Gender and redemption

In all of Achebe's novels, with their different settings and thematic emphases, sexism and misogyny are an important index of masculine fallibility. In *Arrow of God*, as we saw in chapter 3, the community of Umuahia comes to grief, in large part, because it is mired in over-competitive masculinism, and Okonkwo's demise in *Things Fall Apart* is strongly linked to the same idea. In *No Longer at Ease* and *A Man of the People*, the unfitness (for nation-building) of Obi Okonkwo and Odili Samalu is not framed in quite the same way, but sexual arrogance is still placed at the heart of their problems. The short story 'Girls at War' reprises this idea again in a different context. In this sense, then, it comes as no surprise to see how Achebe develops the gendered dimension in *Anthills*. Chris, who as we learn in chapter 5 likes his women 'easy on the eye' like a 'tastefully produced book' (*AS*, 59) is given a humiliating back-story in England, married to a white woman who in his eyes was 'so bent on proving she had a mind of her own she proved ... totally frigid in bed' (*AS*, 59). If we are invited, here, to read between the lines, Beatrice's sarcastic commentary on his sexual performance later in the novel carries the same implication. 'What's the bedbug's excuse', she asks him, 'for biting without bothering to sing first?' (*AS*, 191). In chapter 17, moreover, Chris's ideological redemption is once again coded in sexual-political terms, as he tries to prevent a rape. His act – bounding forward to intervene on behalf of a helpless girl – is clearly an expression of masculinity. In this scene, however, Achebe is careful to present his display as one of unflinching moral courage rather than of competitiveness and egotism. While men all around laugh at the girl's predicament, Chris calls on her attacker, a police sergeant, to remember the responsibilities of his position, offering his own undefended chest as a (Christ-like) symbol of the man's duty to protect the defenceless and to subjugate his own selfish desires.

In Ikem's case, there is a parallel transformation. Highly intelligent and cultured as he is, early scenes nonetheless depict him as a selfish and egotistical lover. Having had sex with his working-class girlfriend Elewa, he refuses to let her sleep in his flat, justifying it to her face on the flagrantly sexist grounds that 'I no want make you join all the loose women of Bassa who no sleep for house ... I wouldn't want a sister of mine to do that, you see' (*AS*, 33). To the reader, he admits rather differently that 'I simply detest the very notion of waking up and finding beside you somebody naked and unappetising' (*AS*, 34). Claiming that his car battery is flat, he puts Elewa in a taxi late at night despite her fears of robbery, while simultaneously confirming these by checking its registration number and the driver's face, 'just in case' (*AS*, 33). Later however, having been berated by Beatrice for his unexamined chauvinism, he is provoked into changing his ideas.

Within Achebe's narrative, this transition is made manifest in the 'strange love letter' Ikem reads in chapter 7. At the heart of the letter is a parallel between Judeo-Christian and Igbo cultural traditions. It likens the biblical story of the Fall in which woman's greed brings about the loss of paradise, to ancient Igbo myths in which she is responsible for a similar atrocity, by cutting off pieces of the sky to put in her soup pot, cracking the sky with her pestle or wiping her 'kitchen hands on the sky's face' (AS, 92). In each, as Ikem suggests, woman is scapegoated as the root of man's misfortunes. In the New Testament, he finds a different, but no less objectionable chauvinism. Having picked up woman 'from right under his foot where she'd been since Creation' man now carries her (as the Virgin Mary) 'to a nice, corner pedestal' (AS, 93) where she will be revered, but remain excluded from power and social affairs. Again a parallel is found in the beliefs of more recent Igbo ancestors, and specifically in the notion of *Nneka* or 'Mother is Supreme'. This is an idea that readers of Achebe's fiction will recall from *Things Fall Apart*, in which Okonkwo's uncle Uchendu explains to a gathering of his kinsmen why Nneka is one of the commonest names given to their daughters. 'It is true that a child belongs to its father. But when a father beats his child, it seeks sympathy in its mother's hut. A man belongs to his fatherland when things are good and life is sweet. But when there is sorrow and bitterness he finds refuge in his motherland' (TFA, 95). Uchendu goes on to castigate Okonkwo for believing himself the greatest of sufferers, by holding up the example of his daughter Akeuni, who has borne many pairs of twins and endured seeing them thrown away in the bush. Like the Virgin Mary who bears the spectacle of her son's crucifixion, she presents motherhood as a model of silent suffering.

To both of these, Ikem offers a different model of female divinity from pre-colonial culture. Initially in the novel, this is associated with the Goddess Idoto, before being developed more concertedly in relation to the powerful figure of Idemili. What Beatrice comes to see (in line with ethnographers of the 1980s such as Ifi Amadiume) as an equal transaction between masculine and feminine, Ikem sees in terms of living with 'contradictions' which 'if well understood and managed can spark off the fires of invention' (AS, 93). Woman is still the muse of the artist, it seems, but no longer to be entirely dismissed. Although on a political level he 'can't tell ... what the new role for Woman will be' (*AS*, 95) Ikem recognises a need to suspend orthodox thinking and '*reform*' (*AS*, 94) social consciousness in a way that places femininity in a completely different position. There is, he intuitively grasps, no room for fanaticism or single-mindedness in 'the complex and paradoxical cavern of Mother Idoto' (*AS*, 96).

Here, through the mouth of Ikem, Achebe makes reference to the work of Christopher Okigbo, in which the presence of Idoto is an important one. Despite his Christian upbringing and education, Okigbo like Achebe became increasingly committed to understanding the traditional belief system of his ancestral community the Ojoto. In his case, the gendered nature of these beliefs was central from the start. Even the river in which he played as a child, only a few miles from Achebe's home village, was dedicated to Idoto and carried her shrine. As Obi Nwakanma says in his biography *Christopher Okigbo: Thirsting for Sunlight*:

> Like most river-dwelling communities among the Igbo, it is apparent that generations of Ojoto people depended on their powerful water deity for all ritual meaning. During Okigbo's childhood in the 1930s, even at the height of the influence of the Christian missionaries and the European 'civilizing mission,' most of Idoto's awesome presence could still be felt, and its worship remained intact.[39]

Within their clan, Okigbo's family itself was the one that provided candidates for the guardianship of Idoto, and had his parents not converted to Christianity, Okigbo himself would have been, as Nwakanma says, 'the rightful successor to the traditional priestly functions of the Ajani shrine'.[40] In his writing, this calling echoes repeatedly, for example in 'The Passage', in which the poet is envisaged as a supplicant at Idoto's altar on the river:

> Before you, mother Idoto
> Naked I stand;
> Before your watery presence,
> A prodigal
> Leaning on an oilbeam
> Lost in your legend.
> Under your power wait I

> On barefoot,
> Watchman for the watchword
> At Heavensgate;
> Out of the depths my cry:
> Give ear and hearken.[41]

In *Anthills*, it is easy to see how Achebe borrows the idea of the lost 'priest within'. However, it is not to Ikem that he gives this role, but to Beatrice. What the novel also takes from Igbo traditional culture, moreover, is a gendered understanding of power in which masculine and feminine are correlative, rather than hierarchised. Within Ojoto cosmology, as Nwakanma says, Idoto was one half of a two-sided Godhead, 'consecrated as the spirit of all life with her twin-consort – Ukpaka Oto – the male archetype and alter-ego to the feminine'.[42] Unlike the essentially masculinist concept of *Nneka*, in which femininity is revered only as a site of suffering and endurance, in other words, Idoto represents an understanding of power in which masculine and feminine principles exist in a dialectical unity, opposing but reinforcing each other. In this sense, what Achebe allows Ikem to 'see through a glass darkly' is something of the shift in gender consciousness that *Anthills* as a whole seems to be working towards.

In matters of gender balance, nevertheless, Ikem is relatively naïve, struggling to grasp ideas which it will then become Beatrice's role to piece together. In chapter 8, indeed, Beatrice's significance as the carrier of a new/ancient understanding of power and its gendered nature begins to emerge more clearly. In some of his earlier fiction, as we saw with *Arrow of God* in particular, there are serious discrepancies between Achebe's representation of gender in traditional Igbo ontology and the way it has been understood by subsequent historians. In that novel the Goddess Idemili, conventionally understood as representing the sacred feminine in Igbo thought, is oddly masculinised. Achebe's research for his early novels was, by his own admission, informal and interest-driven, and his portrayal of Idemili as a competitive, pugilistic male figure in *Arrow of God* would tend to suggest that, at that time in the mid-1960s, his understanding of gender in traditional Igbo culture was much more limited than that of some others such as Okigbo. More than twenty years later in *Anthills*, however, it is clear that his interest in the connotations of Idemili's feminine divinity is very much more developed. In 'Daughters: Idemili', he provides us with an account of the Goddess and her origins:

> In the beginning Power rampaged through our world, naked. So the Almighty, looking at his creation through the round undying eye of the Sun, saw and pondered and finally decided to send his daughter, Idemili, to bear witness to the moral nature of authority by wrapping around Power's rude waist a loincloth of peace and modesty. (*AS*, 97)

Initially here, Idemili's role is somewhat Christ-like in that, as the child of God, her function seems to be to mediate His awesome power through care, gentleness and restraint. When she sees the people thirsty, she sends a stream across the land to their parched communities, just as Jesus feeds the starving and attends to the sick in the Gospels. As we begin to understand, however, the Idemili of Igbo tradition is very far from being a sacrificial 'lamb of God'. Neither – it is worth noting – does she carry the connotations of meekness and purity associated with the Christian figure of the Virgin Mary.

As the work of scholars like Ifi Amadiume, Gloria Chuku and Madhu Krishnan make clear, Idemili is in fact quite a mobile and ambivalent figure in Igbo culture, who manifested differently in different community traditions. A guardian of order, she was ascribed the power to deal out sudden death to those whose swollen ambitions threatened clan stability. At the same time, according to Krishnan, 'as an enchantingly beautiful mermaid protected by her totem, the python, Idemili was believed by certain Igbo communities, particularly around the market town of Onitsha, to be the mother of creation to whom offerings must be made to promote prosperity and health'.[43] Further, as a counterpoint to her fearsome power, Idemili was also figured as a temptress 'leading men astray and stealing their wealth and luck through her manipulation of sexuality' as well as 'bestowing health and fertility upon those who worship at her altar'.[44]

In *Anthills* Achebe picks up on many of these differing connotations, especially through Beatrice, whose symbolic status is left fittingly multiple. In chapter 8, she is depicted leading a supplicant Chris through a journey of sexual self-discovery that is figured unambiguously as a rite of Idemili. This time, her ecstatic cry becomes 'a command or password into her temple', a portal leading to 'streams of clear blue water' (*AS*, 108). In 'Daughters: Idemili', meanwhile, the Goddess is explained less in terms of seduction than as a fearsome controlling and restraining power, in the face of which ambitious men are forced to subjugate themselves. Here, Idemili's importance within Igbo social organisation begins to be explained. In traditional Igbo culture, as Achebe stresses in many of his writings, a system of democratic checks and balances worked to ensure that no individual could become too wealthy and powerful, thereby threatening the equilibrium of the clan. The taking of honorific titles such as *ozo*, for example, traditionally involved huge expenditure of the candidate's wealth, ensuring that those who rose in social stature had to accept a reciprocal diminution in economic power. As the author explained to American students in the early 1970s in a seminar quoted by Robert Wren, the reasons why the highest title of all was rarely if ever taken was because it required the taker to utterly impoverish themselves, by paying the debts of every single member of their community.[45] In this section of *Anthills*, however, Achebe goes on to show how this principle of restraint was embodied on the level of the spiritual by the figure of Idemili. Capable of nurturing and protecting, but also of killing without mercy, Idemili is presented here as the guardian of the community against its own members' over-competitive ambitions. If a man 'who has achieved wealth of crop and livestock' (*AS*, 98) wanted to elevate himself by entering the *ozo* hierarchy, we learn, he first had to humble himself before the Goddess, so that his fitness to become a titled man could be judged:

> His first visit is no more than to inform the Daughter of the Almighty of his ambition. He is accompanied by his daughter or, if he has only sons, by the daughter of a kinsman; but a daughter it must be.

> This young woman must stand between him and the Daughter of the Almighty before he can be granted a hearing. She holds his hand like a child in front of the holy stick and counts seven. Then she arranges carefully on the floor seven fingers of chalk, fragile symbols of peace, and then gets him to sit on them so lightly that not one single finger may be broken.
>
> If all has gone well thus far he will then return to his compound and commence the elaborate and costly ceremonies of *ozo* with feasting and dancing to the entire satisfaction of his community and their ancient custom. Then he must go back to the Daughter of the Almighty to let her know that he has now taken the high and sacred title of his people. (*AS*, 98–9)

If the man cannot demonstrate the gentleness that the affairs of the titled – such as judging community disputes – would require, he is deemed unworthy. If his behaviour is such as might subject the Goddess's 'sacred hierarchy' to 'contamination and scandal' (*AS*, 99) she will not merely reject him but summarily take his life. If he is deemed worthy, the man must simply wait and try to infer his acceptance as a titled man from the fact that, having dared to approach the Goddess, he is still alive. 'Such is Idemili's contempt', the narrator informs us, 'for man's unquenchable thirst to sit in authority on his fellows' (*AS*, 99).

In *Anthills* as a whole, the Idemili story resonates powerfully through the stories of the four protagonists. As far as the three men are concerned, of course, the inference we are invited to draw is that neither Sam, Chris nor Ikem has been judged worthy to claim the exalted positions they have each presumed to take. In their own ways, as we have seen, each is driven by a measure of arrogance and masculine disdain. Notwithstanding Chris's and Ikem's attempts at self-transformation, each of them has a record to defend in which thoughtless privilege and self-indulgence (both material and intellectual) have taken precedence over the plight of their countrymen. In a moral universe in which Idemili, as the embodiment of the sacred feminine, demands that the titled be models of humility and temperance, it can be seen as no scandal that each of them is cut down at the height of his powers.

In terms of her record of moral conduct, of course, Beatrice too is faulted. As the following section 'Daughters: Nwanyibuife' reminds us, she has only recently disgraced herself by making an ill-judged sexual advance at the President. She is, like the others, a privileged been-to with a full-time servant who, at times, she feels free to berate and demean. Idemili, however, is not to be questioned and, in the world of the novel, it is Beatrice who is chosen to survive, carrying with her a new model of power and community. 'According to the leitmotif of the novel', as Elleke Boehmer says in an essay on *Anthills*, 'in the anthill that survives after the fires of the harmattan, Beatrice is queen, keeping the colony together'.[46] She is, as we have already discovered, the bearer of the story itself, the one who has gathered together the 'broken pieces' (*AS*, 78). At the end of the novel, she will bring these together in symbolic fashion, signalling the birth of a redemptive new order.

A new order?

As many critics including Boehmer have noted, Achebe's/Beatrice's framing of *Anthills'* final scene quite deliberately suggests a metonymy with a fresh beginning for Kangan. In her flat, Beatrice has gathered a microcosm of the nation's diversity – intellectuals, market traders and villagers, civilians and military, men and women, young and old, before receiving a vision in the image of Chris's death:

> The change in her when it came was sudden. A deep breath audible through the room and a melting down of the statuesque told of her return ...
> 'I can't thank you enough, Emmanuel, for being there and bringing back the message. And you too, of course, Adamma.' She looked at each in turn with a strained smile on her countenance. 'Truth is beauty, isn't it? It must be you know to make someone dying in that pain, to make him ... smile. He sees it and it is ... How can I say it? ... it is unbearably, yes *unbearably* beautiful. That's it! Like Kunene's Emperor Shaka, the spears of his assailants raining down

on him. But he realised the truth at that moment, we're told, and died smiling ... Oh my Christ!' (*AS*, 223)

The revelation Achebe gives Beatrice here, as the final note of the novel, is interestingly hybrid, combining an explicit invocation of Christ's self-sacrifice with the death of the Zulu emperor Shaka the Great. Both figures share the distinction of having been betrayed by those close to them, and Achebe draws an implicit parallel between the symbolism of their deaths. In the gospels of Matthew and Mark, the keynote of Jesus' final moments is one of doubt and despair, as he cries out 'My God, my God, why hast thou forsaken me?' (*Matthew*, 27:47, *Mark* 15:35). The underlying message here, however, is still one of hope, in that Jesus will rise again and provide a path of redemption for the people. In Shaka's case, the mood of his last moment is not so much despair as a sense of bleak self-satisfaction as, dying, he foresees that his betrayers will fall. Again, nevertheless, as Jane Wilkinson says in an interview with Achebe soon after *Anthills'* emergence, the keynote is triumphant: Shaka's children shall 'rise, scatter the dust of our enemies and make our earth free'.[47] Through the mouth of Beatrice, Achebe translates in political terms: 'Chris was sending us a message to beware. This world belongs to the people of the world not to any little caucus, no matter how talented' (*AS*, 222). The ultimate aim of the elite, we clearly understand, must be to abolish itself.

If Beatrice is the celebrant of a new beginning, the congregation she has brought together includes a soldier, Abdul Medani, who has proved he can weigh actions against their ethics and Elewa, the daughter of a market trader nursing the child of Ikem, an intellectual. Emmanuel and Braimoh are political activists, who stand alongside Agatha, a Christian and an elder from a traditional village. As the latter, Elewa's uncle, says of the baby, 'When I asked who named her they told me All of Us. May this child be the daughter of all of us' (*AS*, 219). In miniature, the novel suggests, what we see assembled is a model of the pluralism that the nation must encompass if it is to survive the 'embittered history' (*AS*, 211) of a state like Nigeria, with its past so overshadowed by tribalist struggle and corruption. Clearly, the gesture Achebe makes here seems utopian. As Boehmer says, like the upright stick that, in its crudeness and simplicity, alludes to the sublime beauty and power of Idemili in her pillar of water, so the humbleness of Beatrice's gathering alludes to the grand, but necessary national transformation that must be wrought.

At the end of *Anthills* Achebe does not explicitly prescribe a solution to Nigeria's ills, as he attempted to do in *The Trouble with Nigeria*. What he certainly does do once again, however, is to make a clear political gesture. How realistic or adequate is this gesture, it is fair to ask, in the context within which he was living in the mid-1980s, under conditions of military dictatorship? The defining feature of the Kangan that the characters of *Anthills* attempt to imagine here is that it is a community that transcends class and ethnic divisions. It is, in a sense, the antithesis of the Nigeria which, from before independence to Babangida's day, had been plagued by competition between ethnically based interest groups, each solidified into its own class hierarchy. By stark contrast to this, the model of community born in Beatrice's flat at the end of the novel is based on an idea of 'the people' (*AS*, 222) in which all of these differences have been put aside, a people in other words which needs no differentiation or elaboration.

Who or what is 'the people' in the world of *Anthills*, however? Let us try, once again, to situate Kangan within the real political geography of West Africa. If the country Achebe describes in *Anthills* represents Nigeria, then as Kortenaar suggests, the most reasonable assumption to make is that the dissident province of Abazon can be taken as representing Igboland – which had tried to break away from the Federation and go its own way in 1967. The people of Abazon speak Igbo, and have Igbo names such as Ikem Osodi. Culturally, their heritage is Igbo, as Kortenaar observes. 'Ikem writes that the ancestors used to say *Nneka*, Igbo for "Mother is supreme". The Abazonians speak of Agwa, the Igbo *arusi* or spirit of divination, and refer to a man's chi or personal god, a concept familiar to readers of *Things Fall Apart*.'[48] Ikem is writing a play about the 1929 Women's War, a landmark in the history of Igbo resistance against the colonising

British. There are some indications that Kangan encompasses some diversity: there are four provinces which it is implied, like Abazon, each have their own identity. When speaking to the students of Bassa, Ikem accuses them of forming 'tribal pressure groups' (*AS*, 153). From a cultural point of view, nevertheless, there is something that does not fit. In an odd way, as Kortenaar acutely observes, all of the key cultural coordinates of Achebe's Kangan are *also* Igbo ones:

> Whenever an African language is spoken in the text, it is Igbo. Elewa's child is called Amaechina, Igbo for 'May-the path-never-close.' Elewa's uncle performs the christening with the kolanut ritual of Igboland. Abdul is the only one who needs a translation, and he gets one from Emmanuel, who does not belong to the same ethnic group as Chris, who in turn is not of the same ethnic group as Ikem; however, all three men understand Igbo. In the traditional dialect of the capital, *Ife onye metalu* is said to mean 'What a man commits': the traditional dialect of Bassa is therefore Igbo, the same language that is spoken in Abazon! Similarly, Braimoh, whose name suggests a Northern Nigerian, uses the Igbo word *inyanga* to mean 'showing off.'
>
> Beatrice is not from Ikem's Abazon, yet her name is Nwanyibuife, Igbo for 'a female is also something.' She is from the country between Omambala and Iguedo, where the goddess Idemili has a stream flowing from her lake to Orimili, 'the great river which in generations to come strange foreigners would search out and rename the Niger.' Orimili is the Igbo name for the Niger. Among Beatrice's people, as among the Igbo, the hierarchy is called *ozo*, the python or *Eke-Idemili* is sacred, and markets are held every four days.[49]

The implication of all this is simple: in terms of the cultural references Achebe uses to describe it, Kangan is not really Nigeria at all, as most readers and critics have assumed. Culturally, Kangan is Igboland.

As we have seen throughout this book, the history of Nigeria from its inception at the beginning of the twentieth century is one dominated by ethnic tension. In 1966, anti-Igbo sentiment in Western and especially Northern Nigeria was so severe that it escalated into pogroms that left an estimated 30,000 Igbo professionals and their families dead, with hundreds of thousands displaced. The civil war, which cost the lives of over two million Igbo children, was fuelled by Igbo determination to found a nation on their own terms and the equally implacable determination of Yoruba and Hausa-Fulani power blocs in Western and Northern Nigeria to defeat those aspirations. In the post-civil war era, attempts were made to lessen the political influence of tribalism by dividing Nigeria into a larger number of smaller regions, but under Shehu Shagari in particular, as I suggested earlier in this chapter, the rival ambitions of ethnically based interest groups were powerful enough to preclude any serious attempt to legislate for national development. Oil, throughout the post-civil war period, dominated Nigerian politics, further skewing the nation's development towards forces of patronage and corruption. What of the Nigerian people themselves? Although we do not have specific social attitudes surveys of the period to go on, the evidence provided by general elections suggests that, in general in this period, ordinary Nigerians were just as tribalist in orientation as their political representatives. Even when the political parties themselves were forced to present themselves as 'national' in 1979 and 1983, as Godfrey Mwakikagile reports, Nigerians whether of Igbo or Yoruba origin voted overwhelmingly for presidential candidates from their own ethic group.[50] At the time Achebe wrote *Anthills*, in other words, tribalism remained as much of an entrenched problem as it had always been. Indeed, as he wrote quite explicitly in *The Trouble with Nigeria*, '[n]othing in Nigeria's political history captures her problem of national integration more graphically than the chequered fortune of ... tribe'.[51] In that work, with good reason, tribalism is identified as a fundamental obstacle to Nigeria's healthy development. As Achebe goes on, identifying the manifestations of ethnic bigotry that remained ubiquitous in the 1980s:

> Everyone agrees that there are manifestations of tribal culture which we cannot condemn; for example, peculiar

habits of dress, food, language, music, etc. In fact many of these manifestations are positive and desirable and confer richness to our national culture.

But to prevent a citizen from living or working anywhere in his country, or from participating in the social, political [and] economic life of the community in which he chooses to live is another matter altogether ... Prejudice against 'outsiders' or 'strangers' is an attitude one finds everywhere. But no modern state can lend its support to such prejudice without undermining its own progress and civilization ... [A]lthough we may not be able to legislate prejudice and bigotry out of the hearts and minds of individual citizens, the state itself and all its institutions must not practice, endorse or condone such habits.[52]

In *Anthills*, where has this critique disappeared to? Looking back to *Things Fall Apart*, it is possible to see that Achebe's presentation of a small Igbo community and its response to invasion had had a resonance that was both particular to that community and to a larger history of colonial struggle throughout Africa. In this sense, the way in which that novel's presentation of the Igbo experience has been seen as metonymic is unproblematic: if the example Achebe offers is typical of many others' experience, this only adds to the power and relevancy of his portrayal. With *Anthills*, however, we have a different case. Achebe's Kangan may be a West African nation on the Niger, with a history closely resembling Nigeria's, but it cannot be read in the same way as Nigeria-and-many-nations-like-it. It cannot even be read as Nigeria, in its fundamentals, but rather as a country unencumbered by the fundamental problematic – tribalism – that had run to the heart of the civil war and so many of Nigeria's problems. Kangan is a nation whose elements can all come together in a vision of a better, united future, because Kangan's people were always-already part of a blissfully oil-free Igbo nation. In this sense, the political gesture of Achebe's last novel is indeed utopian, in the full sense of that word. What it is not, by any stretch of the imagination however, is a programme for Nigeria's redemption.

6

The balance of stories: critical overview and conclusion

On 3 April 1957 a group of young Nigerian radio producers were sent by the Nigerian Broadcasting Service for training at the BBC in London. The aim of their trip, as conceived by the NBS's British Director Tom Chalmers, was to boost the service's credibility by 'building them up as national figures'[1] that a sceptical Nigerian public would be able to recognise and look up to. In the eyes of the departing colonial government, the central purpose of the NBS itself was to promote the One-Nigeria political model, and the role of Achebe and his colleagues was to produce programming that expressed that agenda in the most attractive way possible. When he passed through customs on arrival in London, Achebe's passport still designated him as a 'British Protected Person'.[2] In his own view, however, as he writes in *Home and Exile*:

> That was an arrogant lie because I never did ask anyone to protect me. And to protect someone without his request or consent is like the proverbial handshake that goes beyond the elbow and begins to look like kidnapping. Now my passport calls me a 'Citizen of Nigeria.' In today's circumstances Nigeria might not sound altogether like an unqualified piece of good news. But I have never thought it was. Which is precisely what it means to have my work cut out for me.[3]

In this essay, entitled 'Today, the Balance of Stories', Achebe repeats a traditional saying that, in a roundabout way, sheds light on what he means here by having his 'work cut out' for him with Nigeria. 'It went like this: Until the lions produce their own historian, the story of the hunt will glorify the hunter.'[4] This is, of course, precisely the framework through which his own works have most often been read. In the face of colonial distortion (perpetuated in the English literary canon by authors such as Joseph Conrad and Joyce Cary) Achebe is the lion that tells the story of his people, setting right the historical record. In this reading, Achebe is usually characterised as a cultural nationalist, who reclaims the living culture of the people in a way that crystallises their aspirations towards independent nationhood. As Achebe's essay makes clear, however, this is not quite the way he himself came to see things. Although he had often used the proverb of the lion 'to light up an audience for me or enliven a discourse', he says, 'in a rather strange way, I also recognized fairly quickly that there was something about it that did not fully agree with my deepest intent'.[5] The lion, as the bringer of truth, carries 'too strong an aura of strength', and as he had realised over many years as a crafter of stories, 'I did not really want to see the score of narratives between me and my detractor settled by recourse to power, other than the innate power of stories themselves. And I recognized that this choice of weapons was determined for me not by logic or philosophy but by mere temperament ... the fact, for example, that I have never held a gun in my life.'[6] In what Achebe calls 'the war between dispossession and its nemesis', the responsibility of the writer is not to join with, but to resist the forces that would see words turned from tools into weapons, and 'ploughshares ... beaten back into spears'.[7] Dialogue rather than monologue, and what he calls the 'balance of stories' in place of ideology, are what are needed:

> [M]y hope for the twenty-first [century] is that it will see the first fruits of the balance of stories among the world's peoples. The twentieth century for all its many faults did witness a significant beginning, in Africa and elsewhere in the so-called Third World, of the process of 're-storying' peoples who had been knocked silent by the trauma of all kinds of dispossession. I was lucky to be present at one theatre of that reclamation. And I know that such a tremendously potent and complex human reinvention of self – calling, as it must do, on every faculty of mind and

soul and spirit; drawing as it must, from every resource of memory and imagination and from a familiarity with our history, our arts and culture; but also from an unflinching consciousness of the flaws that blemished our inheritance – such an enterprise could not be expected to be easy. And it has not been.[8]

In Achebe's fiction, as we have seen throughout this book, the idea of a balance of opposing perspectives, not necessarily brought to a comforting ideological closure, is crucial to understanding the dynamics of his work. Before he became a writer, as we saw in chapter 1, his early professional life was defined by the needs of an employer, the NBS, to find and create young Nigerians who could forward its strong ideological commitment to a particular (One-Nigeria) model of independence. In his late twenties and early thirties, his emergence as an international literary figure was again defined in important ways by the needs of Heinemann Educational Books, who wanted to build a new canon of fresh, teachable African writing that could be sold to the education ministries and examination boards of newly independent states. In these contexts, as I have argued, it is not in the least surprising that some of the public addresses and non-fictional writings of his early career, such as 'The Novelist as Teacher', reflecting the needs of his collaborators and facilitators, strike a somewhat didactic and campaigning tone. In the world of his fiction, by contrast however, we see little or nothing of the doctrinaire or prescriptive. At the magic moment of Nigerian independence, this is an author who was willing with *Things Fall Apart* and *No Longer at Ease* to paint a picture of his nation as an abortive colonial project terminally mired in corruption. As a young writer celebrated as a reclaimer of indigenous culture, in *Arrow of God* he presented readers with a thoroughly disquieting image of the Igbo, self-destructively locked in masculine competitiveness, falling too easily to colonialism and its missionary confederates. In the mid-1960s, established as the darling of a liberal middle-class readership, he was content with *A Man of the People* to show martial law as the only solution for a nation let down by its political and intellectual classes. Courtesy of numerous college and university curricula Achebe would increasingly, over the years, be read according to affirmative doctrines of 'the empire writ[ing] back' and 'narrating the nation'. Ironically however, his fiction itself seems to do everything possible to resist such ideologisation.

In *The Education of a British-Protected Child*, Achebe characterises the ethos of the Igbo as that of 'social managers rather than legal draftsmen. Our workplace is', he says 'not a neat tabletop but a messy workshop.'[9] In the wealth of interpretation that has accumulated around his work, a recurrent criticism from feminist scholars is that far too little space in this workshop is given over to balanced representations of women. In the wave of African writing from the late-1950s onwards concerned with cultural reclamation, this was seen as a common problem. As Kirsten Holst Petersen wrote in *Kunapipi* in 1984, while work like Achebe's might be laudable for its assault on cultural imperialism, it was often also guilty of ignoring or sidelining women's social importance, resistance and liberatory aspirations. Referring to *Things Fall Apart*, Petersen argued that 'Achebe's much praised objectivity with regard to the merits and flaws of traditional Ibo society becomes less than praiseworthy seen in this light: his traditional women are happy, harmonious members of the community, even when they are repeatedly beaten and barred from any say in the communal decision-making process and constantly reviled in sayings and proverbs.'[10] A decade later, in a major study of gender dynamics in contemporary African writing, Florence Stratton would make a comparable attack. Although in *Things Fall Apart*, Achebe is unhesitating in exposing problematic aspects of Igbo culture (such as infanticide), she argues, when it comes to the question of the injustices done to women he is entirely complacent:

> The women of Umuofia ... are content with their lot. In their silence they assent to their status as the property of a man and to their reduction to a level lower than a barn full of yams in their role as signifiers of their husbands' wealth. So, too, does Achebe. For although he exposes, through the defection of *osu*, the injustice of Umuofia's social class

system, he remains silent (mute like his women) on its gender hierarchy. And while critics continue to eulogize Achebe for the balance he has achieved in his portrayal of Umuofia's strengths and weaknesses, they have generally avoided pointing to the subjugation of women as one of those weaknesses or to the novel's failure to make the same point. This critical silence on the work's sexism can be attributed to the same cause as that to which Achebe assigns responsibility for the silence on Conrad's racism: sexism 'is such a normal way of thinking that its manifestations go completely undetected'.[11]

In 2002, the author's daughter Nwando Achebe would attempt to redeem her father's record on gender representation, by pointing up the importance of the 'female principle'[12] within *Things Fall Apart* and the world it conjures. In Igbo traditional culture, she observes, the spiritual and the physical are not ontologically separable, but closely entwined domains in which male and female are also balanced. Achebe does, she implicitly admits, make a mistake in referring to the supreme deity Chukwu as a 'Him' (*TFA*, 127) analogous to the Christian God-the-Father. In current understanding Chukwu is, she says, 'neither male nor female'.[13] In the novel, however, the earth is strongly feminised in the powerful figure of *Ani*, who the clan must strive not to offend at all costs. In Achebe's depiction of day-to-day life, women cultivate major foodstuffs like cassava, cocoyam and corn, as well as owning and running the marketplace. In the cultural domain, moreover, they also 'act as the griotes of the society – transmitting history from one generation to the next',[14] as we see when children assemble for stories of the earth and sky in the huts of their mothers. At the very beginning of *Things Fall Apart*, indeed, the importance of women could hardly be signalled more strongly with the news that the clan are about to go to war because '[t]hose sons of wild animals have dared to kill a daughter of Umuofia' (*TFA*, 8). Even the community's 'symbol of war and justice is embodied in a female protective medicine called *agadi nwanyi*'.[15]

Notwithstanding Nwando Achebe's defence of her father's first novel, in *Arrow of God* there is no doubt that Achebe gets some things wrong in his representation of the gendered economy of Igboland. In that novel, as we saw in chapter 3, even the goddess Idemili – who returns to full force in *Anthills of the Savannah* – is oddly masculinised, and against the yardstick of subsequent ethnographic research, Achebe's minimal presentation of the female presence in the spiritual and political realms is questionable, to say the least. As his daughter's subsequent research would go on to show, it was far from impossible for a women in the era Achebe describes to gain power within or lead a clan. Her biography of Ahebi Ugbabe documents the career of a woman who became a female headman, negotiated with the colonial British, was appointed a Warrant Chief, and even took the title of king among her people. As she argues, the truly remarkable fact about Ahebi in this respect was that 'she was able to achieve this feat in a society in which kings had no place; the institution was viewed almost as an affront to the Igbo belief in egalitarianism in which the community led itself'.[16]

Nwando Achebe's study was published in 2011, with the benefit of a quarter of a century of concerted research on gender in traditional Igbo culture to draw on. At the time her father was writing *Arrow of God* in the early 1960s, however, gender history had yet to become an established strand of scholarly work in Nigeria. Insights offered by Sylvia Leith-Ross's study *African Women*,[17] commissioned by the British colonial establishment itself, and by the missionary anthropologist George Basden, were still habitually treated as orthodoxy. In this sense, as I suggested in chapter 3, it is reasonable to assume that when he wrote *Arrow of God*, Achebe's own understanding of gender in Igbo culture was simply not as developed as it would be twenty years later when he wrote *Anthills of the Savannah*. Nonetheless, in defence of the earlier novels it is also important to note that Achebe's depiction of domineering men and self-destructive masculine competitiveness in pre-colonial Igboland is framed as a *critique* rather than a celebration of those aspects of traditional society. From the start, for example, Okonkwo's hyper-masculinism and easy tendency to violence in *Things Fall Apart* is presented as aberrant and problematic rather than typical. It is because he offends the earth goddess by beating his wife in the Week of Peace, and then by killing a clansman, that he is unavailable to aid Umuofia in resisting colonisation when the white man arrives. In the contemporary worlds of *No Longer at Ease* and *A Man of the People*, correspondingly, the weakness of protagonists Obi and Odili, and their unfitness for the high tasks history might have appointed them, is described by Achebe once again through negative masculine traits including sexual over-competitiveness and egotism. As Achebe's *oeuvre* develops through *Girls at War* to *Anthills*, this critique of masculinity begins to be balanced against a much stronger representation of female power, both social and metaphysical. Nevertheless, it is a critique that runs through his fiction from the very beginning. From *Things Fall Apart* to *Anthills*, unbridled masculinism is consistently figured as an index of foolishness and weakness – a failure of society itself, perhaps, to achieve the 'balance of stories'.

In *Anthills*, this sense of the need for a gendered balance is an explicit narrative concern. A feminine principle of 'peace and modesty' (*AS*, 97), but which also encompasses 'contempt for man's unquenchable thirst to sit in authority on his fellows' (*AS*, 99), is introduced through the divine figure of Idemili and her priestly representative Beatrice. Idemili is seen as prizing lightness and balance above all things, but also as capable of wielding power without mercy against arrogance and swollen ambition. Via Ikem, in an undefined way, it is mooted that a 'new role for woman' (*AS*, 95) is on the horizon for women in Africa. If Beatrice exemplifies this by holding a successful party in her flat, however, it is not entirely clear in Achebe's portrayal how the new role might express itself in the public political realm. As with *Arrow of God*, in one sense, the gendered consciousness we see in this novel, tied up with the idea of the feminine as redemptive, is again reflective of its moment. By the late 1980s, feminist scholarship associated with Ifi Amadiume and others was well underway, while Nigerian women writers such as Flora Nwapa and Buchi Emecheta, with whose work Achebe was closely familiar, had placed women and gender in traditional and modern society firmly to the fore in fiction. Black masculinity had also been interestingly recast in relation to traditional conceptions of female empowerment in such texts as Toni Morrison's award winning *Song of Solomon* (1977). In Achebe's portrait of Chris and Ikem with their respective transformations, there are also gentle shades of the 1980s 'new man', crystallised in the refrain of Ian McEwan's Cold War oratorio *Or Shall We Die?* 'Shall there be womanly times, or shall we die? ... Can we have strength without aggression, without disgust, strength to bind feeling to intellect?'[18]

In gender terms, certainly, *Anthills* makes an attempt to achieve a 'balance of stories' in a way that no other text does in Achebe's *oeuvre*. In another area, however, the novel seems to exemplify a stark and surprising lack of balance. Achebe's narrative, set in a postcolonial West African nation on the Niger, invites its readers in all sorts of ways to see Nigeria's present and possible future within its pages. In a way that comes closer than any of Achebe's other fictional works to expressing a nationalist impulse, it even concludes with a symbolic gathering in which all the elements of a redemptive new order are present. Civilians and military, urban and rural, male and female, young and old are represented, as they gather to mark the birth of one who will be the daughter of 'All of Us' (*AS*, 219). As we saw in the last chapter, however, what is glaringly missing from this picture in a Nigerian context is any serious attempt to describe the bridging of the ethnic divides that had defined (and wrecked) the nation's politics since independence. In Achebe's Kangan, the capital city is culturally Igbo, the village is culturally Igbo, even the faraway, rebel province of Abazon is culturally Igbo. Forging a sense of community requires only a collective affirmation, because everybody already belongs to that community. The reclamation of society and culture entails only the realisation that '[t]his world belongs to the people of the world not to any little caucus' (*AS*, 222), because the people already exist in an organic unity that – with the sweeping away of the corrupt neo-colonial state – is already in a state of readiness to reach its moment of becoming.

In *The Ahiara Declaration*, Achebe and his co-authors had described Nigeria as 'a corrupt and rickety structure ... in a perpetual state of powerlessness to check foreign exploitation'.[19] Among its fundamental, ongoing difficulties were not just corruption and domination by neo-colonial interests, however, but also a culture of tribalism that had subverted its national culture from the start. In *The Trouble with Nigeria*, this was a theme that Achebe picked up very explicitly. 'In the lifetime of many Nigerians who still enjoy an active public career', he reminds us, 'Nigeria was called "a mere geographical expression" not only by the British ... but even by our "nationalists" when it suited them to retreat into tribe to check their rivals from other parts of the country.'[20] Years before the British had even left, the dominance of tribal politics had ensured 'the abortion of a pan-Nigerian vision ... a Nigeria in which an Easterner might aspire to be premier in the West and a Northerner become mayor of Enugu'.[21] Even in the 1980s, after the terrible experience of the civil war, when the pernicious effects of tribalism on Nigeria and its people had been demonstrated plainly enough for all to see, he argues:

> [A]ll this self-conscious wish to banish *tribe* has proved largely futile because a word will stay around as long as there is work for it to do. In Nigeria, in spite of our protestations, there *is* plenty of work for *tribe*. Our threatening gestures against it have been premature, half-hearted or plain deceitful.
>
> A Nigerian child seeking admission into a federal school, a student wishing to enter a College or University, a graduate seeking employment in the public service, a businessman tendering for a contract, a citizen applying for a passport, filing a report with the police or seeking access to any of the hundred thousand avenues controlled by the state, will sooner or later fill out a form which requires him to confess his tribe.[22]

Inasmuch as *Anthills* is, more than any of his previous novels, the story of Nigeria as it is, has been and could be, Achebe's elision of the ethnic or tribal dimension in his redemptive 'happy ending' underlines a point that has been made many times in this book: Achebe is never a convincing ideologist.

Never uni-vocal, never content to succumb to 'The One Way, One Truth, One Life menace', as he puts it in *The Education of a British-Protected Child*, his fiction resists 'The Terror that lives completely alone.'[23] Although the Achebe that has trickled down from scholars like Simon Gikandi to study guides and editorials has often been a doctrinaire figure pushing a textbook nationalist agenda, his novels themselves, as I have argued, continually trouble such a reading.

During the 1990s, 'nation' was becoming established as one of the key theoretical coordinates of postcolonial studies, an important pedagogic development which was rapidly to permeate the university and college curriculum. In this context, it is easy to see why a reading of Achebe which placed him in a pleasing alignment with this emerging theme should have been popular with scholars and teachers. As a whole canon of postcolonial criticism will attest, reading through the idea of 'narrating the nation' undoubtedly proved useful in illuminating the strategies of a number of writers including, for example, Salman Rushdie in his early novels *Midnight's Children* (1981) and *Shame* (1983). In the case of Achebe, however, reading his work primarily in relation to nationalism tends inevitably to lead to problems. In Nahem Yousaf's study *Chinua Achebe*, for example, even if the writer's works appear to be predominantly Igbo in focus, it is still assumed that they can be taken as 'representative of Nigeria as a whole'.[24] In the context of a nation in which regional and ethnic diversity and, indeed, conflict shape the cultural landscape in fundamental ways, this represents an enormous leap that is, as I have argued in this book, very difficult indeed to justify from the evidence of the novels themselves.

Often such readings fail to give adequate attention to the tension between statist (in this case, Nigerian) and ethnocultural (in this case, Igbo) nationalisms, the aims and values of which in the realm of culture are strongly divergent. To foreclose this complexity (for example) by arguing as Simon Gikandi does that any articulation of doubts or disenchantment with Nigerian nationhood on Achebe's part can somehow be taken as evidence of his deeper nationalism,[25] has the effect of obscuring, rather than illuminating, the struggles that animate his writing. Achebe's *oeuvre* really cannot, as Yousaf asserts, be read as a continuous and consistent political argument along nationalist lines, comprising 'a "Nigerian" master narrative, the organizing story of a nation'.[26] As I have suggested, it is true that Achebe's public role, especially in his early career, did position him as an unofficial ambassador for Nigeria and for postcolonial Africa as a whole. A few pieces of writing, published for an international audience, are inflected by a certain amount of 'ambassadorial' rhetoric, exhorting writers to 'march right in front'[27] in the struggle against cultural imperialism. Nevertheless, to co-opt Achebe's entire *oeuvre* to a continuous project of 'narrating the nation' fits very awkwardly indeed with his troubled and changing sensibility.

In Gikandi's work, as well as those who followed it, the key theoretical expression of nationalism referenced in relation to Achebe is that of Frantz Fanon, especially in his anti-colonial classic *The Wretched of the Earth*. Here, Fanon describes the position of the 'native intellectual' in relation to colonialism and independence in a way that does, in some respects, provide an illuminating fit with Achebe. Just as Fanon suggests, he was educated within a missionary and colonial school system designed to shape its students' consciousness in terms of European values and assumptions. In common with many of the thinkers and writers with whom Fanon engages, the process of reflecting back on that education clearly did produce a strong anti-colonial reaction, together with a desire to re-engage with his indigenous Igbo culture. However, the fact that Achebe's development accords with this generic pattern does not mean that his work can usefully be thought of as an expression of Fanonian nationalism. For Fanon, nationalism must be more than opposition to colonialism plus a desire to revalue one's culture. It must also include a settled and consistent commitment to the nation-state as the goal and focus of struggle. In Achebe's case, as we have seen, what we actually find is a political sensibility that is much more complex and shifting – and far less programmatic – than this would imply.

As the theorist Benedict Anderson says in his seminal study *Imagined Communities*, since the end of the First World War the modern nation-state has been the pre-eminent political formation worldwide. Recognised by membership of such bodies as the League of Nations after 1918 and the United Nations after 1945, it became 'the legitimate international norm',[28] the definitive licence for peoples to assert their self-determination and to participate formally in global political affairs. Unsurprisingly in this context, the goal of attaining national sovereignty was a cornerstone of nationalist thinking throughout the middle decades of the twentieth century, including in Fanon's work and that of Nnamdi Azikiwe and other anti-colonialist intellectuals who undoubtedly influenced Achebe. For Fanon in particular, the development of national culture is the indispensable condition for any meaningful struggle for self-determination:

> In the colonial situation, culture, which is doubly deprived of the support of the nation and of the state, falls away and dies. The condition for its existence is therefore national liberation and the renaissance of the state. The nation is not only the condition of culture, its fruitfulness, its continuous renewal, and its deepening. It is also a necessity. It is the fight for national existence which sets culture moving and opens to it the doors of creation. Later on it is the nation which will ensure the conditions and framework necessary to culture. The nation gathers together the various indispensable elements necessary for the creation of a culture, those elements which alone can give it credibility, validity, life and creative power. In the same way it is its national character that will make such a culture open to other cultures and which will enable it to influence and permeate other cultures. A non-existent culture can hardly be expected to have bearing on reality, or to influence reality. The first necessity is the re-establishment of the nation in the strictly biological sense of the phrase.[29]

Underlying Fanon's argument here is the idea that national consciousness and the aspiration towards statehood should exist as complementary facets of the same struggle. In Achebe's case, as we have seen however, that is far from being the case.

Even Simon Gikandi, whose nuanced and sophisticated work acknowledges the difficulty of 'nation' as a concept, seems to be blind sighted by this ideological ambivalence and complexity. To sustain his proposal that Achebe is indeed a nationalist, Gikandi is forced to fall back on such a loose conception of Igbo, Nigerian and African identity that these almost become synonymous or interchangeable with each other:

> The important point ... is that in the absence of real signifiers to correspond to the idea of nation, African writers must often invent significant frameworks within which questions of cultural identity can be examined. If Achebe's commitment to Nigeria can be transferred – with ease and integrity – to Biafra, this should not be seen as an indication of the novelist's wavering allegiances, but of the shifting nature of African realities, and of the writer's need to shape his own thinking to come to terms with the African problematic; for Achebe, 'it is in the very nature of creativity, in its prodigious complexity and richness, that it will accommodate paradoxes and ambiguities'. And even when such paradoxes and complexities are signalled by tragic consequences, as in the case of the Nigerian civil war, the writer finds a constant factor in the idea and ideal of an African culture which he must realise in narrative practice. 'Most African writers write out of an African experience and of commitment to an African destiny,' says Achebe.[30]

To treat 'Nigerian', 'Biafran' and 'African', here, as little more than alternative manifestations of the same ideological commitment to 'nation' is (notwithstanding all Gikandi's *caveats*) to give far too little weight to the political contradictions of the period that produced Achebe and his work, I would argue. The rival claims of tribalism, regionalism, pan-Africanism and Nigerian nationhood do not represent subtle gradations of position in the 1950s, 1960s or even the 1980s: they are the fundamental stakes in debates that for many, in Biafra particularly, turned out to be life-and-death affairs.

Among all of Achebe's writings, undoubtedly the most idealistic and doctrinaire is *The Ahiara Declaration*. Nowhere else in his work do we find a comparably unequivocal declaration of values:

> Biafra will not betray the Black man, no matter the odds. We will fight with all our might until black men everywhere can point with pride to this republic standing dignified and defiant, an example of African Nationalism triumphant over its many and age-old enemies.
>
> We believe that God, humanity and history are on our side and that the Biafran Revolution is indestructible and eternal.[31]

Even in Biafra, tasked as he was by a revolutionary leader with producing the 'organizing story of a nation',[32] however, Achebe's fiction disclosed a dissident and questioning sensibility. In his other Biafran story, the children's book *How the Leopard Got His Claws*, for example, the projected future for the community is not triumphant self-realisation but in fact its inverse: a cycle of self-destructive resentment and revenge. In 'Girls at War', meanwhile, we see a Biafra in which the cynical and corrupt survive, while the heroic perish.

As Achebe writes in *The Education of a British-Protected Child*, '[t]he preference of the Igbo is … not singularity but duality. Wherever Something Stands, Something Else Will Stand Beside It.'[33] Achebe was a man from Ogidi, Anambra State, who was thrown headlong into times of extraordinary change. In his own life, as Nigeria's pre-eminent writer, he became part of that story of change. From the very beginning, forces large and small competed to turn him into an ideologue. Working for the national broadcaster, he was paid to promote One-Nigeria. As an author and editor for Heinemann, he was enjoined to produce a new canon expressing the meaning of independence for the classrooms of Africa. As Chair of the National Guidance Committee for Biafra, he was tasked with articulating the principles and values of a fledgling nation. A decade and a half later, as a member of the People's Redemption Party, he was asked to set out the road to redemption for a Nigeria that had bombed and starved that new nation out of existence. Amid such intense, changing ideological demands, as we have seen in this book, however, Achebe found another, un-committed space he could work within. His fiction became that space, where awkward, multidimensional cultural and historical questions could be engaged with seriousness, without succumbing to the 'One Way, One Truth, One Life menace'.[34]

Notes

Chapter 1

1 Chinua Achebe, *The Education of a British-Protected Child: Essays* (London: Penguin, 2009), 40.
2 'Interview with Chinua Achebe', conducted by Dennis Duerden (September 1965). Collected for the BBC African Writer's Club. British Library Sound Archive C143/406.
3 Larry Diamond, *Class, Ethnicity and Democracy in Nigeria: The Failure of the First Republic* (Syracuse: Syracuse University Press, 1998), 26–7.
4 Obi Nwakanma, *Christopher Okigbo: Thirsting for Sunlight 1930–1967* (Woodridge, Suffolk: James Currey, 2010), 32.
5 Benedict Anderson, *Imagined Communities: Reflections on the Origin and Spread of Nationalism*, revised edn (London: Routledge, 1991), 118.
6 Ezenwa-Ohaeto, *Chinua Achebe: A Biography* (Oxford and Bloomington, IN: James Currey/Indiana University Press, 1997).
7 Chinua Achebe, 'There Was a Young Man in Our Hall', *University Herald*, 1952, quoted by Ezenwa-Ohaeto, *Chinua Achebe: A Biography*, 46.
8 'Hiawatha', *University Herald*, 1953, quoted in Ezenwa-Ohaeto, *Chinua Achebe: A Biography*, 48.
9 Achebe, *The Trouble with Nigeria* (Oxford: Heinemann, 1984 [1983]), 5.
10 Ibid., 5–6.
11 Richard Sklar, *Nigerian Political Parties: Power in an Emergent African Nation* (Trenton, NJ: Africa World Press, 2004).
12 Achebe, *The Trouble with Nigeria*, 5.

13 From the opening speech to a Motion appealing for national unity, delivered in the Legislative Council at Kaduna, on 4 March 1958. Nnamdi Azikiwe, *Zik: A Selection from the Speeches of Nnamdi Azikiwe* (London: Cambridge Univeristy Press, 1961), 101.
14 Achebe, *The Education of a British-Protected Child*, 41–2.
15 Ibid., 44.
16 Quoted in *West Africa*, editorial, 19 November 1979, p. 2123.
17 Chinua Achebe, 'The Writer and His Community', in *Hopes and Impediments: Selected Essays* (New York: Anchor, 1990 [1988]), 59.
18 Simon Gikandi, *Reading Chinua Achebe: Language and Ideology in Fiction*, Studies in African Literature (Safrl) (London: James Currey, 1991).
19 Achebe, *The Education of a British-Protected Child: Essays*, 5–6.
20 Ibid., 11.
21 Ibid., 39.
22 Charles Armour, 'The BBC and the Development of Broadcasting in British Colonial Africa 1946–1956', *African Affairs*, 83, no. 332 (1984): 362–3.
23 Ibid., 380.
24 Ibid., 381.
25 Chinua Achebe and Robert Lyons, *Another Africa* (New York: Anchor, 1998), 110.
26 Nwakanma, *Christopher Okigbo: Thirsting for Sunlight 1930–1967*, 104.
27 Ezenwa-Ohaeto, *Chinua Achebe: A Biography*.
28 Ebele Ume-Nwagbo, 'Politics and Ethnicity in the Rise of Broadcasting in Nigeria, 1932–62', *Journalism Quarterly*, 56, no. 4 (1979): 816–21.
29 Ian MacKay, *Broadcasting in Nigeria* (Ibadan: Ibadan University Press, 1964), 32.
30 Ezenwa-Ohaeto, *Chinua Achebe: A Biography*, 57.
31 MacKay, *Broadcasting in Nigeria*, 32.
32 Ume-Nwagbo, 'Politics and Ethnicity in the Rise of Broadcasting in Nigeria, 1932–62', 818.
33 Armour, 'The BBC and the Development of Broadcasting in British Colonial Africa 1946–1956', 395.
34 J. F. Wilkinson, 'The BBC and Africa', *African Affairs*, 71, no. 283 (1972): 180.

35 Ume-Nwagbo, 'Politics and Ethnicity in the Rise of Broadcasting in Nigeria, 1932–62', 820.
36 Wilkinson, 'The BBC and Africa', 180–1.
37 Ezenwa-Ohaeto, *Chinua Achebe: A Biography*, 87.
38 Ibid.
39 MacKay, *Broadcasting in Nigeria*, 86.
40 Achebe, 'The Novelist as Teacher', *Hopes and Impediments: Selected Essays* (New York: Anchor, 1990 [1988]), 41.
41 Ibid., 45.
42 MacKay, *Broadcasting in Nigeria*, 89–90.
43 Ibid., 64.
44 Voice of Nigeria broadcast, 9 July 1967, quoted in A. H. M. Kirk-Greene (ed.), *Crisis and Conflict in Nigeria: A Documentary Sourcebook 1966–70, Vol. II July 1967–January 1970* (Oxford: Oxford Univeristy Press, 1971), 3.
45 Ebele Ume-Nwagbo, 'Broadcasting in Nigeria: Its Post-Independence Status', *Journalism Quarterly*, no. 61 (1984): 590.
46 David Whitaker and Msiska Mpalive-Hangson, *Chinua Achebe's Things Fall Apart* (Abingdon: Routledge, 2007), xi.
47 Nahem Yousaf, *Chinua Achebe* (Tavistock, Devon: Northcote House, 2003), 1.
48 Gikandi, *Reading Chinua Achebe: Language and Ideology in Fiction*, xviii.
49 Vincent Carretta, *Equiano, the African: Biography of a Self-Made Man* (Athens, GA: University of Georgia Press, 2005).
50 Olaudah Equiano, *The Interesting Life of Olaudah Equiano, or Gustavus Vassa, the African, Written by Himself* (London: privately published, 1789), 9.
51 Thomas Jefferson, 'Notes on the State of Virgnia', in *Writings*, ed. Merrill D. Peterson (New York: Library of America, 1984), 266.
52 Equiano, *The Interesting Life of Olaudah Equiano, or Gustavus Vassa, the African, Written by Himself*, 28–9.
53 Rhonda Cobham, 'Making Men and History: Achebe and the Politics of Revisionism', in Bernth Lindfors (ed.), *Approaches to Teaching Achebe's Things Fall Apart*, Approaches to Teaching World Literature: 37 (New York: Modern Language Association of America, 1991), 89.
54 Equiano, *The Interesting Life of Olaudah Equiano, or Gustavus Vassa, the African, Written by Himself*, 5.

55 Ibid., 14.
56 Ibid., 18.
57 Akito Ito, 'Olaudah Equiano and the New York Artisans: The First American Edition of *the Interesting Life of Olaudah Equiano, or Gustavus Vassa, the African*', Early American Literature, 32, no. 1 (1997): 50–74.
58 Ezenwa-Ohaeto, *Chinua Achebe: A Biography*, 4.
59 George Basden, *Among the Ibos of Nigeria: An Account of the Curious and Interesting Habits, Customs and Beliefs of a Little Known African People by One Who Has for Many Years Lived Amongst Them on Close & Intimate Terms* (London: Frank Cass, 1966 [1921]).
60 Sylvia Leith-Ross, *African Women: A Study of the Ibo of Nigeria* (London: Faber and Faber, 1939).
61 Basden, *Among the Ibos of Nigeria*, 9–10.
62 Ibid., 10.
63 Ibid., 27.
64 Ibid., 37.
65 Ibid., 20.
66 Ibid., 17.
67 Ibid., 285.
68 C. L. Innes, *Chinua Achebe*, Cambridge Studies in African and Caribbean Literature: 1 (Cambridge: Cambridge University Press, 1990).
69 Chinua Achebe, 'An Image of Africa', *Massachusetts Review: A Quarterly of Literature, the Arts and Public Affairs*, 18, no. 4 (1977): 788. In subsequent versions this was modified to 'thoroughgoing racist'.
70 Leith-Ross, *African Women: A Study of the Ibo of Nigeria*, 19.
71 Toyin Falola and Saheed Aderinto, *Nigeria, Nationalism, and Writing History* (Rochester, NY: University of Rochester Press, 2010).
72 K. Onwuka Dike, *Trade and Politics in the Niger Delta, 1830–1885* (Oxford: Clarendon, 1956).
73 Toyin Falola, *Nationalism and African Intellectuals* (Rochester, NY: University of Rochester Press, 2001), 232.
74 Falola and Aderinto, *Nigeria, Nationalism, and Writing History*, 29.

75 Isidore Okpeewho, *Once Upon a Kingdom: Myth, Hegemony and Identity* (Bloomington, IN: Indiana University Press, 1998).

76 A. E. Afigbo, *The Abolition of the Slave Trade in Southeastern Nigeria, 1885–1950*, Rochester Studies in African History and the Diaspora (Rochester, NY: University of Rochester Press, 2006).

77 Stephanie Newell, *West African Literatures: Ways of Reading* (Oxford: Oxford University Press, 2006).

78 Achebe, *The Education of a British-Protected Child: Essays*, 14.

79 Ibid., 14.

80 Newell, *West African Literatures*, 103.

81 Pita Nwana, *Omenuko* (Umu Ahia, Nigeria: Methodist Bookstore, 1932).

82 D. N. Achara, *Ala Bingo* (London: Longman, 1958).

83 Cyprian Ekwensi, *When Love Whispers* (Yaba: Chuks, 1948).

84 Cyprian Ekwensi, *People of the City* (London: Longman, 1954).

85 Newell, *West African Literatures*, 98–9.

86 Ibid., 100.

87 Ibid.

88 Gail Low, 'The Natural Artist: Publishing Amos Tutuola's *The Palm Wine Drinkard* in Postwar Britain', *Research in African Literatures*, 37, no. 4 (2006): 22.

89 Ibid., with Low's emphasis.

90 Ibid.

91 Ibid., 23.

92 Alan Hill, *In Pursuit of Publishing* (London: Heinemann, 1988), 130–1.

93 Honor Tracy, 'New Novels', *The Listener*, 26 June 1958, 1068.

94 Ibid.

95 'The Centre Cannot Hold', *Times Literary Supplement*, 20 June 1958, 341.

96 David Chioni Moore and Analee Heath, 'A Conversation with Chinua Achebe: On the Fiftieth Anniversary of *Things Fall Apart*', *Transition: An International Review*, 100 (2009): 16.

97 Hill, *In Pursuit of Publishing*, 122–3.

98 Clive Barnett, 'Disseminating Africa: Burdens of Representation and the African Writers Series', *New Formations*, no. 57 (2005–6): 74–94.

99 See for example, Part IX, 'Language,' in Bill Ashcroft, Gareth Griffiths and Helen Tiffin (eds), *The Post-Colonial Studies Reader* (London: Routledge, 1995).
100 Ibid., 80.
101 Chinua Achebe, 'English and the African Writer', *Transition*, 4, no. 18 (1965): 19.
102 Chinua Achebe, 'The Novelist as Teacher', 45.
103 James Currey, *Africa Writes Back: The African Writers Series and the Launch of African Literature* (Oxford: James Currey, 2008), xvi.
104 Ibid., 4.
105 Ibid., 4–5.
106 Barnett, 'Disseminating Africa: Burdens of Representation and the African Writers Series', 81, quoting from an internal memorandum in the Heinemann Archive, University of Reading.
107 Ibid., 81.
108 Bernth Lindfors, 'Popular Literature for an African Elite', *Journal of Modern African Studies*, 12, no. 3 (1974): 471–86.
109 Toyin Adepoju, 'Mbari Club', in *Encyclopaedia of the African Diaspora: Origins, Experiences and Culture*, ed. Carole Boyce Davis (Santa Barbara, CA: ABS-CLIO, 2008), 665.
110 Abdul Yesufu, 'Mbari Publications: A Pioneer Anglophone African Publishing House', *The African Book Publishing Record*, 8, no. 2 (1982): 53–7.

Chapter 2

1 Gikandi, *Reading Chinua Achebe: Language and Ideology in Fiction*, 4.
2 Ibid., 3.
3 Yousaf, *Chinua Achebe*, 2.
4 Francis Ngaboh-Smart, 'Worldliness, Territoriality and Narrative: *Things Fall Apart* and the Rhetoric of Nationalism', in Ernest N. Emenyonu (ed.), *Emerging Perspectives on Chinua Achebe. Volume 1. Omenka the Master Artist: Critical Perspectives on Achebe's Fiction* (Trenton, NJ: Africa World, 2004), 3.
5 Achebe, *The Education of a British-Protected Child: Essays*, 6.
6 Ibid., 7.

7 Chinua Achebe, 'Named for Victoria, Queen of England', in *Hopes and Impediments: Selected Essays* (New York: Anchor, 1990 [1988]), 38.
8 Chinua Achebe, *Things Fall Apart* (London: Heinemann, 1958), 8. Hereafter referred to in the text as *TFA*.
9 Cobham, 'Making Men and History: Achebe and the Politics of Revisionism', 93.
10 Ibid.
11 *No Longer at Ease* (London: Heinemann, 1962), 3. Hereafter referred to in the text as *NLE*.
12 Ezenwa-Ohaeto, *Chinua Achebe: A Biography*.
13 Armour, 'The BBC and the Development of Broadcasting in British Colonial Africa 1946–1956', 395.
14 James Currey, Alan Hill and Keith Sambrook in conversation with Kirsten Holst Petersen, 'Working with Chinua Achebe: The African Writers Series', in Kirsten Holst Petersen and Anna Rutherford (eds), *Chinua Achebe: A Celebration*, Studies in African Literature (Safrl) (Oxford: Heinemann, 1990), 150.
15 Robert M. Wren, *Achebe's World: The Historical and Cultural Context of the Novels* (Washington: Three Continents, 1980), 83.
16 Arinze E. Agbogu, 'Ogidi Before 1891: A Brief Survey of the Origins, Migration, Settlement, and Intergroup Relations', unpublished research project, mimeographed (University of Nigeria, Nsukka, 1976).
17 Afigbo, *The Abolition of the Slave Trade in Southeastern Nigeria, 1885–1950*.
18 Wren, *Achebe's World: The Historical and Cultural Context of the Novels*, 26–7.
19 Flora Shaw, *A Tropical Dependency: An Outline of the Ancient History of the Western Sudan with an Account of the Modern Settlement of Northern Nigeria* (Cambridge: Cambridge University Press, 2010 [1905]), 348.
20 Afigbo, *The Abolition of the Slave Trade in Southeastern Nigeria, 1885–1950*, 46.
21 Achebe, *The Education of a British-Protected Child: Essays*, 7.
22 F. K. Ekechi, *Missionary Enterprise & Rivalry in Igboland 1857–1914* (London: Frank Cass, 1971).
23 Ibid., 120–1.
24 Herbert Ekwe-Ekwe, *African Literature in Defence of History:*

An Essay on Chinua Achebe (Dakar: African Renaissance, 2001), 105–6.
25 Ibid., 79.
26 Gloria Chuku, *Igbo Women and Economic Transformation in Southeastern Nigeria 1900–1960* (New York: Routledge, 2005), 51.
27 Kalu Ogbaa, *Gods Oracles and Divination: Folkways in Chinua Achebe's Novels* (Trenton, NJ: Africa World Press, 1992).
28 P. N. C. Okigbo, 'Nigerian National Accounts 1950–57', ed. Federal Ministry of Economic Development (Lagos, 1961).
29 Basden, *Among the Ibos of Nigeria*, 20.
30 Achebe, *The Education of a British-Protected Child: Essays*, 7.
31 Innes, *Chinua Achebe*, 24.
32 Ibid.
33 Wren, *Achebe's World: The Historical and Cultural Context of the Novels*, 85.
34 Ibid., 86.
35 Yousaf, *Chinua Achebe*, 4.

Chapter 3

1 A. E. Afigbo, *The Warrant Chiefs: Indirect Rule in Southeastern Nigeria, 1891–1929*, Ibadan History Series (New York: Humanities, 1972), 83.
2 Ibid., 68.
3 Ibid., 69.
4 *Arrow of God* (London: Heinemann, 1964), 107. Hereafter referred to in the text as *AG*.
5 Judith E. McDowell, 'An Interview with Chinua Achebe', in Bernth Lindfors (ed.), *Conversations with Chinua Achebe*, Literary Conversations Series (Lico) (Jackson, MS: University Press of Mississippi, 1997), 8.
6 Wren, *Achebe's World: The Historical and Cultural Context of the Novels*, 116–17.
7 Simon Nnolim, *The History of Umuchu* (Enugu: Eastern Press, 1953).
8 Charles Nnolim, 'A Source for *Arrow of God*', *Research in African Literatures*, 8 (1977): 3.

9   Ibid., 22.
10 C. L. Innes, 'A Source for *Arrow of God*: A Response', *Research in African Literatures*, 9 (1978): 16–18.
11 Don Ohadike, 'The Decline of Slavery among the Igbo People', in Suzanne Miers and Richard Roberts (eds), *The End of Slavery in Africa* (Madison, WC: University of Wisconsin Press, 1988), 448–9.
12 Afigbo, *The Abolition of the Slave Trade in Southeastern Nigeria, 1885–1950*, 52.
13 Ibid., 53.
14 Edward Steel, 'Exploration in Southern Nigeria', *The Geographical Journal*, 32, no. 1 (1908): 6.
15 Ibid., 9.
16 Afigbo, *The Abolition of the Slave Trade in Southeastern Nigeria, 1885–1950*, 47–8.
17 John Oriji, 'Igboland, Slavery and the Drums of War and Heroism', in Sylviane Anne Diouf (ed.), *Fighting the Slave Trade: West African Strategies* (Athens, OH: Ohio University Press, 2003), 125.
18 Michel Fabre, 'Chinua Achebe on *Arrow of God*', in Bernth Lindfors (ed.), *Conversations with Chinua Achebe*, Literary Conversations Series (Lico) (Jackson, MS: University Press of Mississippi, 1997), 48.
19 Romanus Okey Muoneke, *Art, Rebellion and Redemption : A Reading of the Novels of Chinua Achebe*, American University Studies Series XVIII, African Literature (New York: Peter Lang, 1994), 41.
20 Wren, *Achebe's World: The Historical and Cultural Context of the Novels*, 27.
21 Ibid., 28.
22 Ifi Amadiume, *Male Daughters, Female Husbands: Gender and Sex in an African Society* (London: Zed, 1987).
23 Ibid., 122.
24 Lewis Nkosi and Wole Soyinka, 'Conversation with Chinua Achebe', in Bernth Lindfors (ed.), *Conversations with Chinua Achebe*, Literary Conversations Series (Lico) (Jackson, MS: University Press of Mississippi, 1997), 11.
25 Ibid.
26 Ibid.
27 Ibid., 11–12.

28 Chuku, *Igbo Women and Economic Transformation in Southeastern Nigeria 1900–1960*, 207.

29 Ibid., 217.

30 Nigerian Supply Board, Lagos, to Secretary of Eastern Provinces, Enugu, 16 April 1942, and Secretary of Eastern Provinces to Nigerian Supply Board, 4 May 1942, quoted in Chuku, *Igbo Women and Economic Transformation in Southeastern Nigeria 1900–1960*, 215–16.

31 Chuku, *Igbo Women and Economic Transformation in Southeastern Nigeria 1900–1960*, 216.

32 Ibid., 217.

33 Nina Emma Mba, *Nigerian Women Mobilized: Women's Political Activity in Southern Nigeria, 1900–1965*, Research Series (Berkeley: Institute of International Studies, University of California, 1982), 70.

34 Amadiume, *Male Daughters, Female Husbands: Gender and Sex in an African Society*, 34.

35 Ibid., 43.

36 Ibid., 42.

37 Ibid., 123.

38 Ibid., 120.

39 Mba, *Nigerian Women Mobilized: Women's Political Activity in Southern Nigeria, 1900–1965*, 70.

40 Ibid., 28, quoting Margaret Mackeson Green, *Igbo Village Affairs, Etc. (Second Edition.) [with a Map.]* (London: Frank Cass & Co., 1964), 219.

41 Mba, *Nigerian Women Mobilized: Women's Political Activity in Southern Nigeria, 1900–1965*, 28.

42 Ibid., 29.

43 Ibid., 27, quoting Green, *Igbo Village Affairs, Etc. (Second Edition.) [with a Map.]*, 169.

44 Amadiume, *Male Daughters, Female Husbands: Gender and Sex in an African Society*, 140.

45 Mba, *Nigerian Women Mobilized: Women's Political Activity in Southern Nigeria, 1900–1965*, 69.

46 Ibid., 70.

47 Ibid., 72.

48 Ibid., 73.

49 Ibid.

50 Ibid., 76, quoting Adielo Afigbo, 'Revolution and Reaction in Eastern Nigeria 1900–1929', *Journal of the Historical Society of Nigeria*, 3, no. 3 (1966): 553.

51 Judith Van Allen, '"Aba Riots" or Igbo "Women's War"? Ideology, Stratification, and the Invisibility of Women', in Nancy Hafkin and Edna Bay (eds), *Women in Africa: Studies in Social and Economic Change* (Stanford, CA: Stanford University Press, 1976), 60.

52 Adielo Afigbo, *Nigerian History, Politics and Affairs: The Collected Essays of Adielo Afigbo*, ed. Toyin Falola (Trenton, NJ: Africa World Press, 2005).

53 Toyin Falola, *Colonialism and Violence in Nigeria* (Bloomington, IN: Indiana University Press, 2009), 127.

54 Afigbo, *The Warrant Chiefs: Indirect Rule in Southeastern Nigeria, 1891–1929*, 248.

55 Falola and Aderinto, *Nigeria, Nationalism, and Writing History*, 83.

56 Ibid.

57 Nkosi and Soyinka, 'Conversation with Chinua Achebe', 12.

58 Madhu Krishnan, 'Mami Wata and the Occluded Feminine in Anglophone Nigerian-Igbo Literature', *Research in African Literatures*, 43, no. 1 (2012): 6.

59 Ibid., 8.

60 Amadiume, *Male Daughters, Female Husbands: Gender and Sex in an African Society*, 100.

61 Chuku, *Igbo Women and Economic Transformation in Southeastern Nigeria 1900–1960*, 25.

62 Tejumola Olaniyan, 'Chinua Achebe and an Archaeology of the Postcolonial African State', *Research in African Literatures*, 32, no. 3 (2001): 26.

63 Amadiume, *Male Daughters, Female Husbands: Gender and Sex in an African Society*, 101.

64 *Anthills of the Savannah* (London: Penguin, 2001 [1987]), 99. Hereafter referred to in the text as *AS*.

65 Fabre, 'Chinua Achebe on *Arrow of God*', 46.

66 Ibid.

67 Amadiume, *Male Daughters, Female Husbands: Gender and Sex*

in an African Society, 121, quoting George Basden, *Niger Ibos: A Description of the Primitive Life, Customs and Animistic Beliefs of the Ibo People of Nigeria* (London: Frank Cass, 1966 [1938]).

68 Ibid., 121.

Chapter 4

1. Armour, 'The BBC and the Development of Broadcasting in British Colonial Africa 1946–1956', 380.
2. MacKay, *Broadcasting in Nigeria*, 64.
3. Toyin Falola and Matthew Heaton, *A History of Nigeria* (Cambridge: Cambridge University Press, 2008), 158.
4. Ibid., 159.
5. Ibid.
6. Ibid.
7. Max Siollun, *Oil, Politics and Violence: Nigeria's Military Coup Culture (1966–1976)* (New York: Algora, 2009), 18.
8. Ibid., quoting a memorandum from Samuel E. Belk of National Security Council Staff to the President's Special Assistant for National Security Affairs, Washington, 30 December, 1964.
9. 'The Fragile Stability', *Time*, 21 January 1966.
10. Bernth Lindfors, 'Achebe's African Parable', *Presence Africaine: Revue Culturelle du Monde Noir/Cultural Review of the Negro World*, 66 (1968): 132, quoting Richard Harris, 'Nigeria: Crisis and Compromise', *Africa Report*, 10, no. 2 (1965).
11. *A Man of the People* (London: Heinemann, 1966), 147. Hereafter referred to in the text as *MP*.
12. Sklar, *Nigerian Political Parties: Power in an Emergent African Nation*, 118.
13. Achebe, 'The Novelist as Teacher', 44.
14. Ibid., 45, quoting Ezekiel Mphahlele, *The African Image* (London: Faber, 1962).
15. Lindfors, 'Achebe's African Parable', 132.
16. Achebe, 'The Novelist as Teacher', 44.
17. Frantz Fanon, *The Wretched of the Earth*, trans. Constance Farrington, Penguin Classics (London: Penguin, 1967), 188.
18. Ibid., 140.

19 Tony Hall, 'I Had to Write on the Chaos I Foresaw', in Bernth Lindfors (ed.), *Conversations with Chinua Achebe*, Literary Conversations Series (Lico) (Jackson, MS: University Press of Mississippi, 1997), 21.

20 Ibid., 22.

21 Ibid.

22 Fanon, *The Wretched of the Earth*, 166.

23 Ibid., 169.

24 Ibid., 175.

25 Ibid.

26 Chinua Achebe, *There Was a Country: A Personal History of Biafra* (London: Penguin, 2012), 57.

27 Lindfors, 'Achebe's African Parable', 132–3.

28 Ibid., 134.

29 Ibid.

30 Achebe, *There Was a Country: A Personal History of Biafra*, 79.

31 Ezenwa-Ohaeto, *Chinua Achebe: A Biography*, 109.

32 Ibid., 115.

33 Ibid., 116, quoting Peter Enahoro, 'Why I Left Nigeria', *Transition*, no. 3 (1968).

34 Ezenwa-Ohaeto, *Chinua Achebe: A Biography*, 116.

35 Ibid., 118.

36 Ibid.

37 Achebe, *There Was a Country: A Personal History of Biafra*, 69.

38 Ibid., 71.

39 Ibid., 82.

40 Ibid., 96.

41 Phia Steyn, 'Oil Exploration in Colonial Nigeria, c. 1903–58', *Journal of Imperial & Commonwealth History*, 37, no. 2 (2009).

42 Chinua Achebe, '1966', in *Beware Soul Brother* (London: Heinemann, 1972 [1971]).

43 Chinua Achebe, 'Agostinho Neto', in *Collected Poems* (Manchester: Carcanet, 2005), 11.

44 Chinua Achebe, 'Biafra, 1969', in *Collected Poems* (Manchester: Carcanet, 2005).

45 Achebe, *There Was a Country: A Personal History of Biafra*, 100.

46 George Thomson, unpublished letter to Dennis Healey, Secretary of State for Defence, 4 December 1967 (JM10/8 FCO25/251).

47 Michael Leapman, 'British Interests, Nigerian Tragedy', *Independent on Sunday*, 4 January 1998.

48 Ibid.

49 Ibid.

50 Maurice Foley, unpublished letter to John Morris at the Ministry of Defence, 22 January 1969 (DEFE 13/711).

51 John Morris, unpublished letter to Lord Malcolm Shepherd at the Foreign and Commonwealth Office, 13 November 1968 (E/P.O 163/68 DEFE 13/711).

52 Great Britain, Ministry of Defence records, 6 December 1968, ref. E/P.o. 215/68.

53 J. F. Mayne, confidential correspondence as Parliamentary Secretary to the Secretary of State for Defence, 14 November 1968 (FCO25/251).

54 Achebe, *There Was a Country: A Personal History of Biafra*, 193.

55 Ibid., 194.

56 Ibid., 200.

57 Ibid., 201.

58 Chinua Achebe, 'Vultures', in *Collected Poems* (Manchester: Carcanet, 2005).

59 Achebe, *There Was a Country: A Personal History of Biafra*, 210.

60 Ibid., 143–4.

61 Ibid., 144.

62 Chukwuemeka Odumegwu Ojukwu (attrib.), *The Ahiara Declaration: The Principles of the Biafran Revolution* (Geneva: Mark, 1969), 14.

63 Ibid., 11.

64 Ibid., 10.

65 Ibid., 16.

66 Ezenwa-Ohaeto, *Chinua Achebe: A Biography*, 140.

67 Chukwuma Azuonye, 'Reminiscences of the Odunke Community of Artists', *ALA Bulletin*, 17, no. 1 (1989): 23, quoted in Ezenwa-Ohaeto, *Chinua Achebe: A Biography*, 141.

68 Achebe, *There Was a Country: A Personal History of Biafra*, 151.
69 Ibid., 149.
70 Ojukwu, *The Ahiara Declaration: The Principles of the Biafran Revolution*, 23.
71 'Girls at War', in *Girls at War* (Oxford: Heinemann, 1972), 104. Hereafter referred to in the text as GW.
72 Ojukwu, *The Ahiara Declaration: The Principles of the Biafran Revolution*, 7.
73 Chinua Achebe and John Iroaganachi, *How the Leopard Got His Claws* (Somerville, MA: Candlewick, 2011 [1967]), n.p.
74 Ibid.
75 Ibid.
76 Achebe, *There Was a Country: A Personal History of Biafra*, 185.
77 Ibid.
78 Ibid., 52.
79 Fanon, *The Wretched of the Earth*, 120.
80 Ibid.
81 Ntieyong Udo Akpan, *The Struggle for Secession 1966–1970* (London: Frank Cass, 1976 [1971]), 157.
82 Ibid.
83 Achebe, *There Was a Country: A Personal History of Biafra*, 159.
84 Kalu Ogbaa, 'An Interview with Chinua Achebe', in Bernth Lindfors (ed.), *Conversations with Chinua Achebe*, Literary Conversations Series (Lico) (Jackson, MS: University Press of Mississippi, 1997), 71.
85 Onuora Ossie Enekwe, 'Interview with Chinua Achebe', in Bernth Lindfors (ed.), *Conversations with Chinua Achebe*, Literary Conversations Series (Lico) (Jackson, MS: University Press of Mississippi, 1997), 53.
86 Ibid.
87 Ibid., 54.

Chapter 5

1. Enekwe, 'Interview with Chinua Achebe', 53.
2. Innes, *Chinua Achebe*.
3. Ernest Gellner, *Nations and Nationalism* (Ithaca: Cornell University Press, 1983); Anderson, *Imagined Communities: Reflections on the Origin and Spread of Nationalism*.
4. Fanon, *The Wretched of the Earth*, 120.
5. Yousaf, *Chinua Achebe*, 90.
6. Achebe, *The Education of a British-Protected Child: Essays*, 185.
7. Ibid., 227.
8. Falola and Heaton, *A History of Nigeria*.
9. Ibid., 185.
10. Ibid., 181.
11. Ibid.
12. Afigbo, *Nigerian History, Politics and Affairs: The Collected Essays of Adielo Afigbo*, 438.
13. Tom Forrest, 'The Political Economy of Civil Rule and the Economic Crisis in Nigeria (1979–84)', *Review of African Political Economy*, no. 35 (1986): 5.
14. Ibid.
15. Ibid., 8.
16. Ibid.
17. Achebe, *The Trouble with Nigeria*, 19.
18. Ibid., 1.
19. Ibid., 3.
20. Ibid., 17.
21. Ezenwa-Ohaeto, *Chinua Achebe: A Biography*, 197.
22. Achebe, *The Trouble with Nigeria*, 63.
23. Federal Republic of Nigeria, *Official Gazette*, 71:18 (4 April 1984), quoted in Adegboyega Isaac Ajayi, *The Military and the Nigerian State 1966–1993: A Study of the Strategies of Political Power* (Trenton, NJ: Africa World Press, 2007), 98.
24. Daniel Jordan Smith, *A Culture of Corruption: Everyday Deception and Popular Discontent in Nigeria* (Princeton, NJ: Princeton University Press, 2007), 98.

25 Yousaf, *Chinua Achebe*, 90.
26 Mark Weston, *The Ringtone and the Drum: Travels in the World's Poorest Countries* (Alresford, Hants: Zero, 2012), 269.
27 Micheal Peel, *A Swamp Full of Dollars: Pipelines and Paramilitaries at Nigeria's Oil Frontier* (New York: Tauris, 2011), 48–9.
28 'Parcel Bomb Kills Nigerian Journalist Accused of Plotting', *New York Times*, 20 October 1986.
29 Nwando Achebe, *The Female King of Colonial Nigeria: Ahebi Ugbabe* (Bloomington, IN: Indiana University Press, 2011), 11.
30 'Death Toll at 15 in Nigerian Student Protest', Associated Press Report, International News, 26 May 1986.
31 Neil ten Kortenaar, '"Only Connect": *Anthills of the Savannah* and Achebe's Trouble with Nigeria', *Research in African Literatures*, 24, no. 3 (1993): 62.
32 Jerome Nwadike, *A Biafran Soldier's Survival from the Jaws of Death* (Bloomington, IN: Xlibris, 2010), 56.
33 Chinedu Agbodike, *The Hidden Truth* (Bloomington, IN: Authorhouse, 2004), 12.
34 Ibid.
35 Ibid.
36 Anderson, *Imagined Communities: Reflections on the Origin and Spread of Nationalism*.
37 Fanon, *The Wretched of the Earth*, 119.
38 Kortenaar, '"Only Connect": *Anthills of the Savannah* and Achebe's Trouble with Nigeria', 62–3, quoting Ernest Gellner, *Nations and Nationalism*, 124.
39 Nwakanma, *Christopher Okigbo: Thirsting for Sunlight 1930–1967*, 2.
40 Ibid.
41 Christopher Okigbo, *Heavensgate* (Ibadan: Mbari, 1962), 3.
42 Nwakanma, *Christopher Okigbo: Thirsting for Sunlight 1930–1967*, 2.
43 Krishnan, 'Mami Wata and the Occluded Feminine in Anglophone Nigerian-Igbo Literature', 4.
44 Ibid.
45 Wren, *Achebe's World: The Historical and Cultural Context of the Novels*, 86.

46 Elleke Boehmer, 'Of Goddesses and Stories: Gender and a New Politics in Achebe's *Anthills of the Savannah*', in Kirsten Holst Petersen and Anna Rutherford (eds), *Chinua Achebe: A Celebration*, Studies in African Literature (Safrl) (Oxford: Heinemann, 1990), 106.

47 Jane Wilkinson, 'Interview with Chinua Achebe', in Bernth Lindfors (ed.), *Conversations with Chinua Achebe*, Literary Conversations Series (Lico) (Jackson, MS: University Press of Mississippi, 1997), 150.

48 Kortenaar, '"Only Connect": *Anthills of the Savannah* and Achebe's Trouble with Nigeria', 68.

49 Ibid., 69.

50 Godfrey Mwakikagile, *Ethnic Politics in Kenya and Nigeria* (New York: Nova Science, 2001).

51 Achebe, *The Trouble with Nigeria*, 75.

52 Ibid., 7.

Chapter 6

1 Armour, 'The BBC and the Development of Broadcasting in British Colonial Africa 1946–1956', 395.

2 Chinua Achebe, *Home and Exile* (Edinburgh: Canongate, 2003 [2001]), 103.

3 Ibid., 103–4.

4 Ibid., 73.

5 Ibid., 74.

6 Ibid., 74–5.

7 Ibid., 78.

8 Ibid., 79–80.

9 Achebe, *The Education of a British-Protected Child: Essays*, 6.

10 Kirsten Holst Petersen, 'First Things First: Problems of a Feminist Approach to African Literature', *Kunapipi*, 6, no. 3 (1984): 38.

11 Florence Stratton, *Contemporary African Literature and the Politics of Gender* (London: Routledge, 1994), 35.

12 Nwando Achebe, 'Balancing Male and Female Principles: Teaching About Gender in Chinua Achebe's *Things Fall Apart*', *Ufahamu: African Studies Journal*, 29, no. 1 (2001): 126.

13 Ibid., 128.
14 Ibid., 130.
15 Ibid.
16 Nwando Achebe, *The Female King of Colonial Nigeria: Ahebi Ugbabe*, 24.
17 Leith-Ross, *African Women: A Study of the Ibo of Nigeria*.
18 Ian McEwan, 'Or Shall We Die?', in *A Move Abroad* (London: Picador, 1983), 23.
19 Ojukwu, *The Ahiara Declaration: The Principles of the Biafran Revolution*, 14.
20 Achebe, *The Trouble with Nigeria*, 5.
21 Ibid.
22 Ibid., 6–7.
23 Achebe, *The Education of a British-Protected Child: Essays*, 5.
24 Yousaf, *Chinua Achebe*, 2.
25 Gikandi, *Reading Chinua Achebe: Language and Ideology in Fiction*.
26 Yousaf, *Chinua Achebe*, 4.
27 Achebe, 'The Novelist as Teacher', 45.
28 Anderson, *Imagined Communities: Reflections on the Origin and Spread of Nationalism*, 113.
29 Fanon, *The Wretched of the Earth*, 196–7.
30 Gikandi, *Reading Chinua Achebe: Language and Ideology in Fiction*, 8.
31 Ojukwu, *The Ahiara Declaration: The Principles of the Biafran Revolution*, 42–3.
32 Yousaf, *Chinua Achebe*, 4.
33 Achebe, *The Education of a British-Protected Child: Essays*, 5–6.
34 Ibid., 5.

Select bibliography

Works by Achebe

Things Fall Apart (London: Heinemann, 1958).
No Longer at Ease (London: Heinemann, 1960).
The Sacrificial Egg and Other Stories (Onitsha: Etudo, 1962).
Arrow of God (London: Heinemann, 1964).
'English and the African Writer', *Transition*, 4, no. 18 (1965): 27–30.
'The Black Writer's Burden', *Presence Africaine*, 59 (1966): 135–40.
Chike and the River (New York: Cambridge University Press, 1966).
A Man of the People (London: Heinemann, 1966).
Achebe, Chinua, and John Iroaganachi, *How the Leopard Got His Claws* (Enugu: Nwamife, 1972; Somerville, MA: Candlewick, 2011).
'Culture and International Understanding', *Daily Times*, 22 May (1971): 7.
The Insider: Stories of War and Peace from Nigeria (Enugu: Nwankwo-Ifejika, 1971).
Beware Soul Brother: Poems (Enugu: Nwankwo-Ifejika, 1971; African Writers Series: 120, London: Heinemann, 1972).
'Girls at War', in *Girls at War* (Oxford: Heinemann, 1972), 103–23.
'This Earth, My Brother', *Transition*, 41 (1972): 69–70.
Christmas in Biafra, and Other Poems (New York: Anchor, 1973).
Morning Yet on Creation Day: Essays (London: Heinemann, 1975).
The Drum: A Children's Story (Enugu: Fourth Dimension, 1977).
The Flute: A Children's Story (Enugu: Fourth Dimension, 1977).
Achebe, Chinua, and Dubem Okafor, *Don't Let Him Die: An Anthology of Memorial Poems for Christopher Okigbo (1932–1967)* (Enugu: Fourth Dimension, 1978).
'The Bane of Union: An Appraisal of the Consequences of Union Igbo for Igbo Language and Literature', *Anu*, 1 (1979): 33–41.
'Metaphor of the Rain and the Clock', *Daily Times* 10 November (1979): 7.
Achebe, Chinua and Arthur Ravenscroft, 'The Uses of African Litera-

ture', *Okike*, 15 (1979): 8–17.

'Why Writers Need an Association', *West Africa*, 3339 (1981): 1692–94.

'The Okike Story', *Okike: An African Journal of New Writing*, 21 (1982): 1–5.

The Trouble with Nigeria (Enugu: Fourth Dimension, 1983; Oxford: Heinemann, 1984).

Achebe, Chinua, and C. L. Innes (eds), *African Short Stories* (London: Heinemann, 1984).

Anthills of the Savannah (London: Heinemann, 1987; London: Penguin, 2001).

Hopes and Impediments: Selected Essays (London: Heinemann, 1988; New York: Anchor, 1990).

Achebe, Chinua, and C. L. Innes (eds), *The Heinemann Book of Contemporary African Short Stories* (London: Heinemann, 1992).

Achebe, Chinua and Robert Lyons, *Another Africa* (New York: Anchor, 1998).

'Africa Is People', *Massachusetts Review: A Quarterly of Literature, the Arts and Public Affairs*, 40, no. 3 (1999): 313–21.

Home and Exile (New York: Anchor, 2001; Edinburgh: Canongate, 2003).

'The Day I Finally Met Baldwin', *Callaloo*, 25, no. 2 (2002): 502–4.

Collected Poems (Manchester: Carcanet, 2005).

The Education of a British-Protected Child: Essays (London: Penguin, 2009).

There Was a Country: A Personal History of Biafra (London: Penguin, 2012).

Criticism and interviews

Abah, Okwute J., '*Anthills of the Savannah*: A Historical Mythology', *Literary Griot*, 4, no. 1–2 (1992): 126–37.

Achebe, Chinua, and Nuruddin Farah, *Chinua Achebe with Nuruddin Farah, Writers in Conversation* (London: ICA, 1986; videorecording, 1 DVD (40 mins.): sd., col.).

Achebe, Nwando, 'Balancing Male and Female Principles: Teaching About Gender in Chinua Achebe's *Things Fall Apart*', *Ufahamu: African Studies Journal*, 29, no. 1 (2001): 121–43.

Acholonu, Rose, 'Outsiders or Insiders?: Women in *Anthills of the Savannah*', in Edith Ihekweazu and Ernest N. Emenyonu (eds), *Eagle on Iroko* (Ibadan, Nigeria: Heinemann, 1996), 311–21.

Adeeko, Adeleke, 'Contests of Text and Context in Chinua Achebe's *Arrow of God*', *ARIEL: A Review of International English Literature*, 23, no. 2 (1992): 7–22.

Aji, Aron, and Kristin Lynne Ellsworth, 'Ezinma: The Ogbanje Child

in Achebe's *Things Fall Apart*', *College Literature*, 19–20, no. 3–1 (1992): 170–5.
Amadiume, Ifi, 'Class and Gender in *Anthills of the Savannah*', *Okike*, no. 30 (1990): 147–57.
Anyadike, Chima, 'Duality and Resilience in Chinua Achebe's *Things Fall Apart*', *Philosophia Africana: Analysis of Philosophy and Issues in Africa and the Black Diaspora*, 10, no. 1 (2007): 49–58.
Awuyah, Chris Kwame, 'Chinua Achebe's *Arrow of God*: Ezeulu's Response to Change', *College Literature*, 19–20, no. 3–1 (1992): 214–19.
Begam, Richard, 'Achebe's Sense of an Ending: History and Tragedy in *Things Fall Apart*', *Studies in the Novel*, 29, no. 3 (1997): 396–411.
Bloom, Harold (ed.), *Chinua Achebe's Things Fall Apart: Modern Critical Interpretations* (Philadelphia: Chelsea House, 2001).
Boehmer, Elleke, 'Of Goddesses and Stories: Gender and a New Politics in Achebe's *Anthills of the Savannah*', in Kirsten Holst Petersen and Anna Rutherford (eds), *Chinua Achebe: A Celebration*, Studies in African Literature (Safrl) (Oxford: Heinemann, 1990), 102–12.
Bonetti, Kay, 'An Interview with Chinua Achebe', *The Missouri Review*, 12, no. 1 (1989): 62–83.
Booker, M. Keith, *The Chinua Achebe Encyclopedia* (Westport, CT: Greenwood, 2003).
Brown, Hugh R., 'Igbo Words for the Non-Igbo: Achebe's Artistry in *Arrow of God*', *Research in African Literatures*, 12, no. 1 (1981): 69–85.
Carroll, David, *Chinua Achebe* (London and New York: Macmillan/St Martin's, 1980).
Cobham, Rhonda, 'Making Men and History: Achebe and the Politics of Revisionism', in Bernth Lindfors (ed.), *Approaches to Teaching Achebe's Things Fall Apart*, Approaches to Teaching World Literature: 37 (New York: Modern Language Association of America, 1991), 91–100.
—— 'Problems of Gender and History in the Teaching of *Things Fall Apart*', *Matatu: Journal for African Culture and Society*, 7 (1990): 25–39.
Criswell, Stephen, 'Colonialism, Corruption and Culture: A Fanonian Reading of *Mister Johnson* and *No Longer at Ease*', *Literary Griot*, 10, no. 1 (1998): 43–64.
—— 'Okonkwo as Yeatsian Hero: The Influence of W. B. Yeats on Chinua Achebe's *Things Fall Apart*', *Literary Criterion*, 30, no. 4 (1995): 1–14.
Davis, Richard S, 'In Search of Agency among Colonized Africans: Chinua Achebe's *No Longer at Ease* and Joyce Cary's *Mister Johnson*', *Journal of Commonwealth and Postcolonial Studies*, 2,

no. 1 (1994): 12–26.

Diala, Isidore, 'Mediating Mythology, Mollifying Women: Achebe's *Anthills of the Savannah*', *Ufahamu: African Studies Journal*, 30, no. 2–3 (2004): 147–67.

Diala, Okeawolam Isidore, 'Mythic Mediation and Feminism: Achebe's *Anthills of the Savannah*', *ARIEL: A Review of International English Literature*, 36, no. 3–4 (2005): 185–202.

Ehling, Holger, G. (ed.), *Critical Approaches to Anthills of the Savannah* (Amsterdam: Rodopi, 1991).

Eko, Ebele, 'Chinua Achebe and His Critics: Reception of His Novels in English and American Reviews', *Studies in Black Literature*, 6, no. 3 (1975): 14–20.

Ekwe-Ekwe, Herbert, *African Literature in Defence of History: An Essay on Chinua Achebe* (Dakar: African Renaissance, 2001).

Emenyonu, Ernest N., *Emerging Perspectives on Chinua Achebe. Volume 1. Omenka the Master Artist: Critical Perspectives on Achebe's Fiction* (Trenton, NJ: Africa World Press, 2004).

Emenyonu, Ernest N., and Iniobong I. Uko, *Emerging Perspectives on Chinua Achebe, Volume 2: Isinka, the Artistic Purpose: Chinua Achebe and the Theory of African Literature* (Trenton, NJ: Africa World Press, 2004).

Enekwe, Onuora Ossie, 'Interview with Chinua Achebe', in Bernth Lindfors (ed.), *Conversations with Chinua Achebe*, Literary Conversations Series (Lico) (Jackson, MS: University Press of Mississippi, 1997), 52–6.

Fabre, Michel, 'Chinua Achebe on *Arrow of God*', in Bernth Lindfors (ed.), *Conversations with Chinua Achebe*, Literary Conversations Series (Lico) (Jackson, MS: University Press of Mississippi, 1997), 45–51.

García Ramírez, Paula, 'Women in Achebe's Short Stories: Akueke, Veronica and Gladys', in *Proceedings of the 20th International Aedean Conference*, ed. P. Guardia and J. Stone (Barcelona, Spain: Universitat de Barcelona, 1997), 467–72.

Gates, Henry L., and Kwame A. Appiah (eds), *Chinua Achebe: Critical Perspectives Past and Present* (New York: Amistad, 1997).

Gikandi, Simon, 'Chinua Achebe and the Invention of African Culture', *Research in African Literatures*, 32, no. 3 (2001): 3–8.

—— 'Chinua Achebe and the Post-Colonial Esthetic: Writing, Identity, and National Formation', *Studies in Twentieth Century Literature*, 15, no. 1 (1991): 29–41.

—— 'Chinua Achebe and the Signs of the Times', in Bernth Lindfors (ed.), *Approaches to Teaching Achebe's Things Fall Apart*, Approaches to Teaching World Literature: 37 (New York: Modern Language Association of America, 1991), 25–30.

―― 'Fifty Years of Things Fall Apart (1958)', *Wasafiri: The Magazine of International Contemporary Writing*, 24, no. 3 [59] (2009): 4–7.

―― *Reading Chinua Achebe: Language and Ideology in Fiction*, Studies in African Literature (Safrl) (London: James Currey, 1991).

Griffiths, Gareth, 'Language and Action in the Novels of Chinua Achebe', *African Literature Today*, 5 (1971): 88–105.

Hall, Tony, 'I Had to Write on the Chaos I Foresaw', in Bernth Lindfors (ed.), *Conversations with Chinua Achebe*, Literary Conversations Series (Lico) (Jackson, MS: University Press of Mississippi, 1997), 18–26.

Hoegberg, David, 'Principle and Practice: The Logic of Cultural Violence in Achebe's *Things Fall Apart*', *College Literature*, 26, no. 1 (1999): 69-79.

Ibironke, Olabode, 'Chinua Achebe and the Political Imperative of the African Writer', *Journal of Commonwealth Literature*, 36, no. 1 (2001): 75.

Ihekweazu, Edith, and Ernest N. Emenyonu, *Eagle on Iroko: Selected Papers from the Chinua Achebe International Symposium, 1990* (Ibadan, Nigeria: Heinemann, 1996).

Ikegami, Robin, 'Knowledge and Power, the Story and the Storyteller: Achebe's *Anthills of the Savannah*', *Modern Fiction Studies*, 37, no. 3 (1991): 493–507.

Innes, C. L., *Chinua Achebe* (Cambridge: Cambridge University Press, 1990).

―― 'A Source for *Arrow of God*: A Response', *Research in African Literatures*, 9 (1978): 16–18.

Innes, C. L., and Bernth Lindfors. *Critical Perspectives on Chinua Achebe* (Washington, D.C.: Three Continents, 1978).

Innes, Lyn, 'Chinua Achebe and the Creation of a Democratic Novel', *Matatu: Journal for African Culture and Society*, 33 (2006): 195–7.

Iyasere, Solomon O. (ed.), *Understanding Things Fall Apart: Selected Essays and Criticism* (New York: Whitson, 1998).

Jabbi, Bu-Buakei, 'Myth and Ritual in *Arrow of God*', *African Literature Today*, 11 (1980): 130–48.

JanMohamed, Abdul, 'Sophisticated Primitivism: The Syncretism of Oral and Literate Modes in Achebe's *Things Fall Apart*', *ARIEL: A Review of International English Literature*, 15, no. 4 (1984): 19–39.

Jeyifo, Biodun, 'An African Cultural Modernity: Achebe, Fanon, Cabral, and the Philosophy of Decolonization', *Socialism & Democracy*, 21, no. 3 (2007): 125–41.

―― 'Okonkwo and His Mother: *Things Fall Apart* and Issues of Gender in the Constitution of African Postcolonial Discourse', *Callaloo*, 16, no. 4 (1993): 847–58.

Jua, Roselyne M., '*Things Fall Apart* and Achebe's Search for Manhood',

Interventions: International Journal of Postcolonial Studies, 11, no. 2 (2009): 199–202.

Kalu, Anthonia C., 'Achebe and Duality in Igbo Thought', *Literary Griot: International Journal of Black Expressive Cultural Studies*, 10, no. 2 (1998): 17–33.

—— 'The Priest/Artist Tradition in Achebe's *Arrow of God*', *Africa Today*, 41, no. 2 (1994): 51–62.

Kanaganayakam, Chelva, 'Art and Orthodoxy in Chinua Achebe's *Anthills of the Savannah*', *ARIEL: A Review of International English Literature*, 24, no. 4 (1993): 35–51.

Khayyoom, S. A., *Chinua Achebe: A Study of His Novels* (London: Sangam, 1999).

Killam, G. D., *The Novels of Chinua Achebe* (London and New York: Heinemann/Africana Pub. Corp., 1969).

—— *The Writings of Chinua Achebe* (London: Heinemann, 1977).

Kortenaar, Neil ten, 'Beyond Authenticity and Creolization: Reading Achebe Writing Culture', *PMLA: Publications of the Modern Language Association of America*, 110, no. 1 (1995): 30–42.

—— 'Chinua Achebe and the Question of Modern African Tragedy,' *Philosophia Africana*, 9, no. 2 (2006): 83–100.

—— 'How the Centre Is Made to Hold in *Things Fall Apart*', *English Studies in Canada*, 17, no. 3 (1991): 319–36.

—— '"Only Connect": *Anthills of the Savannah* and Achebe's Trouble with Nigeria', *Research in African Literatures*, 24, no. 3 (1993): 59–72.

—— 'Things Fall Apart in History', *Interventions: International Journal of Postcolonial Studies*, 11, no. 2 (2009): 166–70.

Lindfors, Bernth, 'Achebe at Home and Abroad: Situating *Things Fall Apart*', *Literary Griot*, 10, no. 2 (1998): 10–16.

—— 'Achebe's African Parable', *Presence Africaine*, 66 (1968): 130–6.

—— *Approaches to Teaching Achebe's Things Fall Apart*, Approaches to Teaching World Literature: 37 (New York: Modern Language Association of America, 1991).

—— 'A Checklist of Works by and About Chinua Achebe', *Obsidian: Black Literature in Review*, 4, no. 1 (1978): 103–17.

—— 'Chinua Achebe: Novelist of Cultural Conflict', *America*, 175, no. 2 (1996): 23–5.

—— (ed.), *Conversations with Chinua Achebe*, Literary Conversations Series (Lico) (Jackson, MS: University Press of Mississippi, 1997).

—— *Early Achebe* (Trenton, NJ: Africa World Press, 2009).

—— 'Popular Literature for an African Elite', *Journal of Modern African Studies*, 12, no. 3 (1974): 471–86.

Lindfors, Bernth, and Bala Kothandaraman, *South Asian Responses to*

Chinua Achebe (New Delhi: Prestige, 1993).

Machila, Blaise N., 'Ambiguity in Achebe's *Arrow of God*', *Kunapipi*, 3, no. 1 (1981): 119–33.

MacKenzie, Clayton G., 'The Metamorphosis of Piety in Chinua Achebe's *Things Fall Apart*', *Research in African Literatures*, 27, no. 2 (1996): 128–38.

Marcus, James, 'Achebe: *Anthills of the Savannah*. Tyrant's Gambit', *Nation*, 246, no. 15 (1988): 540–1.

Mathuray, Mark, 'Realizing the Sacred: Power and Meaning in Chinua Achebe's *Arrow of God*', *Research in African Literatures*, 34, no. 3 (2003): 46–65.

McLaren, Joseph, 'Missionaries and Converts: Religion and Colonial Intrusion in *Things Fall Apart*', *Literary Griot*, 10, no. 2 (1998): 48–60.

McLeod, John. *Beginning Postcolonialism* (2nd edn) (Manchester: Manchester University Press, 2010).

Moore, David Chioni, and Analee Heath, 'A Conversation with Chinua Achebe', *Transition: An International Review*, 100 (2009): 12–33.

Moore, Gerald, 'Chinua Achebe: A Retrospective', *Research in African Literatures*, 32, no. 3 (2001): 29–32.

Morrison, Jago, 'Chinua Achebe's *A Man of the People*: The Novel and the Public Sphere', in Jago Morrison and Susan Watkins (eds), *Scandalous Fictions: The Twentieth-Century Novel in the Public Sphere* (Basingstoke: Palgrave Macmillan, 2006), 117–35.

—— *The Fiction of Chinua Achebe*, Readers' Guides to Essential Criticism (Basingstoke and New York: Palgrave Macmillan, 2007).

Moses, Michael Valdez, *The Novel and the Globalization of Culture* (New York: Oxford University Press, 1995).

Munro, Ian H., 'Textual Dynamics in Chinua Achebe's *Home and Exile* and *No Longer at Ease*', *International Fiction Review*, 31, no. 1–2 (2004): 54–64.

Muoneke, Romanus Okey, *Art, Rebellion and Redemption: A Reading of the Novels of Chinua Achebe* (New York: Peter Lang, 1994).

Newell, Stephanie, *West African Literatures: Ways of Reading* (Oxford: Oxford University Press, 2006).

Njoku, Benedict Chiaka, *The Four Novels of Chinua Achebe: A Critical Study* (New York: Peter Lang, 1984).

Nkosi, Lewis, and Wole Soyinka, 'Conversation with Chinua Achebe', in Bernth Lindfors (ed.), *Conversations with Chinua Achebe*, Literary Conversations Series (Lico) (Jackson, MS: University Press of Mississippi, 1997), 11–17.

Nnolim, Charles, 'The Artist in Search of the Right Leadership: Achebe as a Social Critic', in Edith Ihekweazu and Ernest N. Emenyonu (eds), *Eagle on Iroko* (Ibadan, Nigeria: Heinemann,

1996), 166–77.
—— 'A Source for Arrow of God', *Research in African Literatures*, 8 (1977): 1–26.
Nwagbara, Uzoechi, 'Changing the Canon: Chinua Achebe's Women, the Public Sphere and the Politics of Inclusion in Nigeria', *Journal of International Women's Studies*, 11, no. 2 (2009): 175–90.
Nwoga, Donatus I., 'Achebe's Vision of a New Africa', in Edith Ihekweazu and Ernest N. Emenyonu (eds), *Eagle on Iroko* (Ibadan, Nigeria: Heinemann, 1996), 152–65.
Obi, Joe, 'A Critical Reading of the Disillusionment Novel,' *Journal of Black Studies*, 20, no. 4 (1990): 399–413.
Ogbaa, Kalu, 'Death in African Literature: The Example of Chinua Achebe', *World Literature Written in English*, 20, no. 2 (1981): 201–13.
—— *Gods Oracles and Divination: Folkways in Chinua Achebe's Novels* (Trenton, NJ: Africa World Press, 1992).
—— 'An Interview with Chinua Achebe', in Bernth Lindfors (ed.), *Conversations with Chinua Achebe*, Literary Conversations Series (Lico) (Jackson, MS: University Press of Mississippi, 1997), 64–75.
—— 'Names and Naming in Chinua Achebe's Novels', *Names: A Journal of Onomastics*, 28, no. 4 (1980): 267–89.
—— 'Of Governance, Revolutions, and Victims: Achebe and Literary Activism in Anthills of the Savannah', in Kalu Ogbaa (ed.), *The Gong and the Flute: African Literary Development and Celebration* (Westport, CT: Greenwood, 1994), 129–47.
—— (ed.), *Understanding Things Fall Apart: A Student Casebook to Issues, Sources, and Historical Documents* (Westport, CT: Greenwood, 1999).
Ogede, Ode, *Achebe and the Politics of Representation: Form against Itself, from Colonial Conquest and Occupation to Post-Independence Disillusionment* (Trenton, NJ: Africa World Press, 2001).
—— *Achebe's Things Fall Apart* (New York: Continuum, 2007).
—— 'Oral Tradition and Modern Storytelling: Revisiting Chinua Achebe's Short Stories', *International Fiction Review*, 28, no. 1–2 (2001): 67–77.
Ogu, Julius, 'The Concept of Madness in Chinua Achebe's Writings', *Journal of Commonwealth Literature*, 18 (1983): 48–54.
Ogwude, Sophia O., 'Achebe on the Woman Question', *Literary Griot*, 13, no. 1–2 (2001): 62–9.
Ojinmah, Umelo, 'The Man Behind the Priest in Arrow of God', in Ernest N. Emenyonu (ed.), *Emerging Perspectives on Chinua Achebe. Volume 1. Omenka the Master Artist: Critical Perspectives on Achebe's Fiction* (Trenton, NJ: Africa World Press, 2004), 207–16.
Okechukwu, Chinwe Christiana, *Achebe the Orator: The Art of Persua-*

sion in Chinua Achebe's Novels (Westport, CT: Greenwood, 2001).
—— 'Oratory and Social Responsibility: Chinua Achebe's *Arrow of God'*, *Callaloo*, 25, no. 2 (2002): 567–83.
Okpewho, Isidore (ed.), *Chinua Achebe's Things Fall Apart: A Casebook* (Oxford: Oxford University Press, 2003).
Olaniyan, Tejumola, 'Chinua Achebe and an Archaeology of the Postcolonial African State', *Research in African Literatures*, 32, no. 3 (2001): 22–9.
Omotoso, Kole, *Achebe or Soyinka? A Re-Interpretation and a Study in Contrasts* (Oxford: Zell, 1994).
Osei-Nyame, Kwadwo, 'Chinua Achebe Writing Culture: Representations of Gender and Tradition in *Things Fall Apart'*, *Research in African Literatures*, 30, no. 2 (1999): 148–64.
—— 'Gender and the Narrative of Identity in Chinua Achebe's *Arrow of God'*, *Commonwealth Essays and Studies*, 22, no. 2 (2000): 25–34.
—— 'Gender, Nationalism and the Fictions of Identity in Chinua Achebe's *A Man of the People'*, *Commonwealth Novel in English*, 9–10 (2001): 242–62.
Palmer, Eustace, *An Introduction to the African Novel: A Critical Study of Twelve Books by Chinua Achebe, James Ngugi, Camara Laye, Elechi Amadi, Ayi Kwei Armah Mongo Beti and Gabriel Okara* (London: Heinemann, 1972).
Parker, Michael, and Roger Starkey, *Postcolonial Literatures: Achebe, Ngugi, Desai, Walcott* (New York: St Martin's, 1995).
Petersen, Kirsten Holst, 'First Things First: Problems of a Feminist Approach to African Literature', *Kunapipi*, 6, no. 3 (1984): 35–47.
Petersen, Kirsten Holst, and Anna Rutherford (eds), *Chinua Achebe: A Celebration*, Studies in African Literature (Safrl) (Oxford: Heinemann, 1990).
Ravenscroft, Arthur, *Chinua Achebe*, Writers and Their Work: 209 (Essex: Longmans, Green, 1969).
Reddy, Indrasena, *The Novels of Acheb and Ngūgū: A Study in the Dialectics of Commitment* (New Delhi: Prestige, 1994).
Rogers, Philip, '*No Longer at Ease*: Chinua Achebe's "Heart of Whiteness"', in Michael Parker and Roger Starkey (eds), *Postcolonial Literatures: Achebe, Ngugi, Desai, Walcott* (New York: St Martin's, 1995), 53–63.
Sabor, Peter, '"Structural Weaknesses" and Stylistic Revisions in Achebe's *Arrow of God'*, *Research in African Literatures*, 10 (1979): 375–9.
Samway, P. H., 'An Interview with Chinua Achebe', *America*, 164 (1991): 684–6.
Scafe, Suzanne, '"Wherever Something Stands, Something Else Will Stand Beside It": Ambivalence in Achebe's *Things Fall Apart* and

Arrow of God', *Changing English*, 9, no. 2 (2002): 119–31.
Serumaga, Robert, 'Chinua Achebe Interviewed', *Cultural Events in Africa*, 28 (1967): 1–4.
Simola, Raisa, *World Views in Chinua Achebe's Works* (Frankfurt am Main: Peter Lang, 1995).
Stratton, Florence, *Contemporary African Literature and the Politics of Gender* (London: Routledge, 1994).
Taiwo, Oladele, *Culture and the Nigerian Novel* (New York: St. Martins, 1976).
Thiongo, Ngũgũ wa, *Homecoming: Essays on African and Carribean Literature* (London: Heinemann, 1972).
Udumukwu, Onyemaechi, 'Achebe and the Negation of Independence', *Modern Fiction Studies*, 37, no. 3 (1991): 471–91.
—— 'Ideology and the Dialectics of Action: Achebe and Iyayi', *Research in African Literatures*, 27, no. 3 (1996): 34–49.
—— 'Language Games in the Post-Colonial Narrative: Achebe's *Arrow of God'*, *Neohelicon*, 21, no. 2 (1994): 235–59.
—— 'Reading Ideology in the Nigerian Novel: *Things Fall Apart* and *Sozaboy'*, *Literary Griot*, 10, no. 1 (1998): 65–88.
Ugah, Ada, *In the Beginning: Chinua Achebe at Work* (Ibadan: Heinemann, 1990).
Whitaker, David, and Msiska Mpalive-Hangson, *Chinua Achebe's Things Fall Apart* (Abingdon: Routledge, 2007).
Wilkinson, Jane, 'Interview with Chinua Achebe', in Bernth Lindfors (ed.), *Conversations with Chinua Achebe*, Literary Conversations Series (Lico) (Jackson, MS: University Press of Mississippi, 1997), 141–54.
Witte, Arnd, '*Things Fall Apart*: The Portrayal of African Identity in Joyce Cary's Mister Johnson and Chinua Achebe's *No Longer at Ease'*, in Anthony Coulson and Eda Sagarra (eds), *Exiles and Migrants: Crossing Thresholds in European Culture and Society* (Brighton, England: Sussex Academic, 1997), 126–35.
Wolfe, Andrea Powell, 'Problematizing Polygamy in the Historical Novels of Chinua Achebe: The Role of the Western Feminist Scholar', in Harold Bloom (ed.), *Chinua Achebe's Things Fall Apart: Bloom's Modern Critical Interpretations* (New York: Infobase, 2010), 153–76.
Wren, Robert M., 'Achebe's Odili: Hero and Clown', *Literary Half-Yearly*, 21, no. 1 (1980): 30–9.
—— 'Achebe's Revisions of *Arrow of God'*, *Research in African Literatures*, 7 (1976): 53–8.
—— *Achebe's World: The Historical and Cultural Context of the Novels* (Washington: Three Continents, 1980).
—— 'From Ulu to Christ: The Transfer of Faith in Chinua Achebe's

Arrow of God', *Christianity and Literature*, 27, no. 2 (1978): 28–40.
—— 'Mister Johnson and the Complexity of *Arrow of God*', in C. D. Narasimhaiah (ed.), *Awakened Conscience: Studies in Commonwealth Literature* (New Delhi: Sterling, 1978), 50–62.
Yousaf, Nahem, *Chinua Achebe* (Tavistock, Devon: Northcote House, 2003).

Further reading

Achara, D. N., *Ala Bingo* (London: Longman, 1958).
Achebe, Nwando, *The Female King of Colonial Nigeria: Ahebi Ugbabe* (Bloomington, IN: Indiana University Press, 2011).
Afigbo, Adielo, *The Abolition of the Slave Trade in Southeastern Nigeria, 1885–1950*. Rochester Studies in African History and the Diaspora (Rochester, NY: University of Rochester Press, 2006).
—— *Nigerian History, Politics and Affairs: The Collected Essays of Adielo Afigbo*, ed. Toyin Falola (Trenton, NJ: Africa World Press, 2005).
—— *The Warrant Chiefs: Indirect Rule in Southeastern Nigeria, 1891–1929*, Ibadan History Series (New York: Humanities, 1972).
Agbodike, Chinedu, *The Hidden Truth* (Bloomington, IN: Authorhouse, 2004).
Agbogu, Arinze E., 'Ogidi Before 1891: A Brief Survey of the Origins, Migration, Settlement, and Intergroup Relations', unpublished research project, mimeographed (University of Nigeria, Nsukka, 1976).
Ajayi, Adegboyega Isaac, *The Military and the Nigerian State 1966–1993: A Study of the Strategies of Political Power* (Trenton, NJ: Africa World Press, 2007).
Akpan, Ntieyong Udo, *The Struggle for Secession 1966–1970* (London: Frank Cass, 1976 [1971]).
Amadiume, Ifi, *Male Daughters, Female Husbands: Gender and Sex in an African Society* (London: Zed, 1987).
—— *Re-Inventing Africa: Matriarchy, Religion, and Culture* (London: Zed Books, 1997).
Anderson, Benedict, *Imagined Communities: Reflections on the Origin and Spread of Nationalism*, revised edn (London: Routledge, 1991).
Armour, Charles, 'The BBC and the Development of Broadcasting in British Colonial Africa 1946-1956', *African Affairs*, 83, no. 332 (1984): 359–402.
Azikiwe, Nnamdi, *Zik: A Selection from the Speeches of Nnamdi Azikiwe* (London: Cambridge Univeristy Press, 1961).
Barnett, Clive, 'Disseminating Africa: Burdens of Representation and the

African Writers Series', *New Formations*, no. 57 (2005–6): 74–94.
Basden, George, *Among the Ibos of Nigeria: An Account of the Curious and Interesting Habits, Customs and Beliefs of a Little Known African People by One Who Has for Many Years Lived Amongst Them on Close & Intimate Terms* (London: Frank Cass, 1966 [1921]).
—— *Niger Ibos: A Description of the Primitive Life, Customs and Animistic Beliefs of the Ibo People of Nigeria* (London: Frank Cass, 1966 [1938]).
Chuku, Gloria, *Igbo Women and Economic Transformation in Southeastern Nigeria 1900–1960* (New York: Routledge, 2005).
Currey, James, *Africa Writes Back: The African Writers Series and the Launch of African Literature* (Oxford: James Currey, 2008).
Diamond, Larry, *Class, Ethnicity and Democracy in Nigeria: The Failure of the First Republic* (Syracuse: Syracuse University Press, 1998).
—— 'Fiction as Political Thought'. *African Affairs*, 88, no. 352 (1989): 435–45.
Dike, K. Onwuka, *Trade and Politics in the Niger Delta, 1830–1885* (Oxford: Clarendon, 1956).
Ekechi, F. K., *Missionary Enterprise & Rivalry in Igboland 1857–1914* (London: Frank Cass, 1971).
Ekwensi, Cyprian, *People of the City* (London: Longman, 1954).
—— *When Love Whispers* (Yaba: Chuks, 1948).
Enahoro, Peter, 'Why I Left Nigeria', *Transition*, no. 3 (1968): 27–30.
Ezenwa-Ohaeto, *Chinua Achebe: A Biography* (Oxford, England and Bloomington, IN: James Currey/Indiana University Press, 1997).
Falola, Toyin (ed.), *African Wirters and Their Readers: Essays in in Honor of Bernth Lindfors* (Trenton, NJ: Africa World Press, 2002).
—— *Colonialism and Violence in Nigeria* (Bloomington, IN: Indiana University Press, 2009).
—— *Nationalism and African Intellectuals* (Rochester, NY: University of Rochester Press, 2001).
Falola, Toyin, and Saheed Aderinto, *Nigeria, Nationalism, and Writing History* (Rochester, NY: University of Rochester Press, 2010).
Falola, Toyin, and Matthew Heaton, *A History of Nigeria* (Cambridge: Cambridge University Press, 2008).
Fanon, Frantz, *Black Skin, White Masks* (New York: Grove, 1967).
—— *The Wretched of the Earth* [*Les damnés de la terre*], trans. Constance Farrington (London: Penguin, 1967 [1961]).
Forrest, Tom, 'The Political Economy of Civil Rule and the Economic Crisis in Nigeria (1979–84)', *Review of African Political Economy*, no. 35 (1986): 4–26.
Green, Margaret Mackeson, *Igbo Village Affairs* (London: Frank Cass, 1964).
Hill, Alan, *In Pursuit of Publishing* (London: Heinemann, 1988).

Ike, Vincent Chukwuemeka, *Sunset at Dawn : A Novel About Biafra* (London: Collins and Harvill, 1976).
Kehinde, Ayo, 'Rulers against Writers, Writers against Rulers: The Failed Promise of the Public Sphere in Postcolonial Nigerian Fiction', *Matatu: Journal for African Culture and Society*, 39 (2011): 221–51.
Krishnan, Madhu, 'Mami Wata and the Occluded Feminine in Anglophone Nigerian-Igbo Literature', *Research in African Literatures*, 43, no. 1 (2012): 1–18.
Leith-Ross, Sylvia, *African Women: A Study of the Ibo of Nigeria* (London: Faber and Faber, 1939).
Lindfors, Bernth, 'A Checklist of Works by and about Chinua Achebe', *Obsidian: Black Literature in Review*, 4, no. 1 (1978): 103–17.
Lindfors, Bernth, and Bala Kothandaraman, 'A Checklist of Indian Scholarship on Achebe', in Bernth Lindfors and Bala Kothandaraman (eds), *South Asian Responses to Chinua Achebe* (New Delhi: Prestige, 1993), 185–98.
Low, Gail, 'The Natural Artist: Publishing Amos Tutuola's *The Palm Wine Drinkard* in Postwar Britain', *Research in African Literatures*, 37, no. 4 (2006): 15–33.
MacKay, Ian, *Broadcasting in Nigeria* (Ibadan: Ibadan University Press, 1964).
Mathuray, Mark, *On the Sacred in African Literature: Old Gods and New Worlds* (Basingstoke, England: Palgrave Macmillan, 2009).
Mba, Nina Emma, *Nigerian Women Mobilized: Women's Political Activity in Southern Nigeria, 1900-1965* (Berkeley: Institute of International Studies, University of California, Berkeley, 1982).
Mwakikagile, Godfrey, *Ethnic Politics in Kenya and Nigeria* (New York: Nova Science, 2001).
Nwadike, Jerome, *A Biafran Soldier's Survival from the Jaws of Death* (Bloomington, IN: Xlibris, 2010).
Ohadike, Don, 'The Decline of Slavery among the Igbo People', in Suzanne Miers and Richard Roberts (eds), *The End of Slavery in Africa* (Madison, WC: University of Wisconsin Press, 1988), 437–61.
Ojukwu, Chukwuemeka Odumegwu (attrib.), *The Ahiara Declaration: The Principles of the Biafran Revolution* (Geneva: Mark, 1969).
Okigbo, Christopher, *Heavensgate* (Ibadan: Mbari, 1962).
Okpeewho, Isidore, *Once Upon a Kingdom: Myth, Hegemony and Identity* (Bloomington, IN: Indiana University Press, 1998).
Oriji, John, 'Igboland, Slavery and the Drums of War and Heroism', in Sylviane Anne Diouf (ed.), *Fighting the Slave Trade: West African Strategies* (Athens, OH: Ohio University Press, 2003), 121–31.
Peel, Micheal, *A Swamp Full of Dollars: Pipelines and Paramilitaries at Nigeria's Oil Frontier* (New York: Tauris, 2011).
Petersen, Kirsten Holst, 'West African Politics and Politicians from

a Literary Point of View', in Dieter Riemenschneider (ed.), *The History and Historiography of Commonwealth Literature* (Tübingen: Narr, 1983), 176–88.

Petersen, Kirsten Holst, James Currey, Alan Hill, and Keith Sambrook, 'Working with Chinua Achebe: The African Writers Series', in Kirsten Holst Petersen and Anna Rutherford (eds), *Chinua Achebe: A Celebration*, Studies in African Literature (Safrl) (Oxford: Heinemann, 1990), 149–59.

Sallah, Tijan M., and Ngozi Okonjo-Iweala, *Chinua Achebe, Teacher of Light: A Biography* (Trenton, NJ: Africa World Press, 2003).

Shaw, Flora, *A Tropical Dependency: An Outline of the Ancient History of the Western Sudan with an Account of the Modern Settlement of Northern Nigeria* (Cambridge: Cambridge University Press, 2010 [1905]).

Siollun, Max, *Oil, Politics and Violence: Nigeria's Military Coup Culture (1966–1976)* (New York: Algora, 2009).

Sklar, Richard, *Nigerian Political Parties: Power in an Emergent African Nation* (Trenton, NJ: Africa World Press, 2004).

Smith, Daniel Jordan, *A Culture of Corruption: Everyday Deception and Popular Discontent in Nigeria* (Princeton, NJ: Princeton University Press, 2007).

Steel, Edward, 'Exploration in Southern Nigeria', *The Geographical Journal*, 32, no. 1 (1908): 6–21.

Steyn, Phia, 'Oil Exploration in Colonial Nigeria, c. 1903–58', *Journal of Imperial & Commonwealth History*, 37, no. 2 (2009): 249–74.

Tutuola, Amos, *The Palm Wine Drinkard* (London: Faber, 1952).

Ume-Nwagbo, Ebele, 'Broadcasting in Nigeria: Its Post-Independence Status', *Journalism Quarterly*, no. 61 (1984): 585–99.

—— 'Politics and Ethnicity in the Rise of Broadcasting in Nigeria, 1932–62', *Journalism Quarterly*, 56, no. 4 (1979): 816–21.

Van Allen, Judith, '"Aba Riots" or Igbo "Women's War"? Ideology, Stratification, and the Invisibility of Women', in Nancy Hafkin and Edna Bay (eds), *Women in Africa: Studies in Social and Economic Change* (Stanford, CA: Stanford University Press, 1976), 59–85.

Wilkinson, J. F., 'The BBC and Africa', *African Affairs*, 71, no. 283 (1972): 176–85.

Yesufu, Abdul, 'Mbari Publications: A Pioneer Anglophone African Publishing House', *The African Book Publishing Record*, 8, no. 2 (1982): 53–7.

Index

A Man of the People 2–3, 72, 134, 136, 138–60, 175, 179–80, 185, 210, 226–7
　analysis 149–55, 160
　and disillusionment 144–5
　the election 146–8
　ending 148–9, 152, 155
　and gender 143–4, 230
　narrative 140–4
　political context 136–8, 139–40
　predictions/warnings 140, 152, 156
　protagonist 140–4, 153–5
　setting 13–14, 138–9
Aba Riots, the 125
Abraham, William 149
Achara, D. N., *Ala Bingo* 41
Achebe, Chinua 1–3, 28, 47–54, 149, 224–6, 237–8
　broadcasting career 17–30, 56, 93, 96, 135–8, 224, 226
　childhood 3–5, 41, 57–8
　as cultural nationalist 28, 92, 225
　education 7–12, 37, 38, 52
　exile in United States 181, 187
　Igbo affiliation 4, 13, 15–17
　joins People's Redemption Party 191–2
　literary context 30–41
　London secondment, 1957 23, 224
　military coup experiences 157–9
　as Moses 16–17
　nationalism 8–12, 17, 55–8, 180, 233–4
　parents 5, 6, 141
　plagiarism accusations 96–8
　relationship to Nigeria 3–4, 12–17, 224–7, 231–6
　relationship with Heinemann 44–8
　return to Nigeria 182, 188
　see also individual works
Achebe, Nwando 198, 228, 229
Action Group, the 21
Adegbenro, Alahaji 22
Adepoju, Toyin 52
Afigbo, Adielo 40, 74, 76, 76–7, 78, 94, 96, 111, 125, 126, 131, 133, 188
African Writers Series 2, 44, 46–7, 48, 49–52, 53, 99, 207
Afrique 95
Agbodike, Chinedu 202
Agbogu, Arinze 73
Agetua, John 191
'Agostinho Neto' 162
Ahiara Declaration, The 3, 168–72, 174, 175, 177, 178, 179, 180, 231–2, 236–7

Aig-Imhokhuede, Ikpehare 20
Ajayi, Adegboyega 194
Akpan, Ntieyong Udo 180–1
Allen, Judith van 125
Amadiume, Ifi 112–13, 116, 119–21, 122–3, 131, 132, 215
Anambra State University of Technology 199
Anderson, Benedict 7–8, 14, 206, 235
Aniagolu, Emeka 171
Anthills of the Savannah 3, 182, 183–223, 232
   Beatrice's role 208, 214–18, 218–20
   Chris's role 203–5, 210–11, 220–1
   and the elite 199–210
   ending 218–20, 231
   and female divinity 212–18
   gender in 126, 185, 210–18, 229, 230–1
   Ikem's role 205–10, 211–15
   message 218–23
   and military dictatorship 184, 192–9
   nationalism in 205–10
   people of Abazon 220–1
   political background 186–92
   protagonists 183, 200
   and redemption 200, 210–18
   spiritual conflict 129
   themes 183–6
   tipping point 198
   'Wild Sun of April' 207–8
anthropology 35–7
anti-colonial sentiment 3–4, 7, 10–11, 79–84, 118–20, 123–30, 234
Armour, Charles 18–19, 23, 135
Aro-Chukwu expedition, 1901–2 76–7, 78
Arrow of God 17, 40, 72, 93–134, 153, 210, 226
   and clan culture 60, 102–3, 107–8, 112–13
   and colonialism 75–8, 98–113, 133–4
   divine visitation sequence 106–7
   final part 97–8, 106–8
   and gender 114–34, 132–3, 214–15, 228–9
   historical focus 93–6, 101, 130–4
   narrative 102–8
   plagiarism accusations 96–8
   portrayal of colonial officers 96, 104–6, 108–12
   protagonist 102, 106
   and resistance 114–34
   spiritual conflict 127–30
   themes 90, 95–113
Awolowo, Obafemi 139, 187
Azikiwe, Nnamdi 10, 11–12, 56, 145, 150, 179, 235
Azuonye, Chukwuma 172

Babangida, General Ibrahim 186, 194–5, 220
Badejo, Victor 23, 132
Balewa, Abubakar 139, 150
Barnett, Clive 47, 49, 50
Basden, George 35–7, 90, 127, 229
BBC 18–19, 71, 135
Beattie, Angela 20
Beier, Ulli 52
Bende–Onitsha expedition, 1908 99–100
Benson, T. O. S. 26–7
Beware Soul Brother 162
Biafra 2–3, 29–30, 160–72, 175, 177, 202–3
   siege of 167–8, 180–1, 193
'Biafra, 1969' 162–3
Biafran Organization of Freedom Fighters (BOFF) 180, 202–3
Biafran writings 160–78, 236–7

Boehmer, Elleke 218, 220
broadcasting 17–30, 56
Buhari, General Muhammadu 192, 193, 194

Carretta, Vincent 32
Carroll, David 83
Cary, Joyce 31, 37, 90, 225
Cawson, Frank 158
Chalmers, Tom 18, 20, 21, 23, 71, 135, 224
Chinua, Madhu Krishnan 128
Christianity 4–5, 33–5, 62–6, 69, 112–13, 213–14, 215
  resistance to 118–19, 131–2
Chuku, Gloria 82–3, 116, 117–18, 128, 131, 215
Church Missionary Society (CMS) 5, 35, 57–8, 64, 121, 141
Citadel Press 175, 178, 186
'Civil Peace' 179
civil servants, privileged 203–5
civil war, outbreak of 29–30
Cobham, Rhonda 33, 59–60, 60
colonial officers, portrayal of 96, 104–6, 108–12
colonial writers 30–1, 37–8, 47
colonialism 21, 30, 57, 108–13, 153, 234
  in *Arrow of God* 98–113, 133–4
  benefits of 64–5, 82–3
  costs of 71, 90–2
  in *No Longer at Ease* 66–7, 74–5
  in *Things Fall Apart* 64–5
  violence 34–5, 75–7, 111–12, 133
  see also anti-colonial sentiment
Commonwealth and Foreign Office (UK) 3
Commonwealth Literature conference, Kampala, 1964 48–9
Commonwealth Writers Conference, Leeds, 1964 27
Conrad, Joseph 31, 35, 37–8, 225
corruption 55, 64, 68, 70, 74–5, 83, 87–8, 91–2, 145, 150, 178, 194–5
cultural hybridisation 74–5
cultural loss 70–1
cultural nationalism 28, 57, 92, 225
cultural politics 72–5
Currey, James 50–1, 53

decolonisation 1–2, 11
Diamond, Gary 6–7
Diamond, Larry 198
Dike, Kenneth Onwuka 38–9, 40
Diop, David 207
domestic violence 115–17
du Sautoy, Peter 44
Duerden, Dennis 4–5

educated elite, double-consciousness of 142–3, 150, 205–10
Education of a British-Protected Child, The 5, 15–17, 57, 79, 90, 227, 233, 237
Eke, Ifegwu 171
Ekechi, F. K. 79
Ekwe 120–1
Ekwe-Ekwe, Herbert 80–2
Ekwensi, Cyprian 32, 41–2
elite, the, role of 199–210
Emecheta, Buchi 230
Enahoro, Peter 158–9
Enekwe, Onuora 182
'English and the African Writer' 53
English language 48–9, 104, 141–2, 196
Equiano, Olaudah 32–5

European values, resistance to 118–20
Ezenwa-Ohaeto 8, 21, 23, 25–6, 35, 71, 157, 159, 171–2, 191

Faber and Faber 43–4
Fabre, Michel 131
Falola, Toyin 38–9, 125
Falola, Toyin, and Matthew Heaton 136–7, 187–8
Falola, Toyin, and Saheed Aderinto 39, 126
Fanon, Franz, *The Wretched of the Earth* 151, 152–3, 179–80, 205, 206, 233–4, 235
female divinity 127–30, 132, 212–18, 229
femininity 214–18, 230
Foley, Maurice 165
Forde, Daryll 43–4
Forrest, Tom 188–9

Gandhi, Mahatma 192
gender 58–61, 227–31
 in *A Man of the People* 143–4, 230
 in *Anthills of the Savannah* 126, 185, 210–18, 229, 230–1
 in *Arrow of God* 114–34, 132–3, 143, 214–15, 228–9
 in *No Longer at Ease* 68–9, 230
 in *Things Fall Apart* 59–60, 114–15, 116, 227–8, 229–30
genocide 81, 161, 171, 181
Ghana 19, 46
Gikandi, Simon 31, 55–6, 72, 151, 233–4, 236
'Girls at War' 172–5, 177, 210, 237
Girls at War 183–4, 230

Giwa, Dele 198
Goldie, George 6
Gowon, General Yakubu 187, 193
Great Britain 3, 6–7, 18–19, 21, 87
 Biafran policy 161–7, 171
 indirect rule system 93–6, 118
 pacification policy 75–80, 99–101
Guma, Alex la 53

Healey, Dennis 163, 166
Heath, Analee 45
Heinemann Educational Books 2, 28, 31, 44–8, 50, 53, 72, 207, 226, 237
 see also African Writers Series
Higo, Aigboje 50
Hill, Alan 44–8, 50, 72
historical reclamation projects 38–41
Home and Exile 224
How the Leopard Got His Claws 175–8, 187, 237

Ibadan, University College 8–9, 19–20, 37, 38, 52
Idemili 127–30, 132, 214–18, 229, 230
identity 5, 17, 136–7
Idoto 212–14
Ifemesia, Chieka 171–2
Igbo, the 4, 13, 15–17, 35–7, 38, 38–41, 227, 228
 gender relations 116–19
 pacification 2, 75–9, 79–80, 99–101
 tribalism 221–3
Ike, Chukwuemeke 171
imachi nkwu 83
Innes, C. L. 72, 73, 90, 97, 184

intellectuals, role of 191
Iroaganachi, John 175
Ironsi, Major General Aguiyi 157–8
Ito, Akito 34

Jefferson, Thomas 33
Jesus 215, 221
Jones, Arthur Creech 19, 135
journalists, suppression of 193–4

Kano, Mallam Aminu 191–2
kleptocracy 188
kola 84–90, 92, 142
Kortenaar, Neil ten 200-1, 206, 220-1
kotma, native officials 64, 68
Krishnan, Madhu 215

Lagos 20, 68, 87, 149, 158–9, 163
land disputes 73–4
Leapman, Michael 164
Leith-Ross, Sylvia 20, 35, 38, 126, 127, 229
Lindfors, Bernth 52, 138–9, 139–40, 149–50, 156
lion metaphor 224–5
London 23, 224
Low, Gail 43–4
Lugard, Lord 40, 93, 95, 111
'Lugard Lectures' (radio broadcasts) 20

MacKay, Ian 21, 21–2, 27, 29, 136
MacPherson, John Stewart 21
MacRae, Donald 72
Makerere University College, Uganda, conference, 1962 48–9
martial law 192, 226–7
masculinity 59–60, 114–16, 120, 126, 131, 143–4, 210–11, 226, 229–30, 230–1

Mayne. J. F. 166
Mba, Nina 116, 119, 121–2, 123–4, 131
Mbari Artists and Writers Club 52–3
military coup 140, 152, 156–9
military dictatorship 14, 184, 186–99
Moor, Sir Ralph 76, 77, 77–8, 79–80, 98
Moore, David Chioni 45
Morning Yet on Creation Day 184
Morris, John 165–6
Morrison, Toni 231
Mpalive-Hangson, Msiska 31
Muoneke, Romanus Okey 111–12
Mwakikagile, Godfrey 222

'Named for Victoria, Queen of England' 57
national culture 6–7, 151, 235
National Guidance Committee for Biafra 169–70, 171–2, 175, 180, 201–2, 237
National Party of Nigeria (NPN) 189
'national question', the 136–7
national renewal, call for 179–80
nationalism 4, 7–12, 17, 18–19, 55–8, 150–1, 180, 185–6, 205–10, 233–4
nationhood 185–6, 233–6
NCNC (National Council of Nigeria and the Cameroons) 145
Ndem, Eyo 171
neo-colonialism 146, 151
New Statesman 149
Newell, Stephanie 32, 41–3
Ngaboh-Smart, Francis 56
Nigeria 1, 5–9, 46, 89, 92, 188, 221–3

CA's relationship with 12–17,
    178–82, 224–7, 231–6
  independence 8–12, 56, 92,
    144–5, 171
Nigerian Broadcasting
  Corporation (NBC) 22–6,
  29–30, 53, 55, 71, 136–7
Nigerian Broadcasting Service
  (NBS) 1, 18–22, 135–6,
  224, 226
Nigerian Constitutional
  Conference 25
Nigerian Historical Society 126
Nigerian national figures 71
Nigerian National Merit Award
  14
Nigerianisation 1, 3–4, 135–6
Nigerianism 172
'1966' 162
Nkosi, Lewis 114
Nkrumah, Kwame 19
Nneka 212, 214
Nnobi 119–20
Nnolim, Charles 97
Nnolim, Simon 96–8
No Longer at Ease 92, 101, 131,
    138, 175, 185, 210, 226
  and colonialism 66–7, 74–5,
    81–2, 83
  ending 84
  gender in 230
  and kola 85, 86–90, 92, 142
  narrative 66–71
  nationalism 55, 56–7
  relationship to *Things Fall
    Apart* 72–5, 82, 90
  'The Novelist as Teacher' 27–8,
    49–50, 53, 150, 152, 226
Nwadike, Colonel Joe 'Hannibal'
  202–3
Nwakanma, Obi 213–14
Nwana, Pita, *Omenuko* 31–2, 41
Nwapa, Flora 230
Nzeogwu, Major Chukwuma
  Kaduna 157
Nzimiro, Ikenna 171

Obasanjo, General Olusegun 188,
  193
Obiechina, Emanuel 171
Ogbaa, Kalu 85, 181
Ogede, Ode 72
Ogidi 4, 57, 73, 99
Ohadike, Don 99
oil 3, 138, 161–2, 164–5, 171, 187,
  192, 222
Ojukwu, Emeka 3, 29, 168–9,
  169–70, 172, 180, 196–7,
  201–3
Okigbo, Chris 20, 53, 175, 186,
  213–14, 215
Okike 53, 182, 184
Okoli, Christie Chinwe 26
Okonkwo saga 58–9, 66, 70–1,
  71–5, 79–84
  see also individual novels
Olaniyan, Tejumola 129
Old Africans, theory of the 69
One-Nigeria 10, 11, 21–2, 55,
  135, 137, 226, 237
Onitsha 41, 52
Opara, Ralph 20
Oriji, John 101
Osundere, Niyi 32
ozo 90–1, 216

Peel, Michael 197
People's Redemption Party 191,
  237
Petersen, Kirsten Holst 72, 227
Phelps, Gilbert 71
publishing industry 1–2, 41–54

Ravenscroft, Arthur 83
redemption 200, 217–18, 230
Regent's Lecture 14–15
religion, traditional 112–13,
  127–30

Research in African Literatures 97
resistance 64, 65–6, 82, 98–9, 100, 114–34, 131–2, 133
Royal Niger Company 5–6, 11
Rushdie, Salman 233

Schools Broadcasting Unit 18
Shagari, Shehu 14, 189, 191, 192, 222
Shaw, Flora 5–6, 74, 77
Shaw, Thurston 38–40
Shepherd, Lord Malcolm 165–6
Siollun, Max 137–8
Sklar, Richard L. 10, 145
slaves and slavery 32, 34–5, 74, 77, 78, 171
Smith, Daniel Jordan 194–5
Society of Nigerian Authors 2, 155–6
Soyinka, Wole 52, 53, 114
Steel, Lieutenant Edward 100
stereotypes 43–4
Steyn, Phia 161–2
Stratton, Florence 227–8
student unrest 199–200
Suez crisis 162
Sunday Nation 152

There Was a Country 3, 155–6, 160–2, 163, 167, 168, 169, 180, 186, 202
Things Fall Apart 31, 37, 42–4, 45, 71–2, 92, 96, 111, 138, 153, 154, 185, 210, 212, 223, 226
  biblical motifs 33, 34
  and clan culture 58–61, 113
  and colonialism 79–84, 98
  ending 65–6, 70
  gender in 59–60, 114–15, 116, 227–8, 229–30
  historical referents 62–6, 73, 75–9, 130–1
  and kola 84–7
  nationalism 55–7
  ozo 91
  part one 58–61, 63, 73–4
  part two 61–5, 74, 75
  relationship to *No Longer at Ease* 72–5, 82, 90
Thompson, Tunde 193–4
Thomson, George 163–5
'Today, the Balance of Stories' 224–6
Trabor, Nduka 193–4
traditional practices 64, 102–3, 106
tribalism 221–3, 232, 236
Trouble with Nigeria, The 8, 182, 188, 189–91, 197, 220, 222–3, 232
Tutuola, Amos, *The Palm Wine Drinkard* 32, 43–4

Ume-Nwagbo, Ebele 21, 22, 24–5, 30
Umuahia Government College 5, 8
Umuchu 96–8
United States of America 181, 187

vernacular African languages 22, 48
Voice of Nigeria 2, 26–30, 93, 136–8, 149
'Vultures' 167

Wali, Obi 48, 49
Warrant Chiefs 94–6, 110, 123, 133
Welch, James 19–20
'What Is Nigeria to Me?' 4, 12–13, 14, 17
Whitaker, David 31
Wilkinson, J. E. 23–4, 25
Wilkinson, Jane 219

Wilson, Harold 163, 164, 165, 166, 171
women 116, 117, 132, 185, 212–13, 227–8, 230
  anti-colonial sentiment 118–20, 123–30, 132
  power and influence 120–3
  resistance 118–20, 123–30, 132, 133
Women's War, the 125
Wren, Robert 40–1, 73, 75–6, 90–1, 96, 112, 131, 216

Yesufu, Abdul 52
Yousaf, Nahem 31, 56, 72, 186, 195, 233, 234

EU authorised representative for GPSR:
Easy Access System Europe, Mustamäe tee 50,
10621 Tallinn, Estonia
gpsr.requests@easproject.com

www.ingramcontent.com/pod-product-compliance
Lightning Source LLC
Chambersburg PA
CBHW052103230426
43671CB00011B/1921